MEDITERRANEAN PARADOXES

Politics and Social Structure in Southern Europe

INTERNATIONAL PERSPECTIVES ON EUROPE
Series Editor: John Trumpbour

Previously published:

Volume 1, The Dividing Rhine: Politics and Society in Contemporary France and Germany

MEDITERRANEAN PARADOXES

Politics and Social Structure in Southern Europe

Edited by

James Kurth and James Petras

BERG

Providence / Oxford

Published in 1993 by

Berg Publishers, Inc.

Editorial offices:
221 Waterman Street, Providence, RI 02906, U.S.A.
150 Cowley Road, Oxford OX4 1JJ, UK

**A CIP catalogue record for this book is available from the British
Library.**

Library of Congress Cataloging-in-Publication Data
A CIP record for this book is available from the Library of Congress

ISBN 0 85496 968 3 cloth
ISBN 0 85496 336 7 paper

ISSN: 0956-2583

Printed in the United States by Edwards Brothers, Ann Arbor, MI.

CONTENTS

NOTES ON CONTRIBUTORS

RONALD CHILCOTE is Professor of Political Economy at the University of California, Riverside. He is the author of numerous books and articles on Portugal and Brazil and on Latin American development. He is the author of *Portuguese Africa, Emerging Nationalism in Portuguese Africa,* and *The Brazilian Communist Party.* He is the editor of the quarterly, *Latin American Perspectives.*

JAMES KURTH is Professor of Political Science at Swarthmore College in Pennsylvania. He is the author of many professional articles on Europe, the United States, and international politics. His research has focused upon the political economy of industrialization and the role of industrial sectors in political change.

DIARMUID MAGUIRE is Lecturer in Government at the University of Sydney in Australia where he teaches European and international politics. His Ph.D. dissertation (Cornell University, 1990) is a study of the British and Italian peace movements, and he is the author of several professional articles on leftist parties and peace movements in Britain, Ireland, and Italy.

JAMES PETRAS is Professor of Sociology at the State University of New York, Binghamton. He is the author of many books and professional articles. His most recent book is *Latin America in the Time of Cholera.* He has published articles in *Le Monde Diplomatique, El País.* and *the Guardian.* He is the former director of the Institute of Mediterranean Studies in Athens.

EVANGELOS RAPTIS AND SERGIO SARAFOPOULOS are researchers on Greek politics in Athens. Their research projects have also included Spanish politics (Raptis) and the politics of economic change in the Balkans (Sarafopoulos).

JOHN TRUMPBOUR is an instructor in History at Harvard University. He is a general editor for Berg's International Perspectives on Europe series.

1 PREFACE: SOUTHERN EUROPE – PAST AND PRESENT

In this volume of Berg's "International Perspectives" series on contemporary Europe, James Petras and James Kurth have brought together social scientists from three continents to explore the evolution of the Southern European political order. Petras and Kurth each represent distinct traditions of social science. Petras practices a critical sociology designed to investigate how ideological and economic interests are refracted through politics. Previously known for his many studies of Latin American politics and social structure, he has recently produced critiques of Southern European socialism that have generated debates from Madrid to Athens. Kurth is a political scientist rooted in traditions of historical sociology in the grand manner of Barrington Moore, Perry Anderson, and Theda Skocpol. In search of the broad historical sweep, the terrain of the middle and long *durée*, he pursues that elusive ideal identified by E.H. Carr in *What is History?*: ". . . the more sociological history becomes, and the more historical sociology becomes, the better for both."[1]

KURTH ON SOUTHERN EUROPE

Kurth's contributions to this volume make the case for studying modern Southern Europe as a unit. Historically there have been many obstacles to such a project. Most comparative social science in North America and Western Europe has busied itself with North Atlantic, northern European civilizations or, alternatively, the great powers of the twentieth century: the U.S., France, Great Britain, Russia, Germany, and occasionally China and Japan. In perpetuating the neglect of Southern Europe as a unit of study, Anglo-Saxon social science hardly stands alone. Southern Europeans themselves resist efforts at assimilating their diverse nationalities and regions into a single whole and, moreover, have a long, sometimes lively history of stressing the incompatibility of their cultures. This resistance can be found at many levels: from popular wis-

---

1. Edward Hallett Carr, *What is History?* (New York, 1963), p. 84.

dom such as the Portuguese aphorism that "De Espanha ni bom vento ni bom casamento" ("From Spain, there is neither good wind nor good marriage"); to government pronouncements such as Olivares's reference to the Portuguese as "canaille," "rogues . . . who pay less in taxes than any people in Europe"; to the bombast of nineteenth-century national- ists who blamed Spanish rule for most things retrograde, including "that pompous and crippled style [with which] the flamboyant character of the Spanish corrupted the simple elegance of Italian letters"; to modern ide- ologues of Hellenic revival who sometimes claimed filiation from a clas- sical tradition of Athenian liberty in contrast to the authoritarianism of Rome from the Empire to the Holy See. Even with the region blanket- ed in fascism fifty years ago, Mussolini still saw fit to invade his ideolog- ical counterpart in Greece, Metaxas, while Portugal's Salazar harbored deep suspicions of Franco and a revival of Spanish nationalism. At the advanced date of 1992, Portugal denounced Spain for celebrating Columbus without acknowledging the trailblazing accomplishments of the Portuguese navigators of the fifteenth century, only the latest in a long saga of mutual vituperation and recrimination.[2]

Looking beyond such skirmishing, Kurth indicates that the countries of Southern Europe have more in common than just the legacies of Roman imperial rule and submission to Habsburg domination. In the nineteenth and twentieth centuries, he suggests, the region shared a sim- ilar sequence of political development as well as a widespread backward- ness in agriculture and industry that effectively preserved a fossilized social structure (see Appendix A). This came to be reflected in the ubiq- uity of so-called obsolete classes, most notably the persistence of landed elite power in all but Greece until the contemporary epoch. Buttressed by high tariff walls on agricultural goods imposed in the late nineteenth century,[3] and flanked by a bourgeoisie too terrified of working class and

2. For the Count-Duke of Olivares (1587–1645) on Portugal, J.H. Elliott, *The Count- Duke of Olivares: The Statesman in an Age of Decline* (New Haven, 1986), p. 527. For the nineteenth-century quotation of the decline of Italian letters due to Spain, see Eric Cochrane, *Historians and Historiography in the Italian Renaissance* (Chicago, 1985 [1981]), p. x. For an example of Greek ideological resistance to Rome, see Michael Herzfeld, *Ours Once More: Folklore, Ideology, and the Making of Modern Greece* (New York, 1986), p. 40. Herzfeld notes tensions in the Greek tradition: on the one hand, seeking to be part of Europe and embracing Rome against Slavic and Turkish despotism, and on the other, appealing to the superiority of Hellenic ways over the rest of Europe. For the latest row between Portugal and Spain, Alan Riding, "Bedfellows with Spain, Lisbon won't cuddle," *New York Times*, 14 June 1992.

3. This interpretation is a type of Mediterranean *Sammlungspolitik*; among one of its many features, it includes the manner in which tariff policy led to a unity of agrarian and industrial elites. In Spain, Catalan textile owners, with some support from their workers, joined Andalusian and Castilian landlords in the cry for protectionism of industry and a backward agriculture. In Italy, its tariff of 1888 brought together a bloc of textile owners,

peasant insurgencies to challenge their preeminence, the landed elites were prone to a reactionary resolution of the transition to the modern world. While Kurth is himself less preoccupied with this aspect of Southern Europe, the imperial policies of Spain, Portugal, and Ottoman Turkey may have provided some of the foundations for this later outcome. The Spanish occupation of Italy from the sixteenth through the eighteenth centuries strengthened sectors of the Italian aristocracy and coopted urban elites as a counterweight to the fiercely independent and often recalcitrant city-states of the Renaissance. During this period, the secular decline of Italy's urban economy, marked by a textile industry overwhelmed by cheap Dutch, English, and French output, shattered much of the mercantile bourgeoisie and left those in good standing content with retreat into agrarian sources of wealth.[4] The power of the landed elite remained immense throughout the Italian peninsula long after Spain's departure: by the turn of the twentieth century, the Borghese family owned nearly 85 square miles of land within and surrounding Rome; in the province of Bologna, an important agricultural breadbasket, 200–300 landowners held two-thirds or 157,500 out of 232,500 acres of the prime land; and in Sicily nearly 800 landowners, two-thirds

---

steel magnates, sugar beet refiners, and wheat growers. Tariffs on grain allowed large landowners to store grain in the spring and force high prices on the peasantry in the fall when the small landowner and landless laborer had depleted any stored foodstuffs. See Michael Seidman, *Workers against Work: Labor in Paris and Barcelona during the Popular Fronts* (Berkeley, 1991), p. 21, and Richard Webster, *Industrial Imperialism in Italy 1908–1915* (Berkeley, 1975), pp. 15–16. In Greece, a bloc of large landowners from newly acquired Thessaly entered the parliament in the 1880s and successfully clamored for a high tariff on wheat imports. In 1884, the wheat tariff underwent a fivefold leap, those for industrial products a tripling. The large landowner bloc in Greece overall had weaker historical roots than their counterparts in the rest of Southern Europe and eventually lost most of their land, although often with state compensation. See below, especially footnote six. Nicos Mouzelis, *Modern Greece: Facets of Underdevelopment* (London, 1978), p. 164n. For additional background on Greek economic policy, see Mark Mazower, *Greece and the Inter-war Economic Crisis* (Oxford, 1991).

Tariff policy and *Sammlungspolitik* is a staple of German historiography. Helmut Böhme, *Deutschlands Weg zur Grossmacht: Studien zum Verhältnis von Wirtschaft und Staat während der Reichsgründungszeit 1848–1881* (1966) produced the classic study of how the protective tariff of 1879 represented a "refounding of the German Reich." The term *"Sammlungspolitik"* stems, however, from the 1890s. In Böhme's account, Rudolf Delbrück, the orchestrator of Prussian economic policy, is elevated to an historical weight and stature closer to that of Bismarck. See also the writings of H.- U. Wehler, *Bismarck und der Imperialismus* (1969) and *The German Empire: 1871–1918* (Leamington Spa, 1985). For a critique of *Sammlungspolitik*, see Geoff Eley, "*Sammlungspolitik*, Social Imperialism, and the Navy Law of 1898," in Geoff Eley, *From Unification to Nazism: Reinterpreting the German Past* (Boston, 1986) and David Blackbourn and Geoff Eley, *The Peculiarities of German History: Bourgeois Society and Politics in Nineteenth Century Germany* (Oxford, 1984).

4. Stuart Woolf, *A History of Italy, 1700-1860: The Social Constraints of Political Change* (New York, 1986), pp. 23–24.

of whom were non-resident, possessed one-third of the island.[5] In Greece, Ottoman rule wedged into the social structure a tax farming stratum of large landowners whose limited tenure and extravagant levies gave way after independence (ca. 1820-1830) to a small-holder peasantry subsequently preyed upon by new merchant intermediaries and extortionate usurers. The post-liberation disintegration of the Ottoman *chiflik* system led to small-holder peasantries in Greece, Bulgaria, and Serbia, a stark contrast to the latifundista pattern of Southern (S. Italy, Spain, S. Portugal), Central (Prussia, Poland, Hungary), and Eastern Europe (Russia). Neither an impoverished microfundista nor a semi-feudal latifundista agriculture provided a social base ready to glide smoothly toward bourgeois democracy.[6]

Meanwhile, Portugal, the first and last of the European empires (outlasting Spain's by seven decades), fit the closest to Joseph Schumpeter's classic description of modern imperialism as an outgrowth of atavistic military and aristocratic elites. With one out of five of its adult male population in the military and a feudal aristocracy in the South that owned latifundia on average 5,878 acres – some 2,500 times the median size of the plots held by the peasantry of the nation's North, Portugal possessed the essential ingredients for combining imperial domination abroad with repression at home. While Greece and Italy failed in late bids for imperial grandeur, the Iberian powers developed an imperialism that was almost the negation of the standard core-periphery pattern of Great Britain, France, Belgium, the United States, and Japan. This was most acute in Portugal, an underdeveloped economy yoked to an imperial governing order. Observing thirty years ago that "the pattern is the very reverse of an imperial economy," Perry Anderson reflected that in Portugal,

5. Data from Arno Mayer, *The Persistence of the Old Regime* (New York, 1981), pp. 30–31. Martin Clark, *Modern Italy, 1871–1982* (London, 1984), pp. 13–19, gives a more nuanced perspective on the range of land ownership patterns in Italy: the tenacity of the small-holder in regions of Piedmont, Lombardy, Veneto, and Liguria, and the particular prominence of latifundia in the South.

6. The small-holder pattern predominated in Greece, but some regions reverted to previous configurations of land ownership. In Thessaly, reattached to Greece in the years following the Congress of Berlin (1878) at a conference of ambassadors in Constantinople (1881), native Greeks replaced the Turkish owners of huge estates (*chifliks*). They retained their vast estates until 1917 when Venizelos imposed a major land reform. For discussions of this process, see Richard Clogg, *A Short History of Modern Greece* (Cambridge, 1986), pp. 89–91, 100. Perry Anderson, *Lineages of the Absolutist State* (London, 1979 [1974]), pp. 387–394, and L.S. Stavrianos, *The Balkans since 1453* (New York, 1958), pp. 478–479.

As is the case for the English civil war and the French revolution, the class bases of the Greek struggle for independence have always been a focal point of historiographical debate; see Clogg's data disputing the view that its leadership came from a merchant class background, p. 49. Cf. Mouzelis, pp. 12–13, with his distinction between a radicalized, pro-Enlightenment diaspora bourgeoisie and a more traditionalist indigenous bourgeoisie.

With the single exception of cotton for the textile industry, the classic colonial absorption of raw materials for re-export as manufactured products, does not occur. The balance is exactly opposite: quasi-raw material exports (cork, wine, etc. – involving minimal technological intervention), manufactured imports.[7]

As for Spain, despite having greater wealth than Portugal in the modern epoch, it had a similar trade pattern in its relationship with other industrial imperialisms. France, for instance, in 1935 produced 17 times as much pig iron as Spain and over ten times more crude steel. Its wheat yields were double those of Spain. Michael Seidman, in his innovative study of Popular Front era Spain and France, points out that

> The two countries developed the classic trading relation of an industrial to an agrarian nation: the French exported manufactured goods, and the Spanish shipped agricultural products. In 1934, the largest French exports to Spain were in order of importance, automobiles and parts, other motor vehicles, silk, iron and steel, and chemical products. Spain sent to France fruits, sulphur, wine, lead, and fresh vegetables.[8]

In Kurth's own interpretation of Southern Europe, the first significant divergence in modern politics between the Iberian peninsula on the one hand and the Greek and Italian nations on the other came in the region's encounter with a new imperial order, the *pax Americana* imposed in the aftermath of World War II. While Iberian authoritarianism survived into the 1970s, Greece and Italy witnessed the triumph of parliamentarism under the new conditions set by Allied occupation.

Barrington Moore was once asked to explain why he thought social revolutions were a likely prerequisite for the triumph of bourgeois democracy. After all, it had been objected that West Germany and Japan apparently made the transition to parliamentarism in peaceful conditions following World War II. In *Reflections on the Causes of Human Misery* (1970), he called the Allied occupation a form of "*ersatz* revolution." For

---

7. Perry Anderson, "Portugal and the End of Ultra-Colonialism," *New Left Review*, May–June 1962, p. 86. This also includes the data cited above on land distribution in Portugal. The observation on Portugal and Schumpeter's theory, as well as the estimate of male participation in the military, comes from Fred Halliday, "Portugal: Atlantic connection," *New Statesman and Society*, 22 May 1992, p. 25. For more detailed data on the composition of the military that may slightly modify Halliday's estimate, see Kenneth Maxwell, "Regime Overthrow and the Prospects for Democratic Transition in Portugal," in Guillermo O'Donnell, Philippe C. Schmitter, and Laurence Whitehead, *Transitions from Authoritarian Rule: Southern Europe* (Baltimore, 1986), p. 110. He writes: "In 1974... one out of four men of military age was in the armed forces.... The armed forces represented (at a low estimate) a proportion per 1,000 of the population (30.83) exceeded only by Israel (40.09), and North and South Vietnam (respectively 31.63, 55.36); five times that of the United Kingdom, three times that of the United States or Spain."

8. Seidman, pp. 19–20.

Southern Europe, Kurth employs a similar device for explaining the new
configuration of forces that allowed the Greek and Italian departure from
Iberian patterns of dictatorial rule. While the U.S State Department may
well have taken a sympathetic view towards the renewal of right-authoritarian order if the Communist Party had been able to prevail at the bal-
lot box (Italy, 1948) or on the battlefield (Greek civil war, 1946–49),[9]
parliamentarism in these two countries attained hegemony, despite frequent adverse assaults: in Greece during the 1950s, the existence of hundreds of political prisoners, Communist and otherwise, the continued
employment of police and paramilitary repression, and from 1967–74
the rise of the Colonels who predicated their usurpation on the need for
a purification and "rebirth" designed to facilitate the eventual restoration
of democracy; in Italy, the persistence of clientelism and gangrenous
growths of corruption, and in the 1970s the flourishing of extraparliamentary enterprises on both the far right and far left dedicated to tactics
of terror. The Italian political theorist Norberto Bobbio argued at the
time that the closed-door secrecy of the ruling Christian Democrats had
found an eerie parallel in the clandestine, antidemocratic practices of the
counterrevolutionary sects and revolutionary groupuscules:

> I limit myself to the suspicion . . . that state secrecy has been used to protect
> anti-state secrecy. . . . The degeneration of the Italian system began there. . . .
> One of the founders of modern terrorism, Bakunin, proclaimed the necessity
> of an "invisible dictatorship." Whoever joins a terrorist group is forced to go
> underground, wear a mask, and exercise the same art of lying so often
> described as one of the prince's stratagems. He, too, scrupulously follows the
> maxim that power is more effective the more he knows and sees without
> being seen.[10]

9. William Colby in his memoir of CIA service, *Honorable Men* (New York, 1978)
declares that "the very deliberate and conscious policy was made in Washington that no
help of any kind go to the Neo-Fascists or Monarchists. The unanimous view was that...
the United States did not *need* to back right-wing groups in its campaign to stop the rise of
the Communists." (italics mine) For a somewhat different view of U.S. cooperation with
far right and mafia elements, see Roberto Faenza and Marco Fini, *Gli americani in Italia*
(Milano, 1976).

For a critical view of U.S. ties to authoritarian elements in Greece, see Andreas Papandreou, *Democracy at Gunpoint* (New York, 1970). Of the rise of the Colonels in 1967, he
recalls:

"I asked [U.S. Ambassador Phillips] Talbot whether America could have intervened the
night of the coup, to prevent the death of democracy in Greece. He denied that they could
have done anything about it. Then Margaret [Papandreou's wife] asked a critical question:
What if the coup had been a Communist or a Leftist coup? Talbot answered without hes-
itation. Then, of course, they would have intervened, and they would have crushed the
coup."

10. Noberto Bobbio, "Democracy and Invisible Government," in *Telos*, 52, 1982, pp.
54–55. See also Robert Lumley, *States of Emergency: Cultures of Revolt in Italy from 1968 to
1978* (London, 1990), p. 285.

Indeed much journalistic and academic commentary of the late 1970s and early 1980s still judged the prospects for democracy in Southern Europe to be precarious, as a sampling of headlines from over a decade ago concerning the region's wealthiest country might attest: "Italy in Agony" (*Time*), "Italy is Finished" (*Der Spiegel*), and "Le Chaos Italien" (a frequent French newspaper headline, reports *Le Nouvel Observateur*).[11]

But the tide began to change. In 1983, the U.S. liberal weekly the *New Republic* featured Michael Ledeen, who in an article entitled "Craxi's Moxie" saluted Italy's new "sexy leader" as one who "may somehow force the country's politicians to come to grips with the problems they have diligently avoided for the past fifteen years."[12] In a very different spirit from the *New Republic's* abrupt conversion to Italophilia, Joseph LaPalombara published his *Democracy Italian Style* (1987), praising the postwar Italian system for high levels of popular participation and a political machinery that in its own way managed to articulate and respond to public needs. In a special issue devoted to Italy, France's *Nouvel Observateur* (3 May 1990) entitled its cover article, "Les miracles de l'Italie," while *U.S. News & World Report* (18 July 1988) ran with "Europe's sun belt also rises: Not since the Medicis has the Mediterranean shown so much flare." The U.S. media also began an upsurge of coverage favorable to the neoliberal economic experiments in Portugal and Spain, paradoxically under the tutelage of Socialist regimes. Again Ledeen observed that the "selection of Craxi as Italy's prime minister completes the transition of Latin Europe from artereosclerotic conservatism to democratic socialism . . . of a particularly realistic sort." Referring to Italy's Craxi, Spain's Felipe González, and Portugal's Mario Soares, he declared that "In the curious world we now live in, these three men of the left are attempting to remedy the effects of runaway social spending programs carried out by previous governments of the right (or center-right). And in foreign policy, these Eurosocialists are more consistently and coherently concerned about Soviet actions than

11. The U.S., German, and French headlines of gloom are assembled in the *Nouvel Observateur*, 3 May 1990.

12. Michael Ledeen, "Craxi's Moxie," *New Republic*, 5 September 1983, pp. 10–11. The issue also contains an essay praising Gonzalez-era Spain by Morton Kondracke. The Reagan foreign policy team, which later made generous use of Ledeen's skills in engineering the Iran-contra arms for hostages deal, may have felt a special devotion to Craxi, for reasons suggested by Giovanni Agnelli, the president of FIAT, in an interview with *Le Monde* (15 June 1983). Declaring that Craxi aspired to be the Italian Helmut Schmidt, a right-wing social democrat, Agnelli said that "Washington also appreciates him because without the P.S.I. the missile question would not be raised." At the time, the U.S. sought to introduce a modernized range of nuclear Euromissiles, and the Italian Socialist Party controlled the Defense ministry in Italy's Cabinet. The craze for Craxi has gone into permanent retreat, as at this moment he is threatened with the prospect of jail should he be convicted of corruption.

were their predecessors," among whom he may have counted Francisco Franco with his sometimes amicable trade relations with Havana. Early unease about Felipe González's criticism of U.S. foreign policy toward Nicaragua quickly dissipated when on a visit to Ronald Reagan in Washington he declared otherwise. "There was, I think, no fundamental disagreement about Central America," the Spanish prime minister told the American press corps.[13] The U.S. media rewarded González with near unanimous commendation for marshalling support behind NATO in a national referendum of 1986 and later for rallying a divided public behind Operation Desert Storm, billed as Spain's first participation in international conflict since the defeat at the hands of U.S. imperialism in 1898. For those willing to discount Spain's sending of the armed Blue Division to aid Hitler on the eastern front or Spanish military forays into Morocco during the Riff War of the 1910s and 1920s, the interventionist spirit of González was hailed as sign of a new diplomatic maturity. Not to be counted out of the celebration of new-found Iberian virtue was Portugal. The *New York Times* (24 February 1984) gave latter day Lusitania a patronizing pat of approval with an article carrying the headline: "Women Add a Certain Pizazz to Portugal's Politics."

Even the electronic media thought it an auspicious moment to acclaim Southern European life, beyond the annual news routine of showing the Pope's Easter greeting and the bulls running from Pamplona. Melding together an unseemly *ménage* of Reagan era "family values," the spirit of Bitburg, and nostalgia for Southern Europe the way it used to be, NBC produced a mini-series starring George C. Scott on the unknown Mussolini, which, according to *Newsweek* (20 May 1985) "will downplay all that nasty fascist politics and concentrate on the Duce's loving relationship with his children."

The sole exception to the Southern Euphoria concerned the government of Greece's Andreas Papandreou. Tainted with charges of anti-Americanism (by Diane Sawyer on "Sixty Minutes" and by Henry Kamm in a profile in the *New York Times Magazine*), and faulted for not

---

13. *New York Times*, 22 June 1983. For other gestures of PSOE support for Washington's foreign policy, see Thierry Maliniak, "M. Felipe Gonzalez annonce l'achat de 72 avions de combat américains," *Le Monde*, 1 June 1983, and "Les socialistes espagnols multiplient les gestes de bonne volonté à l'égard des Etats-Unis," *Le Monde*, 23 June 1983, the latter of which notes that though González continues to criticize U.S. policy in Central America, Washington is happy because "the points of accord on the policies pursued in Central America 'surpass the points of discord.'" According to Maliniak and Diana Johnstone in *The Politics of Euromissiles* (London, 1984), the PSOE's ardor to please Washington stemmed from a desire to placate the military concerning Morocco, a close ally of the U.S. and a threat to Spain's last outposts in North Africa, Ceuta and Melilla. González hoped to avoid a repetition of the abortive golpe of 23 February 1981 that sought to overthrow his predecessor.

dismantling state programs with the diligence of his Eurosocialist counterparts, Papandreou in the end did nothing to abrogate NATO base
agreements and for good measure rebuilt a central symbol of U.S. inter-
ventionism, a statue of Harry S. Truman blown up by Greek leftists in
anticipation of the arrival in Athens of U.S. Secretary of State George
Shultz. The *New Republic*, always wary of Papandreou for his PLO sym-
pathies and anti-NATO proclamations, conceded that he

> repeats the comfortable catechism of anti-Americanism while doing nothing
> to harm Greece's ties with the United States. . . . We are tempted to applaud
> hypocrisy of this sort. Papandreou's pronouncements have few practical con-
> sequences, and allow the United States to retain access to the Aegean. He is
> preferable to someone who takes his party's platform more literally.[14]

PETRAS'S CRITIQUE OF SOUTHERN EUROPEAN SOCIALISM

Nonetheless, during the 1970s, there emerged an alternative body of literature, most notably that of the prolific Belgian Marxist economist
Ernest Mandel, who argued that with the collapse of authoritarianism in
the South, left parties were squandering a propitious moment for
advancing radical political change. These works decried first Stalinism
and then the social democratization of the major European Communist
parties, the latter trend reflected in the Italian Communist Party's cooperation with Christian Democrat policies of austerity (1976-79), as well
as in the Spanish Communist Party's neo-reformist posturings outlined
in *'Eurocomunismo' y Estado* (*Eurocommunism and the State*, 1977) by its
Secretary General Santiago Carrillo.[15] While mainstream social scientists
lauded conciliation and convergence for averting the resumption of class
and civil warfare, much of the Southern European working class did not
seem eager to adapt to the revisionist ferment of the 1970s. Powerful
surges of working class strike and political unrest convulsed Southern
Europe. In Spain, for instance, the number of working hours lost

14. "Squeaky Greek at the Wheel," *New Republic*, 4 February 1985, pp. 9–10. The article, nevertheless, warns: "The trouble with hypocrites is that they have a way of talking
themselves into a corner." So they concluded that Papandreou remained a potential threat.

15. Ernest Mandel, *From Stalinism to Eurocommunism* (London, 1978) and *Revolutionary
Marxism Today* (London, 1979). For critiques of Eurocommunism from other left traditions, see Carl Boggs and David Plotke, eds., *The Politics of Eurocommunism: Socialism in
Transition* (Boston, 1980) The chief text of revisionism in Spain is Santiago Carrillo, *'Eurocomunismo' y Estado* (Barcelona, 1977). Carrillo placed "Eurocommunism" in quotations, as
the term was invented by anti-communist ideologues in the mid-1970s and only later
adopted by many Communists. See Philip Schlesinger, *Media, State, and Nation* (London,
1991), chapter six, for a history of the term and its many ideological mutations in the
1970s. For an illuminating survey of the literature on Eurocommunism in Spain, see
Patrick Camiller, "The Eclipse of Spanish Communism," *New Left Review*, 147, Septem-
ber/October 1984.

through strikes hurtled from 1.5 million hours in 1965 to 8.7 million in 1970 to 14.5 million in 1975, and then to 150 million in 1976.[16] In Greece, seven years of draconian wage restraint under the Colonels gave way to constant pressure for redress, culminating in dramatic worker demonstrations against high prices in Athens during May 1981. Inheriting the eventual electoral triumphs from those struggles were not the Communists but rather the Socialist parties. After an interlude of conservative democratic rule in Spain and Greece in the late 1970s, the Socialists burst out of opposition, at first quite militant in rhetoric and, in the eyes of much of the Western left, full of potential for achieving radical reform. Whereas Mandel and his co-thinkers had vented frustration at the *social democratization* of the Communist parties of the 1970s, Petras in the 1980s emerged as a leading critic of the Thatcherization and *neo-liberalization* of the social democrats.[17] This great right moving theatre show opened with several thematic innovations: Craxi of the Italian Socialist Party put in charge of the government coalition in hopes that he could better discipline the working class than the Christian Democrats; and Soares of the Portuguese Socialist Party eroding agrarian reform as well as expressing irritation at the Socialist International for supposed over-indulgence toward the Third World, for instance in the Brandt Commission's call for 2 percent of GNP to be transferred from North to South, from the rich to the poorer countries of the world. Spain's *via thatcheriana* brought in its wake unemployment approaching 20 percent amidst vandalized public services, a ravaged physical environment, and large-scale projects designed to slake the thirst for predatory overconsumptionism among the middle and upper classes. For the old party faithful, there was the occasional flare of marxisant rhetoric and revolutionary iconography on the party's posters.

Indeed the combination of radical rhetoric and consumerist extravagance was on display in full baroque regalia during the 1992 Olympics. Armed with nearly $200 million in public funds to construct apartments, the Socialist-run city council of Barcelona had given a solemn pledge in 1986 to sell the proposed units, in words spoken by Mayor Pasqual Maragall, at "low, competitive prices." In 1992, the apartments were unveiled and priced in the vicinity of well-oiled yuppiedom at $350,000 for a three-bedroom. The Olympic Village has ironically been named "Nova Icaria" after the radical communist utopia of Etienne Cabet

16. For strike data in Spain, see Jose Maria Maravell and Julian Santamaria, "Political Change in Spain and the Prospects for Democracy," in O'Donnell, Schmitter, and Whitehead, pp. 77 and 82.

17. Petras in his chapter on Greece and particularly Ronald Chilcote in this volume's essay on Portugal probably go to greater lengths than Mandel to demonstrate the class basis and economic constraints that made the retreat from socialism a likely outcome.

(1788-1856). Even *Time* art critic Robert Hughes, author of the best-seller *Barcelona* and an admirer of the project, conceded in mock-horror: "You might as well call an upscale condo block in Berlin the Rosa Luxemburg Tower." Apparently unbeknownst to Hughes, on Madrid's nouveau chic northwest corner is the Rosa Luxemburg Estate in which a semi-detached home fetches a price of 165,000 British pounds.[18]

In the 1960s and 1970s, North American social democrats such as Irving Howe and Michael Harrington suggested that the Democratic Party of the U.S. would increasingly move toward the place on the political spectrum occupied by Europe's social democrats. If Petras's analysis is on target, European social democracy has instead brought about the Americanization of the continent's politics, featuring exclusive dominance by capitalist parties, election techniques based on the "Brand A, Brand B" sloganeering of the media experts and the advertising industry, and publics whose attentions are diverted into apathetic consumerism and mediatized spectacle.

When Petras's critiques of the Southern European socialist parties appeared in the mid-1980s, some judged them unduly harsh. They have since gained a certain notoriety for prescience after the dizzying spectacle of subsequent revelations and prosecutions piled atop a mound of corruption already grown fetid and rotting. Even Catholic Cardinal Enrique Tarancón, an outspoken critic of Francoism, admits ruefully that the theft and brigandage under the González regime probably exceeds the buccaneering carried out by corsairs in the entourage of the late Generalissimo.[19]

Now there are those political scientists who, following the insight of Sir Lewis Namier on Hanoverian Britain, might represent this as a sort of progress by arguing that corruption can more easily flourish with the decline of dangerously overheated ideological passions. Corruption "was a mark of English freedom and independence," thought Namier, "for no one bribes where he can bully."[20] Moreover, with politicians and their enemies no longer committed to higher, transcendent values that they will

18. Robert Hughes, *Barcelona* (New York, 1992), p. 40. For the Madrid anecdote, and the anti-democratic pratices of the PSOE in the building projects of the 1980s and early 1990s, John Hooper, "Fast track to the Olympics," *Guardian* (UK), 13–14 June 1992.

19. "A lot of rot," *Economist*, 8 February 1992. The correspondent concludes that the charges of the respected Tarancón may be hard to prove. "Socialists," according to *The Economist*, "tend to argue that the exposure of scandal is a sign of health. In the past, they say, the press and the courts were timid." *The Economist* adds in response: "This cheering argument would be stronger were Spain's judiciary more independent. . . . The snag is that in 1982 the improbable happened. The Socialists won an outright majority in parliament and with it unchallenged control of the judiciary committee. Spain's judges still depend too much on political masters." In the elections of 1993, the Socialists won, but lost their majority control.

20. Lewis Namier, *England in the Age of the American Revolution* (London, 1970 [1930]), p. 4.

fight to the death to defend, conflicts can be resolved without the threat of class or civil war. Britain's immediate postwar foreign secretary Ernest Bevin had indeed thought it futile to fund the Spanish opposition to Franco because for him it only risked a new round of calamity and bloodshed.[21]

But given such misrule and malfeasance among the Socialists, there are questions of how they have been able to sustain their rule. Admittedly the Greek electorate voted Papandreou out of office, albeit narrowly, and González barely escaped defeat in the elections of 1993. In Italy, investigation into scandal in Milan has effectively decapitated the Socialists, while the ensuing crisis now threatens the rest of the Italian political class. The Socialists in Italy talk about dismantling their party and forming a brand new organization made up of reformist PSI remnants and flotsam and jetsam from parties of the political center. Should they survive, the Socialists must also worry about desertion from women voters who, after gliding substantially leftward during the feminist mobilization of 1968-1976, express continued disenchantment with the party's abominable record of inclusion: in the Chamber of Deputies elected in 1983, only 1 out of 73 PSI deputies were women, compared to 38 out of 198 for the PCI and 6 out of 255 for the DC.[22] Despite such festering problems, the political success of the Socialists in the overall region has had tangible sources. In sociological terms, late industrialization in Southern Europe had by the 1970s produced the social bases conducive to social democratization.[23] The class structure now vaguely resembled that of Northern Europe during the breakthrough period for social democracy spanning from the interwar period in the Scandinavian countries to 1945 in the United Kingdom. Only in the case of Southern Europe, postmodern elements possessed a much heavier weight in the social structure than that of the North circa the early postwar era (see Kurth, pp. 52–53). Per-

21. Of course, such high-minded concerns did not deter British intelligence from helping Greek rightists during the civil war or the American CIA from funneling resources to the Christian Democrats in Italy in the 1940s and to the Portuguese Socialists in the 1970s when the alternative might be the triumph of a hard-line left. For a discussion of Bevin's dilemmas, see Raymond Carr, "How Franco Made It," *New York Review of Books*, 4 February, 1988. On CIA support for the Portuguese Socialists, Maxwell, p. 130.

22. Donald Sassoon, *Contemporary Italy* (New York, 1986), p. 107. Overall the proporton of women in the lower house of national parliaments in Western Europe during 1990 ranges from a high of 38.1 percent in Sweden to a low of 5.3 percent in Greece. Spain with 13.4 percent and Italy with 12.9 percent lie just below the European median, Portugal with 7.6 percent occupies the basement with the United Kingdom (6.3), France (5.7), and Greece (5.3). Data from Hege Skjeie, "The Uneven Advance of Norwegian Women," *New Left Review*, 187, May/June, 1991, p. 94. For background on women in southern European politics, see Sassoon on Italy, Eleni Stamiris, "The Women's Movement in Greece," *New Left Review*, 158, July/August 1986 and Monica Threlfall, "The Women's Movement in Spain," *New Left Review*, 151, May/June 1985.

23. The discussion that follows owes much to the concluding chapter of Perry Anderson, *English Questions* (London, 1992).

haps relatedly, the South's social democratic parties lacked the same organic links with the labor movement as their northern counterparts, reflected in weaker levels of unionization (with the exception of Italy, typically only 20 percent of the workforce compared to 60-80 percent in Sweden and Austria) and a less active presence in resisting the dictatorships in Spain, Portugal, and Greece than their main rivals on the left, the communist parties. Thus they reached those growing segments of the new middle class who appear content to vote Socialist rather than participate in unions. Heavily weighted toward white collar managers, teachers, doctors, lawyers, state bureaucrats, and scientific and technical workers, the Socialists increasingly grounded their appeal on three yardsticks: 1) efficiency, 2) advance of civil liberties, and 3) modernization.

By all three measures, the Socialists have begun to lose legitimacy and good will, but in Greece, Portugal, and Spain they retain a substantial minority of the electorate. First, on the subject of efficiency, there is a pessimistic sense among the electorate that all parties partake in corruption, and in the case of Greece, as Petras suggests, Papandreou was supported at the polls by many who felt for the first time that they had been given access to goodies from the patrimonial state.[24] In Spain, despite the preponderance of Socialist scandal, officials from the People's Party (the main party of the conservative opposition) also carry with them the stale aroma of corruption, in particular indictments for taking bribes for giving support in local councils to a variety of building projects. In Italy, all of the major parties, including the former PCI, long sailed gracefully upon rivers of corruption and patronage. (However, in contrast to Spain where a government poll at the end of 1992 indicates that only 2 percent regard it as the nation's top problem, recent Italian developments indicate a public more determined that the political swamp be drained of such rampant thievery. The post-Cold War epoch by easing middle class anxieties about Communist triumph has thus eroded support for patronage networks at one time thought necessary to choke off the PCI.)[25] Second, the advances of civil liberties under the Socialists have helped remove the terror and trauma lingering from the reign of the Colonels, Salazar, and Franco. "Andreas took away the fear" is how one Greek peasant woman expressed her support for Papandreou.[26] Greek voters respond favorably to PASOK's populist attacks against U.S. support for

24. Angered by austerity and charges of corruption against the right and their Prime Minister Constantine Mitsotakis, the Greek electorate appears likely to propel Papandreou back to power in national elections slated for October 1993.

25. Spanish poll cited by John Hooper, "Spain's pride turns to shame," *Guardian* (UK), 8 March 1993.

26. Oral interview with Dennis Skiotis, historian of modern Greece, Harvard University, summer 1991.

13

JOHN TRUMPBOUR

the authoritarianism of the Colonels and the regime in Turkey. There is
a widespread sense of gratitude to the Socialists in the domain of civil liberties, despite occasional abuses which in Spain today include continued
police torture of Gypsies and suspected supporters of the ETA, stepped-
up crackdowns on Arab immigrants, and now González's move to clamp
restrictions on the right to strike, the last one ironic because as a young
lawyer he fought to wrest this privilege from the Francoist apparatchiks.
Third and finally, the Socialist parties have associated themselves with
modernization and all that seems positive in this word. Mitterrand of
France with the slogan of "changer la vie" and pursuit of colossal projects of hyper-modernity (the TGV, the Louvre pyramid, the Tolbiac
library, La Defense) is the pacesetter in this regard, but the Spanish, Portuguese, and Greek socialists have all combined the slogan of change
("cambio" and "allaghi") with ambitious state plans for modernized
infrastructure. This is where they break from Thatcher, who relied more
on private capital than the state for such enterprises. In the United States,
Clinton in his triumph over the Republicans similarly unified the slogan
of "change" with emphasis on infrastructure, muting the stress on social
justice and welfare that alienates middle class publics safely bunkered in
suburbia and hostile to what might loosely be called a politics of compas-
sion. Despite Clinton's and the Socialists' vast discharge of rhetorical
vapor on the need to improve public transit, the infusion of infrastructural spending favors the automobile complex, as González, for instance,
spends almost five times more on highways over rail.[27] Many regions still
experience grindingly atrocious, nineteenth-century rail service. That,
however, is not what is noticed in the mediatized society of the spectacle
mastered so brilliantly by the Socialists.

As rickety, dilapidated buildings are bulldozed away in favor of a
Marks and Spencer in Lisbon, as potholed goat trails give way to modernized thoroughfares in Salonika, as 21st-century bullet trains link
Madrid with González's hometown of Seville and tracks blocking access
to the coast in Barcelona are placed underground and reveal six new
shimmering beaches, those who speak out against the pollution, the congestion, and the overdevelopment in the worst of these projects are
scorned as neo-Puritans holding Southern Europe back from its appointed destiny of attaining relative equality with the wealthier nations of the
European Community.[28] "In Spain," writes the *Economist* (25 April

27. "Spain: Mitteleuropa on the Med" (A Survey), *Economist*, 25 April 1992, p. 8.
28. Opponents of the Seville bullet train often use the Socialists' own Euro-rhetoric in
denouncing the project. Rather than link Spain with France, they say, it allegedly leads
Spain backward to the south. Spanish television also found it worthy of mild ridicule: in
the early days of the TGV, they enjoyed showing clips of empty passenger cars. A more
sinister charge emerged in early 1993 when, as John Hooper reports, "the German multi-

14

1992), "'the right' is associated with the fascist past, 'the left' with progress." Among the left constituency in Southern Europe, there may be a certain parallel with the findings of Peter Winn in his classic study of the Chilean working class, *Weavers of Revolution* (1986). Winn argued that compared to their parents' generation the younger working class generation exhibited both (1) a greater political militancy, due to new forms of community and their formation in the midst of sixties protest movements and new left intellectual currents, and (2) a greater attraction to consumer affluence partly as a result of exposure to the new media and music culture. Whereas the movements associated with the Unidad Popular of Allende had channeled these new energies and aspirations toward the first, the struggle for social justice, the converse occurred in Southern Europe, where the Socialists decided to put the stress on the second: the new materialism and consumerism. They saw themselves appealing to those Jean-Luc Godard had christened "the children of Marx and Coca-Cola." As a favorite chant of libertarian-left activists in Italy during the 1970s would have it, in an inversion of the Leninist slogan ". . . all power to the soviets": "Free radios are a provocation – all power to the television!" (*"Le radio libere sono provocazione – tutto il potere alla televisione."*)[29]

The golden age of the Latin and Hellenic Socialist parties is over: Mitterrand, ailing and aging, suffered one of the most resounding political defeats in modern French history during the parliamentary elections of 1993; Soares, the president of Portugal, has cohabited with the dominant center-right Social Democrats whose leader Cavaco Silva holds the post of prime minister; and Craxi of Italy, González of Spain, and Papandreou of Greece all carry pockmarks from a politics of *pistonnage* well-greased by graft and payola. There are, however, two potentially contradictory forces that may allow for at least partial survival of Socialist power: (1) the politics of integration and (2) voter realignment from regionalist and separatist movements.[30] It is apparent that the recent history of the world's advanced industrial nations has been one of domination by con-

national Siemens [had] handed over several million pounds to three firms run by former officials in the Socialist party and government. The payments were for services in connection with Spain's first high-speed train link . . . Siemens, which headed a consortium awarded a 440 million pound contract, said the payments were for 'technical and commercial advice.'" A High Court judge has discovered a network of PSOE-linked firms with what Hooper describes as "skeleton staffs" who from the end of 1989 to the end of 1990 billed Spain's ten largest companies and banks 4.4 million pounds for consulting. When the judge asked to see the studies said to cost as much as 500,000 pounds, the firms claimed the reports had been (conveniently) misplaced or destroyed. *Guardian* (UK) 8 March 1993.

29. Lumley, p. 303.

30. Incidentally, many of the regionalist and separatist movements do not regard integration and regional autonomy as contradictory. The Italian Leagues employ the slogan: "Away from Rome, closer to Europe." Carlo Ruzza and Oliver Schmidtke, "The Making of the Lombard League," *Telos*, 90, Winter 1991–92, p. 69.

servative parties, at least at the presidential or prime ministerial level: Japan, Germany, Great Britain, the U.S., and Italy. Spain may represent a successful break from this pattern. This development has been reinforced by integration and regionalism: first, at the level of integration, the Socialists have proven adept at gaining EC resources for the so-called poor four (Spain, Ireland, Greece, and Portugal), which has been further facilitated by the Socialist leadership of the EC in the person of Jacques Delors. Until recent charges of corruption squelched enthusiasm for his candidacy, Felipe González was himself long rumored to be the frontrunner to succeed Delors at the EC helm. Now there remain considerable obstacles to future EC benificence toward the South, the new German insularity and Spain's own advancing wealth. Of the last, some economists believe that if Spain's substantial underground economy were to undergo proper calculation, the nation would have surpassed the 90 percent of per capita EC GNP used as an aid threshhold as well as the standard of living in the United Kingdom. These gains face erosion in the current recession, with job lay-offs and galloping inflation bringing new threats of a major labor offensive against the EC's single market: witness the general strike of 28 May 1992 in Spain that shut hundreds of factories, and the rallies and near riots of 2 October 1992 in Rome against the austerity package of Italy's Socialist Prime Minister Giuliano Amato.

Still there remains a sense in Spain and elsewhere among middle-class publics that the Socialist technocrats can best deliver the goods from their Eurocrat counterparts in Brussels. It is such considerations that provoke Denis MacShane's observation that the "Spanish Socialists are the most Eurofanatic of the Continental left."[31] In Greece, with the largest proportion of self-employed petty bourgeoisie in the EC, there are outbreaks of anti-Brussels protests based on the efforts to terminate state

31. Denis MacShane, "The Pain in Spain," *New Statesman and Society*, 1 May 1992. Attitudes among different middle classes within EC nations have many variations. In Italy and Spain, EC integration is sometimes hailed for imposing austerity on what are seen as irresponsible and spendthrift governments, and in Greece there is the occasional joke that after 400 years of Ottoman rule from Constantinople, it may be time to submit to Brussels. Contrary to the view that the EC fosters austerity, others believe that Papandreou did not feel uncomfortable with huge deficits because he ultimately thought that the EC could bail his government out of a crisis. In the meantime, the petty bourgeoisie of Greece continues to exhibit opposition to the EC, as political scientist Nikiforos Diamandouros remarks: "The self-employed small timers - and there is a greater percentage of them than anywhere else in the EC - are deeply opposed to further integration in Europe. . . . They see the opening of borders as a threat to the country's national identity and are fearful of its consequences, because it will necessitate a clampdown on excessive state protectionism." Diamandouros, quoted by Helena Smith, "Crossroads of East and West," *Guardian* (UK), 26 November 1990.

subsidies and fear of German multinational corporations overwhelming small fry enterprises (over 85 percent of all manufacturing enterprises in Greece had less than ten employees in 1984).[32] Even here, however, fear of Turkey recuperates substantial support for a politics of European integration.

Second, regionalist and separatist movements at times may leave the Socialists as their greatest beneficiary. Simply stated, the regionalist movements have tended to divert votes from the national conservative parties, thus damaging prospects for a right resurrection. To resume again with Spain, the conservative People's Party runs close to the Socialists in most regions of Spain, but its popularity drops off dramatically to single figures in Catalonia and the Basque country where normally right-leaning voters pull the lever for Jordi Pujol's Catalan nationalists and Xabier Arzallus's Basque Nationalists. The millions of votes siphoned from the conservative forces allow for continued Socialist triumphs. Contrary to some theories that suggest ethnic separatism is based on internal colonization and economic deprivation, Catalonia and the Basque country are generally wealthier than most of Spain and, in ordinary circumstances, would not appear to be a natural constituency for "left of center" parties. The Spanish right's association with Franco's assaults against regional identity is a legacy that will continue to harm conservative prospects for recapturing control of the Spanish Cortes. In Italy, the two pillars of postwar order have been the ruling Christian Democrats and the opposition Communist Party. With the rise of the Leagues, which employ such slogans of slashing self-ridicule as "Pay, you Lombard jackass" to object to the Christian Democrat tradition of draining resources from the North to the underdeveloped South, this may wreak havoc with the traditional DC plurality in parliament. Unlike Spain, however, the Socialists squandered whatever opportunity they had to overtake the DC as the main governing party. Gianfranco Miglio, the grand theoretician of the *Lega Nord*, observes that the Leagues possess the same social base as the DC: "workers, artisans, businessmen, small and medium entrepreneurs, professionals, teachers, intellectuals, and many young people," who are "breaking with the Catholic party as a result of growing secularization." As it declines in the North, the DC, he predicted in 1991, "will consolidate its role as the leading party in Central and Southern Italy. . . . The Socialists, who continue to receive support in all Italian provinces, could become the typical federal party, i.e., a party which, because of its ideological orientation, takes responsibility for safeguarding solidarity between the various Italies." The latter has not

---

32. Data from Rinn S. Shinn, ed., *Greece: A Country Study* (Washington, 1986), p. 180.

been borne out by subsequent developments: the Socialists have fallen into even greater disgrace than the heavily tarnished DC in the ongoing corruption scandal. Moreover, the PCI's transformation into the PDS, a kind of hybrid social democratic party, has allowed them to hold on to voters who in the rest of Southern Europe would probably have drifted toward the Socialist parties. Italy's divergent pattern owes much to the long entrenched social democratization of its main communist party: in Greece, Portugal, and Spain, the Communist parties have kept more of their Stalinized structures intact. In some sense, therefore, Miglio's conclusion about the trajectory of the left parties in Italy has been almost vindicated (despite his failure to forecast the impending implosion of the PSI): "It is highly unlikely that the supporters of the former Communist Party and other smaller parties, which also draw support from all parts of the country, could do anything other than complement the Socialist Party."[33] It could take years before the latest and greatest of quagmires in postwar Italian politics leads toward resolution.[34]

Already the global recession and renewed despair about the region's political class has plunged Southern Europe into an age of uncertainty. The triumphalist, celebratory literature about the achievements of progress in Southern Europe has given way to renewed cadences of Europessimism and songs of retreat.

Southern Europe continues to live in the shadow of two pervasive images. The first is cast from the distant past: the legacies of antiquity and the Renaissance, epochs said to resound with triumph and glory. Samuel Johnson claimed that "Almost all our religion, almost all our law, almost all the arts, almost all that sets us above savages, has come to us from the Mediterranean."[35] Italian civic humanism from Bruni to Machiavelli regarded classical antiquity as the lodestar to national regeneration, while in Portugal its literary vanguard, Camões (1525–1580), Vieira

33. Gianfranco Miglio, "Towards a Federal Italy," *Telos*, 90, Winter 1991–92, p. 22. Milan's continued investigation into the alleged corruption of Bettino Craxi and the abysmal Socialist performance in the Italian elections of 13 and 14 December 1992 involving 55 communes and approximately 1 million voters indicates a much more rocky future for the PSI than anticipated by Miglio. Compared to the April 1992 general elections, the Socialists lost 3.6 percent of their support, the Christian Democrats, 4.8 percent, while the ex-Communist Democratic Party of the Left slid only 1.9 percent. Meanwhile, the Northern League posted a 3.4 percent leap, along with gains for the anti-Mafia Network (+2.7 percent) and the neo-fascist Italian Social Movement (+1.7 percent). "A plague on the parties," *Economist*, 19–25 December 1992.

34. For a pessimistic view of the reform referendum of April 1993, see Tobias Abse, "The Triumph of the Leopard," *New Left Review*, 199, May/June 1993.

35. Samuel Johnson quoted by James Boswell in George Birkbeck Hill, ed., *Boswell's Life of Johnson* (vol. III, Life 1776-1780), (New York, 1921 reprint ed.), p. 42.

(1608–1697), Garrett (1799–1854), Eça de Queiroz (1845–1900), and Pessoa (1888–1935), instead rejoiced in the fifteenth century as the pinnacle of human achievement. As the Jesuit Vieira proclaimed in his *História do Futuro*: "In those happy times . . . nothing was read of in the World except the navigations and conquests of Portuguese. That history was the silence of all [other] histories. Enemies read in it their ruin, rivals their envy and only Portugal its glory."[36]

Nevertheless, there is another image of Southern Europe that lingers from the more recent past. That is, the view of Southern Europe as a region mired in banditry, backwardness, and barbarity. Northern Europeans look upon modern Southern Europeans with disappointment for somehow not resembling the classical philosopher-kings or Periclean and Ciceronian statesmen so celebrated in the public schools and Gymnasium. The great Russian poet Pushkin called the modern Greeks "the legal heir of Homer and Themistocles"; but when he finally got around to meeting members of the Greek merchant class he declared their land "a nasty people of bandits and shopkeepers." Churchill labeled the ELAS forces "miserable Greek banditti" and "the most treacherous filthy beasts." A British officer during World War II judged the Italians a "people who live in squalor and have made a mess of their country, their administration and their lives."[37] In the postwar period, the most acutely felt episode of derision likely surrounds Lyndon Johnson's rebuke of Greek ambassador Alexander Matsas:

> America is an elephant, Cyprus is a flea. Greece is a flea. If these two fellows continue itching the elephant, they may just get whacked by the elephant's trunk, whacked good. . . .[38]

In response to this longstanding humiliation, Southern Europe has picked up the gauntlet of progress, part of a dash toward Europe so urgent that its leaders seem ready to forsake past loyalties and solidarities. Despite itself spending nearly 1.5 billion ECU on development and humanitarian aid to Latin America from 1976-1989, the European Community has called on Spain and Portugal to terminate their special

36. Vieira quoted by Ronald W. Sousa, *The Rediscoverers: Major Writers in the Portuguese Literature of National Regeneration* (University Park and London, 1981), p. 74. In particular, Camoes's *Os Lusíadas*, the national epic of Portugal, was a standard text in the school curriculum, especially under Salazar.

37. Pushkin and Churchill quoted by Clogg, pp. 55 and 149. British officer quoted by Paul Ginsborg, *A History of Contemporary Italy: Society and Politics, 1943-1988* (London, 1990), p. 1.

38. LBJ quoted by Christopher Hitchens, *Cyprus* (London, 1984), p. 61. His speech began with a few choice expletives about the Greek parliament and Constitution. He added for good measure, "Don't forget to tell old Papa-what's-his name what I told you — you hear?," a reference to then Greek Prime Minister George Papandreou.

relationships and immigration privileges for Latin America.[39] Some of the new policy is designed to placate the least savory political elements, notably the leader of France's Front National Jean-Marie Le Pen, who in wilder moments of oratory alleges that Paris's main refuge for prostitution, the Bois de Boulogne, is filled with Brazilians because of Portugal's laxity in enforcing immigration restrictions.[40]

It is the politics of race and European identity that have reared what appears to be an increasingly ugly head. Snarling barbarism redolent of the interwar years is once again ascendant. For the discontents of modernity, the idea of progress carries a very different meaning from that of the sober technocrats of the EC, and for many Europeans, northern and southern, this means the resumption of the cold war in the longer and original definition of the term. In the fourteenth century, the Spaniard Don Juan Manuel coined the couplet "cold war" to refer to the permanent struggle against the Arab.[41] As Southern Europe now stands at the front line of the continent's boundaries, the pressure mounts to expel the rising Arab and Third World presence in the Iberian peninsula and beyond. Such developments starve and imperil further growth of a democratic politics in Western Europe.

Creeping repression, wedded to an economics of Thatcherism, is not likely to augur well for the future. Petras's essays give jarring testimony to the political decay and depredations of the market in Southern Europe

39. For data on EC aid to Latin America, see the EC booklet *The European Community and Latin America* (Brussels, 1991). This does not include the substantial European contributions to Catholic programs in Latin America; see "Trente ans en Amérique latine: Rapport de l'Aide à l'Eglise en Détresse 1962-1992," *Aide à l'Eglise en Détresse Bulletin* (Belgium), no. 6, September 1992.

40. In Spain, the recent murder of Lucrecia Perez, a black woman from the Dominican Republic, has called attention to the rise in hate crimes against Third World peoples. "Un guardia civil y jóvenes nazis, acusados de dos crímenes racistas: ocho detenidos por los asesinatos de inmigrantes en Madrid," *El País* (edicion internacional/weekly), 30 November, 1992. In the same edition, see their special feature "La crisis de los refugiados: La invasión que hace temblar a Europa." King Juan Carlos in his annual *mensaje de Nochebuena* has condemned the rise of xenophobic violence. See "El Rey llama a la solidaridad y condena 'los malos vientos de xenofobia' que soplan en Europa," *El País* (edicion internacional/weekly), 28 December 1992.

Italy, which sent 26 million Italians abroad between 1861 and 1973 (with less than 25 percent permanently returning), became a net importer of labor in the 1970s for the first time in the modern epoch. Labor from the Philippines, Egypt, and the Horn of Africa have emerged as targets of anti-immigrant ideologues. For data on immigration and emigration flows, see Sassoon, p. 98.

41. For discussions of the origin of the term cold war, see Fred Halliday, *The Making of the Second Cold War* (London, 1986), p. 5, and his article, "Spanish customs," *New Statesman and Society*, 15 February 1991. For the latest on repression of Arabs, including the practices of "a beefed-up Spanish Customs Service that is now being advised by the U.S. Border Patrol," John Ross, "Quincentennial Deja-Vu - Spain Expels Arabs All Over Again," *Z Magazine*, October 1992.

well underway in the 1980s. The ongoing investigation of corruption in Italy has disgraced the political class and led to calls for wholesale privatization, often by "reformist" Socialists who propose a fire sale of national assets in desperate hopes of retaining power. And yet, Diarmuid Maguire's guarded but positive balance sheet on the postwar achievements of Italian democracy and James Kurth's conclusion may suggest other possibilities. In Eastern and Central Europe, economic advisors hail Anglo-American traditions of laissez-faire and free markets as the only alternative to the torpor of decades of state socialist management and misrule. However, in the face of negative growth rates and explosive levels of unemployment, the beleaguered denizens of the regions are beginning to echo that query of a backbench Tory MP during the first Thatcher recession: "We were supposed to see the economy rise like the phoenix from the ashes. Well, we've got the ashes all right. Now where's the bloody phoenix?"[42] They are therefore increasingly open to other visions of political economy. For instance, Italy's earlier postwar success, craftily mixing state supported enterprise with a measure of protectionism, has attracted followers in Hungary who admire its prospects for the revival of the region's frozen economies.[43] In such an event, Southern Europe might no longer be thought of as a backward zone that simply follows the lead of the wealthy north. For in spite of rampant clientelism, and the persistence of Lombard opulence and squalor in the Mezzogiorno, the Italian model may yet undergo resurrection. Among its partisans, the postwar economic miracle repudiates Anglo-American orthodoxies about the market as the sole arbiter of progress and, in that extraordinary phrase of Francis Fukuyama, as the end of history.[44]

42. Quoted by Simon Hoggart in *Observer Sunday*, 16 February 1992.

43. For a critical look at the Italian model and Hungary, see Erik Izraelewicz, "La Hongrie, un 'capitalisme du goulasch,'" *Le Monde*, 28 July 1992. "Hungary looks instead for its model in Europe," writes *Le Monde*, "between Italy and Austria." Sarolta Bartucz, who advises the government on enterprises in the public sector, discusses a holding company that could orchestrate state planning and investment, what she calls "a type of Italian IRI [Istituto per La Recostruzione Industriale]." Opponents on the right worry that it will create "a vast industrial public sector that is non-competitive," observes *Le Monde*; the left fears that the Italian model may prove compatible with a Hungarian Mezzogiorno: there exist massive inequalities between the relatively well off Budapest and Transdanubian regions on the one hand and the impoverished southeast and northeast on the other. For a critique of the common view that Eastern Europe is undergoing a transition to capitalism, see Simon Clarke, "Privatization and the Development of Capitalism in Russia," *New Left Review*, 196, November/December, 1992. As for the recent lacklustre performance of the IRI, see Robert Graham and Haig Simonian, "A Behemoth goes to the block," *Financial Times*, 15 June 1993.

44. In fairness to Fukuyama, he argues that the so-called mixed economies of Scandinavia fit within his model of nations that have achieved the end of history. It is the more extreme champions of anti-communism and the virtues of free markets who have claimed the end of history for undiluted neoliberalism.

Concerning the Italian model, a combination of a patrimonial state with a mixed market capitalist economy, there is skepticism that a similar "miracle" of the 1950s and 1960s could be repeated in the late capitalist 1990s. The relatively closed economies of the 1950s stand in sharp contrast to the transnational enterprise and extraordinary mobility of capital that characterize the capitalist social order of the 1990s. Capital today is better equipped to flee and elude a political and economic order willing to grant patrimonial coatings of protection to domestic industries and labor.

Still it should not be forgotten that Italy's industrial and political leadership in the aftermath of WWII, though often quite cooperative with U.S. policymakers, created nationalized corporations such as petroleum maverick ENI (Ente Nazionale Idrocarburi – 1953) in the face of active howls of protest from Standard Oil, the State Department, and the U.S. media elite. Secretary of State John Foster Dulles warned Italy's President Giovanni Gronchi, a representative of the "social" wing of the DC, that the U.S. did not grant foreign aid to allow nationalized enterprises to compete with the U.S. oil giants. The leader of ENI, Enrico Mattei, had previously reminded Italians that discovering petroleum at Caviaga in 1946 and later at Cortemaggiore "were the first rays of hope in the otherwise bleak panorama of the Italian economy. For the first time in its history, our country has found that it is not condemned to poverty, as has been predicted for many years." As ENI spread its operations from Italy to Morocco to Libya, C.L. Sulzberger of the *New York Times* scorned Mattei as a "condotierre," a mercenary in the pay of powerful princes. See Harvey O'Connor, *World Crisis in Oil* (New York, 1962), pp. 392–395, Paul Frankel, *Mattei, Oil and Power Politics* (New York, 1966), and Daniel Yergin, *The Prize* (New York, 1991), the last which treats the mysterious plane crash that killed Mattei in late 1962. The post-Mattei ENI probably did not fulfill its early promise as politicians, most notoriously Craxi, later converted it into a milk cow for themselves and their political allies. By the mid-1970s, Italy's three largest corporations in volume of production had the state as owner or part-owner: the industrial group IRI, followed by ENI, and then chemical group Montedison. Sassoon, p. 140. For a critical analysis of ENI and IRI, see Harvey B. Feigenbaum, *The Politics of Public Enterprise: Oil and the French State* (Princeton, 1985), Chapter 5 which is titled "Public Enterprise in Comparative Perspective."

For perspective on the magnitude of Lombard opulence and poverty in the Mezzogiorno, see Sassoon, p. 214. He publishes data from the *Financial Times* (13 July 1981) on inequality throughout the Italian peninsula. If 100 is the median for per capita GNP for Italy as a whole, Valle d'Aosta (157) and Lombardy (133.2) rank one and two respectively out of twenty regions, while Campania (64.8) and Calabria (53.1) stand at the bottom. According to data for 1990, the *Economist* (26 June 1993) reports little change in these grim figures, although Lombardy has overtaken Valle d'Aosta as national leader in per capita GNP.

APPENDIX A: A NOTE ON POLITICS AND THE COMPOSITION OF SOUTHERN EUROPEAN SOCIAL STRUCTURE

Charting the components of the social structure of these four nations is sometimes rendered difficult by the dearth of detailed sociological data available elsewhere, as Martin Blinkhorn points out in his essay, "The Iberian States," in Detlef Mühlberger, *The Social Basis of European Fascist Movements* (London, 1987). Nevertheless, the work of P. Sylos Labini, *Saggio sulle classi sociali* (1974) on interwar Italy demonstrates how its major social groupings diverged substantially from northern European countries such as Great Britain and Germany:

THE MAJOR SOCIAL GROUPINGS IN ITALY, 1921–36 (BY PERCENTAGE)

	1921	1936
Haute bourgeoisie (upper class)	1.7	1.6
Subtotal	1.7	1.6
White-collar petty bourgeoisie	3.2	5.0
Independent rural petty bourgeoisie	37.0	35.6
Independent urban petty bourgeoisie	10.3	11.5
Other petty-bourgeois elements	2.8	2.7
Subtotal	53.3	54.8
Wage-earning agricultural workers	21.8	16.2
Wage-earning industrial workers	19.6	21.4
Others	3.6	6.0
Subtotal	45.0	43.6
TOTAL (percentage)	100	100

P. Sylos Labini table reproduced in Mühlberger, p. 7.

As for Greece, its social immobility is most starkly indicated by data comparing nearly six decades from 1861–1920. The sectoral distribution of the population remained nearly frozen.

COMPOSITION OF ECONOMCALLY ACTIVE POPULATION
(PERCENTAGES)

	1861	1920
Agriculture	74.0	70.0
Industry and Handicrafts	10.0	13.1
Commerce and Transport	6.1	9.2
Public Administration	4.4	2.0
Professional and Other	5.5	4.8

SOURCE: A.F. Freris, *The Greek Economy in the Twentieth Century* (London, 1986), p. 36.

Marco Revelli, in his chapter on Italy in the Mühlberger volume cited above, points out that Germany and Great Britain had a vast decline in workers from the traditional middle classes including both urban and rural petty bourgeoisie, elements replaced by "a new class of white-collar workers integrated into the technological structure of modern companies." Comparing Thomas Geiger's data on Weimar Germany where the traditional middle class stood at 34 percent of the population to those of Italy, with a figure exceeding 53 percent, Revelli notes that these "obsolete" elements of the Italian middle class had a very substantial rural component. "If to this we add the fact that the bulk of the proletariat was made up of wage-earning agricultural workers (21.8 percent as compared with 19.6 percent of wage-earning industrial workers)," he concludes, "we gain some idea of the enormous pockets of social immobility and resistance to change which existed in Italy, an expression of economic practices and life-styles which were in many respects antagonistic to the basic demands for rationalisation exerted by the new industrial processes and bound to react radically to the threats being posed to the social status quo." Whether rural and urban petty bourgeois resistance to rationalization is the locomotive of political reaction remains a subject of controversy; see Richard Hamilton, *Who Voted for Hitler?* (Princeton, 1982). Hans Speier in *German White-Collar Workers and the Rise of Hitler* (New Haven, 1986) indicates that the supposedly progressive new middle class was in reality a significant source of German political reaction, as the vast majority embraced ferocious anti-Semitism, strident nationalism, strong opposition to trade unions, and general contempt for blue collar workers and Weimar democracy. For Latin America, James Petras in his *Politics and Social Structure in Latin America* (New York, 1970), particularly part I, attacks U.S. social science and State Department planners for their faith in the new middle class as the vanguard of social progress. For an incisive critique of the common association of the rural with reaction, see Raymond Williams, *The Country and the City* (New York, 1973).

As for postwar Italy, Donald Sassoon in *Contemporary Italy* (New York, 1986) discusses the debates over P. Sylos Labini's data and traces the transformation to a more postmodern social structure in the present. Three scholarly interventions on the subject of Italian social structure include the following: Antonio Chiesi, "Alcune note sulla distribuzione dei redditi e la struttura di classe in Italia nel periodo postbellico," *Quaderni di Sociologia*, vol. 24, no. 3, 1975, Carlo Trigilia, "Sviluppo, sottosviluppo e classi sociali in italia," *Rassegna Italiana di Sociologia*, vol. 17, no. 2, 1976, and Paolo Ammassari, *Classi e ceti nella società italiana* (Turin, 1977). The last work decries the absence prior to 1968 of serious sociological inquiry into Italian social structure.

Turning to the Iberian peninsula in the interwar years, Blinkhorn suggests that the right-authoritarian politics of Spain and Portugal did not take the radical fascist turn of Italy for several reasons: (1) weaker pressures from industrialization; (2) the absence of dislocation and political upheaval from World War I because of Iberian non-participation in the conflict; (3) regional hostility to Spanish nationalism in Catalonia, the Basque country, and Valencia that channeled much urban petty bourgeois support toward anti-centralist, pro-democratic movements and parties (i.e, left-wing Catalanismo, the Basque Nationalist Party, and the Autonomous Republican Party dominant in Valencia); and (4) right social Catholicism in small-town Castile, Leon, and Aragon that remained suspicious of anti-Church radicals in the fascist Falange. As Blinkhorn concludes, "The effective conquest of Spanish society's middling layers by, variously, demo-republicanism, regional nationalism and social Catholicism made unlikely the appearance of an autonomous fascist movement during the early 1920s, and was to create serious problems for those that did eventually emerge in the 1930s." (p. 325) Raymond Carr and Juan Pablo Fusi in *Spain: From Dictatorship to Democracy* (London, 1981) show how Franco had to exercise a sometimes delicate balancing act among the different "families" supportive of his regime: (the institutional families) the Falange, the Church, the army, as well as (the political families) the integral Francoists, the monarchists, the technocrats and the professionals.

Blinkhorn's portrayal of a social base, riddled with ideological fissures and regional loyalties, can be regarded as a premonition of why the

Spanish state seemed less destined to evolve into a totalitarianism on the scale of Mussolini's fascist order.

For more on Portugal, consult Blinkhorn, and for Greece, see the individual works of Mouzelis, Freris, Clogg, and Stavrianos cited above.

2 A TALE OF FOUR COUNTRIES: PARALLEL POLITICS IN SOUTHERN EUROPE, 1815–1990

James Kurth

"Europe stops at the Pyrenees," said Talleyrand. That Italy is only "a promontory which links Europe to Africa" was a familiar observation of his contemporaries. And Greece, added Metternich, lies "beyond the pale of civilization." To the statesmen of the early nineteenth century, the politics of the countries of Southern Europe were somehow different than the politics of the countries to the north.

So it seems even now, a century and three-quarters later. It was only in the last generation that Portugal, Spain, and Greece established democratic regimes, and today they, with Italy, still maintain the least legitimate political systems and the least equitable social structures within the European Community. And in the intervening 175 years there have been many political phenomena which have shown that politics in Southern, or Mediterranean, Europe has moved on a different path and at a different pace than politics in Central and Northern Europe. Examples are the military coups and civil wars in nineteenth-century Spain and Portugal, the foreign rule and wars of independence in nineteenth-century Italy and Greece, the strength of the anarchist movement in Spain and Italy at the turn of the century, the early acceptance of authoritarian regimes in the 1920s, the Spanish and Greek civil wars in the 1930s and 1940s, the persistence of authoritarian regimes in Portugal, Spain, and Greece until the mid-1970s, and the peculiarities of the socialist governments in these same countries in the 1980s. Indeed, some of these phenomena, such as military coups and authoritarian regimes, demonstrate that politics in Southern Europe has had more in common with politics in more distant regions of the world, especially Latin America.[1]

---

1. Politics in Southern Europe has also had much in common with politics in Eastern Europe between the two world wars, particularly with politics in Poland, Hungary, Romania, Bulgaria, and Yugoslavia. Greece can be seen as the country that links the southern and eastern peripheries of Europe. This is discussed in greater detail in the last chapter of the present volume.

This chapter is an effort to examine and explain the distinctive features of the politics of four countries in Southern Europe: Portugal, Spain, Italy, and Greece. The first section will be a brief comparative survey of the political development of these countries during the 175 years since the end of the Napoleonic Wars. The emphasis will be on the two larger states, Spain and Italy, with comparative references to the two smaller ones, Portugal and Greece.

The next two sections will bring to bear two analytical models that have often been used to explain the politics of one or more Southern European countries. One model is that of patrimonial authority, derived from the work of Max Weber and Richard Morse, as well as the related concept of patron-client politics.[2] The second model is that of delayed development, derived from the work of Alexander Gerschenkron and Albert Hirschman, and the related concept of dependent development.[3] The application of the concepts of delayed development and dependent development to the politics of Southern Europe has been less explicit than that of patrimonial authority and patron-client politics. However, for much of the last 175 years, Southern Europe has been in the twilight zone of semidevelopment, seen by observers either as the least developed of the advanced economies or as the most advanced of the underdeveloped economies.

I. THE POLITICAL DEVELOPMENT OF SOUTHERN EUROPE

There have been many periods in which the countries of Southern Europe have shared a common history, of which the Roman Empire is only the most obvious example. More recently, in the seventeenth century Spain, Portugal, and much of Italy were ruled together by the Spanish Habsburgs. However, the conventional milestone marking the beginning of the modern era in Southern Europe is the Napoleonic Wars, which brought new invasions, new institutions, and new ideas to each of these old lands. Although the defeat of Napoleon brought about

2. Max Weber, *The Theory of Social and Economic Organization*, ed. Talcott Parsons (New York, 1964), especially pp. 341–58 (on Weber, see also Reinhard Bendix, *Max Weber: An Intellectual Portrait* (Garden City, N.Y., 1962), especially pp. 329–84); Richard M. Morse, "The Heritage of Latin America," in *The Founding of New Societies*, ed. Louis Hartz (New York, 1964), pp. 123–77; Sidney G. Tarrow, *Peasant Communism in Southern Italy* (New Haven, Conn., 1967); Keith R. Legg, *Politics in Modern Greece* (Stanford, Calif., 1969).

3. Alexander Gerschenkron, *Economic Backwardness in Historical Perspective* (Cambridge, Mass., 1962); Albert O. Hirschman, *A Bias for Hope: Essays on Development and Latin America* (New Haven, Conn., 1971), especially pp. 91–114; Fernando Henrique Cardoso and Enzo Faletto, *Dependency and Development in Latin America* (Berkeley, Calif., 1978); Peter F. Klarén and Thomas J. Bossert, eds., *Promise of Development: Theories of Change in Latin America* (Boulder, Colo., 1986), part 2.

a temporary restoration of the old regimes, by 1820 all four countries were in revolt. In the ensuing 170 years, Portugal, Spain, Italy, and Greece have undergone processes of political development that have been similar to each other in many ways.

It is possible to discern six broad phases of development in each country. The periods of maximum convergence among the four states were from the 1870s to the 1930s, a period which included three phases of political development, and the 1980s, the period of the most recent phase. There was also much in common among the four countries in both the initial phase lasting roughly from the 1810s to the 1870s and the phase lasting from the 1940s to the 1970s, but in these cases it is useful to distinguish two patterns, a western one emphasizing similarities between Spain and Portugal, and an eastern pattern emphasizing similarities between Italy and Greece.

Spain and Portugal (1820s–1870s): Pronunciamentos and Civil Wars

Spanish politics from 1820 to 1876 has been called both the era of pronunciamentos and the era of the Carlist Wars. The former refers to the numerous occasions when military officers, usually middle class and politically liberal, "pronounced" against the existing government in order either to overthrow it or to achieve some more particular demand. The first of the liberal pronunciamentos began in Cádiz in 1820; in later years, many were initiated in the commercial city of Barcelona. The counterpoint between governments in Madrid and pronunciamentos in Barcelona made much of Spanish politics in the nineteenth century "a tale of two cities."

The second form of political violence was the Carlist Wars. These were the three savage civil wars (1833–39, 1845–48, 1872–76) fought between liberal central regimes on one hand and regional and traditional forces on the other. The former fought in the name of one branch of the Spanish Bourbons, that of Isabella II and later Alfonso XII; the latter, the Carlists, fought in the name of another branch, that of a prince known as Don Carlos.[4] Called wars between "the Red and the Black," they were also "Wars of the Spanish Succession," fought over which branch should succeed to the throne. In each of these struggles, which they lost to the central government, the Carlists often resorted to the tactics of *guerrilleros*, or social bandits.[5]

4. On the Carlists and on the complicated dynastic question in Spain, see Stanley Payne, "Spain, " in *The European Right: A Historical Profile*, eds. Hans Rogger and Eugen Weber (Berkeley, Calif., 1965), pp. 168–207; and Gerald Brenan, *The Spanish Labyrinth: An Account of the Social and Political Background of the Civil War* (Cambridge, 1950), pp. 203–14.

5. On social bandits, see E. J. Hobsbawm, *Primitive Rebels: Studies in Archaic Forms of Social Movement in the 19th and 20th Centuries* (New York, 1965).

Portuguese politics from 1820 to about 1853 showed a similar pattern of military uprisings and civil wars. The 1820 revolution in Spain led to contacts between Spanish and Portuguese liberals and thence to a liberal military uprising in Porto that same year, the first of many military uprisings that were to begin in that commercial city against governments in Lisbon. Even more than Spanish politics, Portuguese politics in the nineteenth century was "a tale of two cities."

The Portuguese also had their counterpart to the Carlist Wars. One major civil war (1832–34, overlapping with the beginning of the First Carlist War) was fought between liberal and traditional forces. Similar to the Spanish pattern, the former fought in the name of one branch of the ruling Braganças, that of Maria II; the latter, the Miguelists, fought under the name of another branch, that of a prince known as Dom Miguel.[6] As in Spain, the liberals were the victors. A second civil war (1846–47, overlapping with the Second Carlist War in Spain) took the form of a conflict between a modernizing regime and a millenarian rebellion, the Maria da Fonte movement, which was eventually suppressed.

During this phase of Spanish and Portuguese political development, France and Britain intervened in several of the major political conflicts. The liberal revolution of 1820 in Spain was put down in 1823 by a French army, "the 100,000 sons of St. Louis," and the absolutist king, Ferdinand VII, was restored to his full powers. Conversely, a decade later, the liberal government ruling in the name of the child-queen Isabella II received substantial military aid from the British and the French during the First Carlist War. At about the same time, the British and French also gave substantial military aid to the liberals in Portugal against the Miguelists. During the Maria da Fonte rebellion, the British and the Spanish both undertook various military actions to aid the Portuguese government.

The two modes of political violence, military coups and civil wars, reflected the two main political forces in Spain and Portugal at that time. One force was the middle classes, more *clases medias* composed of officials than a bourgeoisie composed of entrepreneurs. An important form of middle-class political organization was the secret society, in particular the Masonic society, e.g., the *Grande Oriente* in Spain and the *Sinédrio* in Portugal. The secret societies included as members many military officers, some of whom had been indoctrinated as Masons by British or French military officers during the Peninsular War. Similar secret societies also existed in Italy (e.g., the *carbonari*). These societies played a

6. On the Miguelists and on the dynastic question in Portugal, see A. H. de Oliveira Marques, *History of Portugal*, vol. 2, *From Empire to Corporate State* (New York, 1972), pp. 55–64.

major role in organizing liberal military uprisings in Southern Europe in the early nineteenth century. In many ways, Freemasonry was the "international" of the revolutionary middle class in the post-Napoleonic period.

The middle-class reformers called themselves liberals. The name itself was Spanish in origin;[7] many of their ideas, however, were imported: constitutional monarchy from Britain, centralized administration from France, and the expropriation and redistribution of church and communal lands from both. In the Spanish and Portuguese context, such ideas also meant new offices and new lands for the middle class. The Spanish liberals took the occasion of the First Carlist War to confiscate and, between 1835 and 1837, auction the lands of the Catholic church off to the wealthy (and not to the small peasant), creating a new group of large landowners, and thereby reinforcing the old landed upper class. The Portuguese liberals took the occasion of the Miguelist defeat to do the same (1834).

The ideas and interests of the liberals put them in conflict with the second major political force, that of corporate orders and local communities intent on preserving their traditional rights, privileges, and immunities (*fueros*) against a centralizing, modernizing, and secularizing regime. In Spain, these traditional forces also included the rural areas of the northern, peripheral regions that retained their own fueros, i.e., the Basque lands, Navarre, Aragon, and Catalonia. Traditional forces organized themselves soon after the liberal revolutions of 1820, in Spain first as the *Apostólicos* and then as the Carlists, and in Portugal as the Miguelists.

The Carlists were splendid reactionaries, probably the most reactionary movement in Europe. They did not want to return to the modernizing monarchies of the French or Spanish Bourbons of the eighteenth century; they wanted rather to return to the monarchy of the Spanish Habsburgs of the seventeenth century or even before, ideally to the confederal monarchy of "Their Most Catholic Majesties," Ferdinand and Isabella. The Carlists were also splendidly consistent. As late as the 1870s, they destroyed trains and railroad stations as "accursed novelties," and as late as the early years of the twentieth century, they put forward as the first of their political demands the restoration of the Inquisition, "that most august tribunal, brought down by angels from heaven to earth."[8]

Defeat in war seems to have changed the character of the Carlists less than victory changed the character of the liberals. With the acquisition of

---

7. The first use of the term "Liberal" for a political group was in Spain in 1810, in the Constituent Cortes at Cádiz.

8. Brenan, *Spanish Labyrinth*, p. 205, 211.

the church lands by the liberal middle class in the 1830s and with the victory of the central regime in the First Carlist War, liberalism ceased to have much meaning or weight in Spanish politics. The 1840s saw the rise to power of two military strong men; the first was Baldomero Espartero, who had been the central government's victorious general in the war against the Carlists and who has been called "Spain's first military dictator."[9] He was followed by the more conservative Ramón Narváez, whose slogan was "use the stick and hit hard" and who founded the national rural police force, the Guardia Civil, in 1844, doubtless to secure the hold of the old liberals on their new lands.

In Portugal, the 1840s similarly witnessed the rise of two strong men, first António da Costa Cabral, then João Carlos Saldanha. After the Maria da Fonte rebellion, Portugal also entered a period of less meaningful party labels. In addition (and unlike in Spain), the military coups subsided after the mid-1850s. The political parties began to rotate in office with a certain symmetry, a pattern that came to be called "rotativism," which would last essentially until the end of the nineteenth century.

The last years of this phase of political development were more troubled in Spain. In the 1860s, Spain undertook a number of foreign adventures which turned into defeats or disasters (Santo Domingo, Mexico, and Peru). In 1868, a military coup overthrew the Bourbon monarchy of Isabella II, issuing in a chaotic period that was to last for seven years and saw the brief monarchy of an Italian prince, Amadeo (1870–73), the Third Carlist War (1873–76), and the First Republic (1873–74). Finally, yet another military pronunciamento brought about a Bourbon restoration in 1875 under a new monarch, Alfonso XII, and Spain, like Portugal, entered into a new and more peaceful political phase.

Italy and Greece (1820s–1870s): Liberation and Unification

The politics of Italy and Greece from the 1820s to the 1870s shares some features with that of Spain and Portugal, such as a number of military uprisings and popular insurrections. There is, however, a basic difference: the politics of Italy and Greece were dominated by the effort to achieve national unification (the Risorgimento in Italy, the Megali Idea or "Great Idea" in Greece), whereas the central governments of Spain and Portugal needed only to preserve it.

The Congress of Vienna left Italy divided into several states with restoration regimes under Austrian protection. Between 1820 and 1848 there were several popular revolutions in the various Italian states that were put down by Austrian intervention. These revolts came in waves; a

9. William C. Atkinson, *A History of Spain and Portugal* (Baltimore, 1960), p. 282.

revolution in one state would set off a similar rebellion in another (the Kingdom of the Two Sicilies and Piedmont in 1820, the Papal States and Piedmont in 1831–33, all of the Italian states in 1846–48).

It was with good reason that Austria, adhering to a domino theory, followed a policy of containment. During the Napoleonic Wars, many Italian military officers serving in Napoleon's armies had been initiated as Masons by their French comrades. With the end of the wars, these demobilized officers returned to Italy and immediately began to organize into secret societies with revolutionary purposes, such as the carbonari. In 1820, as in Portugal, a revolt by liberal military officers against the Bourbon monarchy in Spain provoked similar rebellions of liberal military officers in the Bourbon Kingdom of the Two Sicilies and in Piedmont. In each of the four revolutions, the would-be revolutionaries proclaimed as their constitution a variant of the liberal Spanish constitution of 1812. The revolutions in the Two Sicilies and Piedmont were put down by Austrian military intervention, just as the revolution in Spain was put down by the French.

This saw the end of the military uprisings by the carbonari, but in 1831–33 and again in 1846–48, there were popular insurrections in various Italian states. These insurrections coincide roughly in time with the First and Second Carlist Wars in Spain and with the Miguelist War and the Maria da Fonte rebellion in Portugal, but there does not appear to be any causal connection. Finally, through the political leadership and military conquests by Piedmont, the process of unification was largely accomplished from 1859 to 1870; the major annexation milestones were Lombardy in 1859, Tuscany, the Papal States (except Rome), and the Two Sicilies in 1860, Venetia in 1866, and Rome in 1870.

The Piedmontese conquest of the Papal States and the Kingdom of the Two Sicilies in 1860 brought about not only the unification of much of Italy but also political phenomena in many ways comparable to those in Spain and Portugal. With the conquest, the Piedmontese liberals confiscated church and communal lands, redistributed them to the wealthy and favored among the middle classes, and thereby reinforced an old class of landlords. And for half a decade after the conquest of Two Sicilies, the centralizing, modernizing, and secularizing Piedmontese regime was engaged in putting down "the Brigandage" in southern Italy, the movement of social bandits who fought in the name of the old Bourbon king and who are reminiscent of the Carlists in Spain and the Miguelists in Portugal.[10]

10. The Risorgimento is discussed by Arthur James Whyte, *The Evolution of Modern Italy* (New York, 1965). Social bandits in southern Italy are discussed by Hobsbawm, *Primitive Rebels*, pp. 13–56.

Just as Piedmont formed the political center around which the unification of Italy took place, so did Attica and the Peloponnesus form the political center for the unification of Greece. In 1827, with the assistance and protection of Russia, Britain, and France, these regions won their independence from the Turks. After six years, which began with a republic and ended in anarchy, the three protecting powers in 1833 established a monarchy with a Bavarian prince as King, Otto I. Otto imported Bavarians to serve as administrators and soldiers, and the major political factions were known as the "Russian" party, "English" party, and "French" party. In 1843, a revolt by Greek military officers forced the expulsion of the Bavarian troops and the establishment of a parliament; the revolt can be interpreted as primarily a guarantee of more patronage for the growing Greek middle classes. In 1862, another military revolt forced Otto's abdication, and the protecting powers appointed a Danish prince as King George I. He was to rule in relative domestic peace for almost fifty years, while Greek politics continued to be dominated by the Megali Idea or unification effort. The process of unification for Greece began later and lasted longer than in Italy; the major milestones were the annexation of the Ionian Islands in 1864, of Thessaly in 1881, of Crete, Macedonia, and Epirus in 1913, and of Thrace in 1919.

In summary, Italy and Greece in this phase of their political development experienced military coups, along with Spain and Portugal. Nevertheless, the amount of military intervention in politics was less in Piedmont, the core region of Italy, and in Greece than it was in the two countries of the Iberian peninsula. In Piedmont and in Greece, the monarchies played a more active and more dominant role in politics, in part because of accidents of royal personality, in part because of the primacy of foreign policy as long as the goal of national unification remained unfulfilled.[11]

Southern Europe (1870s–1910s): Trasformismo and Caciquismo

By the mid-1870s, each of the four countries of Southern Europe had entered into an era of relative political calm that was to last in its essentials almost until the eve of the First World War. The military coups, popular revolutions, and civil wars of the earlier phase were left behind, and political change took place within a system whose formal features were constitutional monarchy, parliamentary majorities, frequent elections, and civil liberties. The way the political systems actually worked, of course, was rather more complex.

11. On the role on the monarchy and patronage in Greek politics during the early years of independence, see John A. Petropulos, *Politics and Statecraft in the Kingdom of Greece, 1833–1843* (Princeton, 1968).

Italian politics from 1876 to 1914 has been called the era of *trasformis-mo*, a period in which strong and skillful premiers (Agostino Depretis, Francesco Crispi, and Giovanni Giolitti) and on occasion the king him-self "transformed" opposition deputies into government supporters, with the ample but subtle use of political patronage, government contracts, and personal rewards. The result was the obliteration of differences between the Right and the Left, the two parties which were the heir to the liberals of the Risorgimento, and the institutionalization of a political process devoid of political issues, an early case of "the end of ideology." A similar process characterized the politics of the three other countries.

In Spain, after the Restoration of 1875, the leaders of the Conserva-tive and Liberal parties, Antonio Cánovas del Castillo and Práxedes Sagasta respectively, reached an agreement on *el turno*, "whereby two political parties automatically rotated in power through the mechanism of contrived elections."[12] This agreement, which was sometimes referred to as "the Pact of the Pardo," was coupled with the practice of offering patronage and benefits to reasonable deputies from smaller, more radical, parties, which was known as "the policy of attraction." The result was similar to that of trasformismo in Italy.

In Portugal, as we have already seen, a similar process had begun in the 1850s. By the late 1870s, an arrangement between the Regeneration and Progressive parties was fairly well institutionalized and became known as "rotativism." In both Spain and Portugal, as in Italy, the king on occasion played the central role in the game. And in Greece, a simi-lar process also occurred, with the king having a somewhat greater role in the allocation of patronage and the creation of coalitions.

Trasformismo, then, was one major feature of Southern European politics during this phase. A related feature was caciquism. Caciques were local bosses and patrons in rural areas (the word was originally used in Latin America for the chiefs of Indian tribes). It was through these local bosses that the government "made the election," in a phrase com-mon to all four countries. The methods were often coercive, often imag-inative, in a way familiar to students of "stolen elections" in some regions of the United States. Caciquism was the natural outgrowth of the grafting of the British model of parliamentary elections and the French model of centralized administration onto the reality of rural life in Southern Europe. The British model, including the elected member of parliament, created the need to "make" elections; the French model, including the prefect, created the means with which to make them.

Caciquism was mainly a phenomenon of rural areas, however. Elec-

---

12. Joan Connelly Ullman, *The Tragic Week: A Study of Anticlericalism in Spain, 1875–1912* (Cambridge, Mass., 1968), p. 10.

tions in the cities were more difficult to control and more indicative of the real opinions of the electorate. This meant that eventually caciquism was to have a paradoxical impact on the biggest cacique of all, the king. Since the only real elections were those in the cities, they acquired inordinate importance, far beyond what they would have had there been real elections in both urban and rural areas. Thus it was that republican victories in municipal elections in Portugal in 1908 and 1910 and in Spain in 1931 could bring about the end of monarchies.

Although trasformismo and caciquism can and have existed independently, they have a powerful "elective affinity" for each other. The existence of the caciques (and the corresponding demobilization of the electorate) meant the existence of deputies who could be bought and that a government could therefore find many men in parliament with whom it could strike a deal; it also meant that the major electoral challenges to governments came from those areas in which caciques did not exist. Conversely, the existence of a trasformism parliament meant that the caciques had a number of access points to the central political process, which they might not have had in an authoritarian system or in a system of highly disciplined parties.

What were the conditions that brought about the trasformismo-caciquism systems of Southern Europe in the second half of the nineteenth century? First, the liberal program had been largely fulfilled, and the political class had become fairly homogeneous. In Spain, Italy, and Portugal, with the confiscation and redistribution of church and communal lands, there was a merging of the interests of the old landlords and the old *clases medias*, who were now new landlords. For different reasons, there was a similar merging of interests in Greece. Further, the new industrialists, a growing class in Spain, Italy, and, to a lesser extent, Portugal, were also brought into the existing systems, especially after the 1870s by national tariffs both on industrial products and on particular agricultural ones, a marriage of cloth and wheat comparable to the contemporary marriage of iron and rye in Bismarck's Germany.

Second, the main challengers to the existing systems were excluded by a variety of means. In Spain and Italy, the clerical challengers were largely excluded by their recent defeats, in Spain in the Third Carlist War, and in Italy by the Piedmontese monarchy's conquest of the Papal States and the ensuing papal declaration known as the *non expedit*; this last forbade Catholics from either voting for or serving as public officials of the new national state. The radical (socialist, anarchist, syndicalist) challengers were largely excluded by suffrage restrictions on industrial workers and by their own version of *non expedit* – the Spanish socialists, for example, called it their "policy of blessed intransigence" – which rejected collaboration with bourgeois political parties. Of course, there was always the exclusion imposed by the caciques. These combined exclusions opened a wide gap between "the official country" and the "the real country."

Together, these conditions suggest that the trasformismo-caciquism systems were very fitting for the Southern Europe of that time. Some of the conditions also suggest, however, that the systems could only be temporary, given the industrialization and urbanization that were inevitable.

In the 1890s, the political systems of Southern Europe were confronted with a number of crises and problems. One set was the product of international politics, in particular "the new imperialism" of the major powers. In the course of the decade, each of the four countries suffered a major defeat in foreign affairs. Portugal suffered the first and the mildest of these defeats when, in 1890, it had to yield to a British ultimatum and relinquish its claims to parts of Africa; the result at home was an increase in opposition to the regime and a reactive increase in authoritarian measures. Italy in 1896, in conformity with the contemporary fashion for colonial adventures, sent an army to conquer Abyssinia, only to have the Abyssinians destroy it at the battle of Adowa; this, along with peasant rebellions and urban riots, led to authoritarian measures which lasted until 1900, in the course of which King Umberto I was assassinated. Greece in 1897 went to war with Turkey in order to liberate Crete but was badly defeated, increasing political opposition at home. Spain in 1898 was defeated in war by the United States and was forced to relinquish almost all of its remaining colonial empire, which had been both a source of offices for the Castilian military and a source of markets for Catalan industrialists. Each group, in its own way, became alienated from the regime, especially the latter. Yet within four or five years of their respective foreign crises, the four political systems had already largely reached a new equilibrium, showing not only the vulnerability of the trasformismo-caciquism system but also its powers of recuperation.

A second set of problems was posed by "the agrarian question." In each of the four countries, most especially in Spain and Italy, the commercialization of agriculture on large estates had created a large class of landless laborers (*braceros* in Spain, *braccianti* in Italy) and proletarianized sharecroppers. From the 1890s to the First World War, there were a number of peasant rebellions, especially in regions characterized by this agricultural class (e.g., Andalusia in Spain, Sicily in Italy, the Alentejo in Portugal, and the newly acquired region of Thessaly in Greece). It was among the agricultural laborers of Andalusia that anarchism became an especially strong force. However, these peasant rebellions were forcibly suppressed and did not pose a fundamental or unmanageable challenge to

37

the existing system. The peasants' answer to "the agrarian question" was anarchism and syndicalism; the landlords' answer was the Guardia Civil and the carabinieri.

A third set of problems was posed by "the social question," i.e., by the growing industrial working class. Yet, until the First World War, this was in many ways a problem largely confined to three cities, Barcelona in Spain and Turin and Milan in Italy.

Of course, there is substantial evidence to suggest that the trasformismo-caciquism system would have inevitably collapsed from internal weaknesses, as can be seen from a brief survey of each country in the years just before the First World War. In Portugal, King Carlos I appointed an authoritarian premier, João Franco, who dissolved the Cortes in 1907. The assassination of the king followed in 1908, and republicans won the elections in Lisbon in 1908 and 1910. A secret society (not surprisingly named the *Carbonaria*) soon organized a military rebellion, which easily overthrew the monarchy in 1910 and established a republic. In Spain, in the famous *Semana Trágica* (Tragic Week) of July 1909, industrial workers of Barcelona seized control of the city and burned the property of the church. In Italy, in the "red week" of June 1914, industrial workers and braccianti led by socialists seized control of towns and rural areas in Emilia and the Romagna and destroyed government and commercial property. In Greece, a group of young officers organized the Military League and carried out a coup in 1909, which limited the role of the monarchy and brought to power Eleutherios Venizelos, who represented new urban groups and newly acquired regions, such as Thessaly. Finally, in 1913, King George I was assassinated.

Yet, plausible arguments can be made that all this political turmoil was being contained by the trasformismo-caciquism systems. In Spain and in Italy, the rebellions were readily suppressed, and in these countries it is not difficult to imagine a new "policy of attraction," an "opening to the left," that would have drawn the more moderate leaders of the more skilled workers into supporting the regime. In Greece, the military coup and the new presence of Venizelos in many ways merely reestablished the old patronage system on a broader base. In Portugal, which is the hardest case to argue, the new republic found a certain stability under the hegemony of the Democratic party. It is probably no accident that the two military coups against kings occurred in Greece and Portugal, the least industrialized of the four countries, in which mutual fear of the working class had not yet forced the military and the monarchy into permanent coalition. The Greek coup of 1909 and the Portuguese coup of 1910 can be seen as reversions to the era of liberal pronunciamentos as much as predictions of an authoritarian future.

As late as 1914, the trasformismo-caciquism system of Southern Europe retained considerable strength and flexibility with which to adapt to internal developments, such as a rebellious class of agricultural workers and a growing class of industrial workers. Even in 1920, after the systems had sustained the international shocks of the First World War and the Russian Revolution, many of the old elements remained. The explanation for the final collapse of the trasformismo-caciquism systems is not a simple one.

Southern Europe (1910s–1920s): World War and Political Breakdown

In 1914, on the eve of the First World War, each of the four countries of Southern Europe retained a parliamentary system with a substantial number of contested electoral districts and a considerable realm of meaningful civil liberties. By 1926, a dozen years later, each was ruled by an authoritarian regime. In Italy, Mussolini became premier in 1922 with "the march on Rome" and, far more importantly, with the support of the agricultural and industrial elites, the army, and the king. The authoritarian system was established by degrees, but by 1926 the opposition political parties had been outlawed and the process was complete.

In Spain, General Miguel Primo de Rivera became dictator in 1923 with a coup d'état and also with the support of the agricultural and industrial elites, the army, and the king; the latter referred to Primo de Rivera as "my Mussolini."

In Portugal, Major Sidónio Pais became dictator in 1917 in a military coup; he was assassinated a year later, however, and the republic entered into a period of frequent political turnover and of oscillation between civilian and military rule. A military coup in 1926 brought about a stable authoritarian regime, however, especially after the appointment of António de Oliviera Salazar as finance minister in 1928.

In Greece, a military coup in 1922 forced King Constantine I into exile. Two years later, the military established a republic, and Greece also entered into a period of frequent political turnover and of alternation between civilian and military rule. The Greek Second Republic was almost as unstable as the first a century before, and as its contemporary Portuguese republic. Finally, a military coup in 1935 brought about the restoration of the monarchy; the new king, George II, soon appointed General Ioannis Metaxas as premier, who established a stable authoritarian regime in 1936.

At first glance, the obvious explanation for the collapse of these political systems into authoritarian regimes lies in the effects of the First World War. First, since the Southern European countries were on peripheral fronts of the major European powers, the decision of each to enter the war or not was not made automatically in 1914 by strategic circumstance, but rather was arrived at in 1915 or 1916 by political choice. The political elites in each country were split into two camps: pro-Allies and pro-Germany (Spain and Greece) or at least pro-Allies and proneutrality (Italy and Portugal). The split was especially severe in Italy, where it was deepened by the ignominious defeat by the Austrians at the Battle of Caporetto in 1917, and in Greece, where it was exacerbated by the humiliation of British and French occupation and the temporary expulsion of pro-German King Constantine I in 1917.

Secondly, the war led to rapid increases in industrial production and in the size and demands of the industrial working class; to inflation, speculation, and shortages; and consequently to widespread social disruption. The disruption was especially severe in Spain and in Portugal, where it was deepened by a wave of strikes in 1917. The divisions and disruptions were accentuated by the Bolshevik Revolution in Russia, which sent a wave of millenarian expectation and revolutionary activity through the agricultural and industrial working classes of Europe.

The response to the Bolshevik Revolution was more intense in the three Latin countries (Italy, Spain, and Portugal) than it was in Greece, in part because of the small size of the latter's agricultural and industrial working classes. In Italy, there were land occupations and widespread strikes under the leadership of the Socialists, culminating in "the occupation of the factories" in Milan and Turin in September 1920. In Spain, there were similar land occupations and strikes under the leadership of the Socialists and the anarchists, culminating in a wave of anarchist political assassinations, bombings, and burnings in Barcelona in 1920 and 1921.

At the same time, conservative forces also organized groups for political action. In Italy, demobilized army officers organized the *fasci di combattimento*, also known as the *squadristi*. In Spain, discontented army officers organized the *juntas de defensa* or officers' syndicates. Italy and Spain had become classic cases of competitive political polarization. Portugal went through a similar process in more muted form.

The political elites and parties of the old parliamentary systems, already divided by the war, fragmented further under the new pressures. In Spain, the old establishment parties, the Conservatives and the Liberals, split into several factions; in Portugal the Democrats did the same. In both countries, most cabinets were short-lived and lasted only a few months. In Italy, the old establishment party, the Liberals, lost many seats to the new mass parties, the Socialists and the *popolari* (the Catholic party); here, most cabinets lasted from nine months to a year.

With all of this political turmoil one might have predicted the collapse of the old systems of Latin Europe and the establishment of authoritarian regimes sometime by 1920, the high point of radical strength. After 1920, the millenarian expectations and political force of the socialists, communists, and anarchists rapidly subsided, although anarchist violence in Barcelona continued during 1921. But Mussolini, the first of the right-wing authoritarian leaders, did not come to power until October 1922, and Primo de Rivera did not make his coup until September 1923.

The old parliamentary systems of Latin Europe had in fact been able to contain the new revolutionary movements. The upper and middle classes supported the old systems against attacks from the left, from below. It was this support that gave the old systems their strength. The upper and middle classes would not, however, support the old systems against attacks from the right, from above.

The revolutionary fever of 1917–20 had left its mark. The old systems no longer inspired any affection or respect; rather, they were held in contempt for their little compromises with the left and for the indecorum of their frequent changes in cabinets. And now, in the early 1920s, persons of the upper and middle classes carried in their minds both inherited traditions of civil liberties and recent memories of radical activity. They were sensible in that, in the choice between liberty and order, they knew they should choose order; their error in 1922 and later lay in thinking that they still had to make the choice.

Thus, in Italy, the upper and middle classes built up the Fascists to smash the Socialists long after the Socialists had ceased to be a threat. When the Fascists, having nothing else left to do, demanded power and marched on Rome in November 1922, there were no establishment forces willing to stand in their way.

In Spain, Primo de Rivera's coup had even less to do with a social crisis. In 1921, Moroccan tribes had inflicted a stunning defeat upon the Spanish army, killing seventeen thousand soldiers. A commission of inquiry was due to report its findings to the Cortes in September 1923; it was widely known that the report would show that responsibility for the disaster lay chiefly with King Alfonso XIII, who had frequently involved himself in military affairs. A week before the commission was scheduled to publish its report, Primo de Rivera made his coup and proclaimed himself dictator, with the approval of the king; the report was never published. Similarly, in Portugal, the military coup in 1926 was not in response to any immediate or obvious social crisis.

In addition, a demonstration effect was at work for the authoritarian forces in the 1920s, as it had been for the liberal forces in the nineteenth

41

century (1820, 1831–33, 1846–48). The Spanish coup-makers cited the Italian fascists, and the Portuguese coup-makers cited them both.

In brief, in 1922 and in the next few years, the old parliamentary systems of Latin Southern Europe were like the old churches of Barcelona the morning after they had been gutted by anarchist fires. In the soft early morning light, they still looked, from a distance, almost as they had the day before. With the first cold wind from the north, however, they utterly collapsed.

In Greece, there was for a while a different pattern, one more in keeping with the liberal military coups of an earlier era. In 1922, the Megali Idea or "Great Idea" was turned into the "Great Catastrophe" when the Turks defeated the Greek army in Asia Minor, slaughtered thousands of Greek civilians, burned the city of Smyrna, and put an end to 2,500 years of Greek civilization on the eastern shore of the Aegean Sea. A military coup immediately forced the king into exile and six of his ministers were executed. The disaster and the harsh reprisal caused a sharp cleavage in Greek politics, largely explaining the oscillations of the next dozen years, until the monarchical restoration of 1935 and the Metaxas regime of 1936. However, in the Greece of the early 1930s, just as in the Latin countries in 1917–21, it was an only temporary increase in the strength of the industrial working class and of the communists that frightened the elites into accepting an authoritarian regime.

Southern Europe (1920–1940s): Authoritarian Regimes and Corporate States

The authoritarian regimes of Mussolini in Italy, Primo de Rivera and, later, Franco in Spain, Salazar in Portugal, and Metaxas in Greece had a good deal in common. The political rhetoric of each regime contained much about their new solution to the social question, the organization of society into a "corporate" or "corporative" state. This was especially true in Italy and Portugal, but also the case in Spain and even in Greece. The social significance of the regimes, however, lay not in the formal corporate organizations that they created, but in the traditional corporate interests that created them.

The regimes were supported by, and in large measure represented, the interests of the agricultural elites, the industrial elites, the church, and the military. (In Greece, however, land ownership was more diffuse than in Latin Europe.) These four groups can be looked upon as the four pillars, or corporate orders, of the realm, with the leader of the regime, a sort of *poder moderador*, or moderating power, balancing and adjudicating their competing interests.

These four groups in turn had their natural social oppositions in the agricultural workers, the industrial workers, the intellectuals, and certain liberal professionals, such as lawyers. These last four groups can be looked upon as the four targets of the regimes. With their advent, the essential political instruments of each opposition were abolished: the independent unions and legal strikes of the agricultural and industrial workers and the civil liberties and free press of the intellectuals and liberal professions.

There were also differences from regime to regime, in their approaches to the single party and to foreign policy.

The most important determinant of the role of the single party in the authoritarian system was whether the party existed prior to the regime's formation. The *Unión Patriótica* of the Primo de Rivera regime in Spain and the *União Nacional* of the Salazar regime in Portugal were created after the regimes were established in order to manufacture a vague populist legitimacy for the existing order. The result was not a party state but merely a state party. These official parties soon became merely parties of officials, channels for bureaucratic advancement. An official political party has much the same function as an official cocktail party. Perhaps this is why Metaxas never got around to creating one.

The *Falange* existed in Spain before the Civil War, but it has often been said that the history of the Second Republic from 1931 to 1936 can be written with no mention of it. The Civil War itself brought an enormous but also an amorphous expansion in its membership. It was not long before Franco reduced the *Falange* to yet another official, legitimizing organization. This withering away of the state party much distressed many "old shirts," who looked back with fondness on its brief heroic age.

Italy was the only Southern European country to have a well-organized, right-wing mass party in existence before the establishment of the authoritarian regime, and indeed it was this party which formed the regime. The Fascist party continued to play a more important role in Italy than its counterparts in Spain and Portugal, although even here a withering process occurred.

That Italy initially had such a party and the others did not is the result of two conditions. First, in Italy there were large numbers of demobilized soldiers readily available to form both the core and the shock troops of the party. Second, in Italy there was greater industrialization, resulting both in a larger and more threatening industrial working class and in a larger and more frightened middle class; the resentful members of the latter also filled party ranks. These two conditions together probably suffice to explain the strength of the Fascist party in Italy and the weakness of its counterparts elsewhere.

Another difference between the regimes was in their foreign policies. Few countries have had more prudent foreign policies than Franco's

Spain or Salazar's Portugal. Few countries have had more bellicose or reckless ones than Mussolini's Italy, with his invasions of Abyssinia (1935), Albania (1939), France (1940), and Greece (1940). In the years before each leader took power, Mussolini had already established a reputation for abrupt and dramatic action, while Franco and Salazar had established reputations for calm and prudent calculation. Also, the temptations for new foreign conquests offered to Mussolini by the international situation in 1935–40 surpassed anything ever offered to the Iberian dictators (Primo de Rivera as well as Franco and Salazar) or to Metaxas of Greece.

The authoritarian regimes of Mussolini in Italy, Primo de Rivera and Franco in Spain, Salazar in Portugal, and Metaxas in Greece can be interpreted as a natural form of political system for Southern Europe. We will have more to say in later sections about this question of a natural or "elective" affinity between Southern European societies and authoritarian regimes. Certainly, the longevity of three of the regimes seems to give empirical evidence for the point. The authoritarian regime established in Portugal by the military in 1926 and particularly by Salazar after 1928 endured for nearly half a century; at its demise in 1974, it was, apart from the Soviet Union and Mongolia, the oldest authoritarian regime in the world. The authoritarian regime established in half of Spain in 1936 by Franco and in all of Spain by 1939 also had an impressive duration. Even the authoritarian regime established in Italy by Mussolini lasted for more than twenty years, from 1922 to 1943. Indeed, had it not been for his entry into the Second World War on the German side and for the consequent Allied invasion of Italy, Mussolini and his regime might have lived on into the 1950s, then, like Franco, to be acclaimed by certain Western leaders as a great statesman of Europe and a bulwark against communism. The Metaxas regime also was only overthrown by foreign invasion, in its case, ironically, by the Italians and the Germans.

The major anomaly in this elective affinity interpretation is the collapse of the Primo de Rivera regime in 1930, with the subsequent fall of the monarchy in 1931 and the establishment of the Second Republic.[13]

Since in an authoritarian regime, so much depends upon the qualities of the leader, it is tempting to focus on this idiosyncratic variable. Of the five leaders, Primo de Rivera before coming to power had developed the least reputation for personal force and political skill. He was also in poor health during his last years in power and died six months after his

---

13. On the end of the Primo de Rivera regime, see Stanley G. Payne, *Politics and the Military in Modern Spain* (Stanford, 1967), pp. 224–65.

overthrow. In addition, since Primo de Rivera was deposed in 1930, it is also useful to focus on the impact of the international economic depression, which toppled authoritarian regimes in comparable countries elsewhere (e.g., Ibáñez in Chile), although it more frequently toppled democratic ones (e.g., Yrigoyen in Argentina). In contrast, Mussolini had already initiated a deflationary policy in 1926 and Salazar had done so in 1928; this meant that the impact of the international depression was reduced when it hit Italy and Portugal.

Spain's Second Republic itself lasted for eight years: five years of heated partisan conflict between political extremes followed by three years of civil war, including military intervention by the Italians, the Germans, and even the Portuguese. The fact that the republic was able to endure so long and under such conditions suggests that Southern Europe contained the potential for another kind of stable political system. It is interesting to speculate, however, on what might have happened if the republic had won the Civil War. Within two years, Spain, like France, probably would have been invaded by the Germans; a few years later, like France and Italy, it would have been liberated by the Allies. The end result might have been yet another multiparty system dominated by a conservative Catholic party, as in postwar France and Italy.

Spain and Portugal (1940s–1970s): Habsburg Monarchy and Modern Society

For more than twenty years after the end of the Second World War, the most important differences between the politics of Spain and Portugal, on the one hand, and the politics of Italy and Greece, on the other, derived from the simple fact that the latter two countries had been drawn into the war and the former two had not. In Italy, the war and the German occupation of the north in 1943–45 discredited the army, the monarchy, and their ally, the Fascist party. More importantly, the Italian resistance movement and the American liberation forces insured the renewed participation in the political process of liberal and even radical groups. An ensuing land reform reduced the role of the landed upper class, another main element in the old authoritarian alliance. The American army played the role of a "conquering bourgeoisie," breaking up the coalition between the industrial and agricultural elites, the Italian-style marriage between iron and rye, and imposing a bourgeois revolution from above to fill the place of the absent bourgeois revolution from below.

In Greece, the German and Italian occupation of 1941–44 discredited many elements of the Metaxas regime that had collaborated with the occupiers. The Greek resistance movement and the British intervention forces guaranteed the renewed participation in the political process of

JAMES KURTH

liberal and, briefly in 1944–45, even radical groups. The subsequent American intervention (1947–50) in the Greek Civil War restrained the authoritarian groups from making a complete comeback, at least temporarily.

In Spain and Portugal, however, there was no invading Allied army to conquer the right (and to contain the left), and the old authoritarian regimes continued to rule essentially unchanged until the mid-1970s.

The authoritarian regime in Spain was well described in a famous article by Juan Linz;[14] the authoritarian regime in Portugal was in many ways similar.[15] Both were examples of what Philippe Schmitter, constructing an ideal-type, called "corporatist-authoritarian rule":

> In this syndrome, the political process is dominated by a heterogeneous elite, itself composed of functionally differentiated, bureaucratically organized "orders." These noncompetitive "orders" have been heavily penetrated by the state. Thus the processes of interest representation and leadership selection are controlled from above. Corporatist ideology to the contrary notwithstanding, the orders are not politically equal, for the military establishment is frequently predominant. Vertical, compartmentalized interactions and exchanges are encouraged; horizontal ones on a class or regional basis are discouraged, if not prohibited. The processes of electoral selection and legislative decision making are controlled by a single or dominant party, which neither monopolizes access to influential roles nor enforces rigid ideological conformity. On the contrary, authoritarian regimes deliberately cultivate a multiple legitimacy base – a calculated mixture of traditional, charismatic and legal-rational principles – and demand of their subjects compliance rather than active support or enthusiasm. This complex, often contradictory, basis of legitimacy distinguishes these regimes from narrowly dictatorial and, hence, illegitimate *régimes d'exception*. The decision-making process is depoliticized and deideologized as much as possible. Emergent problems are converted into legal and administrative issues; challenges to prevailing policy are usually answered by co-optation and selective privilege rather than substantial modification or wholesale repression.[16]

The steady liberalization of the Spanish regime after Franco's death in 1975 and *a fortiori* the sudden collapse of the Portuguese regime in the military revolution of 1974 suggest that by the mid-1970s this basis of

14. Juan J. Linz, "An Authoritarian Regime: Spain," in *Mass Politics,* ed. Erik Allardt and Stein Rokkan (New York, 1970), pp. 251–83.
15. See, for example, the description in H. Martins, "Portugal," in *European Fascism,* ed. S. J. Woolf (New York, 1969), pp. 302–36. A comprehensive account of the Portuguese authoritarian regime is given in *Contemporary Portugal: The Revolution and Its Antecedents,* eds. Lawrence S. Graham and Harry M. Makler (Austin, Texas, 1979).
16. Philippe C. Schmitter, "Paths to Political Development in Latin America," in *Changing Latin America: New Interpretations of its Politics and Society,* ed. Douglas A. Chalmers (New York, 1972) pp. 91–92.

46

legitimacy was narrow rather than broad, passive rather than positive. Yet in the three decades after the Second World War, the two Iberian authoritarian regimes showed a remarkable resiliency and capacity to withstand serious strains which were imposed both from within and from without and often in combination. In Spain, these periods of strain were the late 1940s, with the guerrilla resistance in Andalusia and along the Pyrenees and the diplomatic isolation imposed by the liberal states; the mid-1950s, with the social dislocation caused by inflation and resentment in the military caused by the decolonization of Morocco; and the late 1960s and early 1970s, with industrial strikes, Basque nationalism, and the indirect political pressures of the European Economic Community.

In Portugal, the internal pressures were sometimes the product of a peculiar feature of the regime. Since the 1930s, the regime held formal elections at regular intervals, four years between parliamentary elections, seven years between presidential ones. These elections were not free, the opponents of the regime won only trivial victories, and indeed they often withdrew on the eve of the election. However, during the month before the election, censorship was relaxed and criticism of the regime was permitted. Indeed, Mário Soares, who was to become the most important civilian political leader after the 1974 revolution, first established his political reputation as an opposition candidate in these elections. In Portugal, the periods of strain were: the late 1940s, with the 1949 elections and some international pressures from liberal states; 1958–62, with the 1958 presidential election, the uprising in Angola and loss of Goa in 1961, and two attempted military coups in 1961–62; 1968–70, with the transition from Salazar to Marcello Caetano (the regime's "succession crisis"); and finally 1973–74, with the disrupting impact of the colonial wars in Africa upon the army and, again, muted political pressures from the EEC.

There is another sense in which the corporatist-authoritarian regimes of Spain and Portugal were durable. Stanley Payne commented on Franco's Spain:

> it could be argued that *franquismo* was as close as one could get to Carlism in twentieth-century terms. . . . As an "arbiter" of the movement, he reflected the old Traditionalist desire for an unfettered authority which would nonetheless be respectful of the various divergent sectors of conservative interest. The Cortes installed in 1943 was undemocratic and corporative, thereby approximating to a considerable degree the century-old Carlist demand for a "traditional" Cortes. . . . As for clericalism, the 1938 culture and education laws, and the whole structure of Church-state relations, culminating in the 1951 Concordat, granted most Traditionalist demands in

the religious sphere. Franco might even be termed an uncrowned Carlist king.[17]

In many ways, these corporatist-authoritarian regimes were more like the monarchy of the Spanish Habsburgs, or the early Portuguese Braganças, than any other Iberian regime in the intervening centuries. In their authoritarianism, they stood apart from the liberal monarchies and parliamentary systems of the nineteenth and early twentieth centuries, and they stood with the absolute monarchies from before the French Revolution. In their corporatism, however, and especially in their generally congenial relations with the church, they even stood apart from the modernizing, secularizing Bourbon and Bragança monarchies of the eighteenth century. Their truest prototype was the Habsburg monarchy of the seventeenth century and before. It is in this sense that the Carlists, the most traditionalist political movement in Europe and the losers of the three Carlist wars in the nineteenth century, can be said to have won the fourth, the Spanish Civil War, in the twentieth.

The military coup that overthrew the Portuguese authoritarian regime in April 1974 was detonated by conflicts within the military over old policies toward the colonial wars in Africa and, less grandly, over new policies for the promotion of officers. But the regime had already been weakened by the changing perceptions of the Portuguese economic elites, who by 1973 saw their interests lying in closer ties with the EEC, which would require the greater liberalization of Portuguese politics.

The military coup in turn detonated the Portuguese Revolution of 1974–75, which for nineteen months ran as a sort of museum exhibition – and therefore bloodless representation – of the great European revolutions of the past. It turned out, however, that the truest analogy was the liberation in France and Italy between 1944 and 1946. By the 1970s, the socioeconomic structure of the Portuguese population had much in common with that of France and, especially, Italy thirty years before. And as in France and Italy in the 1940s, in Portugal in the 1970s a superficial and ephemeral interlude of revolutionary politics, the politics of "the Lisbon Commune," was followed by a period of cautious and conservative governments, based upon the electoral support of a mass of small farmers, small shopkeepers, and small officials and assisted by economic aid from the major capitalist states of the West. But there was also a special Portuguese touch – a renewal of the old *poder moderador* in the person of President – and General – Ramalho Eanes.

The example of the Portuguese Revolution was one factor propelling the post-Franco regime in Spain toward a liberalization and democrati-

17. Stanley Payne, "Spain," p. 202.

zation which it hoped would preempt a similar revolution or worse. More decisive, however, was the desire of Spanish industrial and agricultural elites to gain admission into the European Community. By the 1970s, Spain had developed a productive and diversified economy, and it appeared that its goods would be highly competitive within the community if Spain were a member. The community, however, would not admit Spain into membership until, in the words of a resolution passed by each of its main institutions in 1975, "freedom and democracy have been established in Spain."

It was remarkable indeed that a liberal democracy was successfully established in Spain by the government of King Juan Carlos I, through a sort of historical compromise between the Socialist party and the Bourbon monarchy. It was the first time in twentieth-century Europe that an authoritarian regime transformed itself into a stable democracy without the violent overthrow of the top leadership. But it was not the first time that political events in Spain have surprised the rest of the world.[18]

Italy and Greece (1940s–1970s): Dominant Party or Dominant Military

The outcome of the Second World War was far different in Italy and Greece than in Spain and Portugal. In the two eastern countries the war created conditions which permitted the reestablishment of liberal parliamentary systems. However, with this the similarity between Italy and Greece largely ends. The Italian political system has weaknesses which are numerous and even notorious, yet it has retained, for more than four decades, civilian rule, electoral competition, and civil liberties. The parliamentary system in Greece was always more frail than its counterpart in Italy, and the military coup in 1967 imposed an authoritarian regime even harsher than its counterparts in Spain and Portugal.

Italian politics after the Second World War gave the appearance of being as volatile as any in Europe; first a kingdom, with two kings in 1945–46; then a republic, with thirty-six governments by 1975; and "hot autumns," "checkerboard strikes," rioting over the location of a regional capital, and political bombings and assassinations in the late 1960s and 1970s.

From a different perspective, however, the most striking feature of Italian politics has been its lack of change. The Christian Democratic

18. The collapse of the authoritarian regimes in Portugal and Spain and the transitions to democratic systems are analyzed in Ronald H. Chilcote et al., *Transitions from Dictatorship to Democracy: Comparative Studies of Spain, Portugal, and Greece* (New York, 1990); Guillermo O'Donnell, Philippe C. Schmitter, and Laurence Whitehead, eds., *Transitions from Authoritarian Rule* (Baltimore, 1986); Raymond Carr and Juan Pablo Fuji Alzpurua, *Spain: Dictatorship to Democracy* (London, 1981); Robert Clark and Michael Haltzel, eds., *Spain in the 1980s: The Democratic Transition and a New International Role* (Washington, 1987).

party has exercised an unbroken hegemony since 1945, normally in coalition with smaller parties but always as the dominant party in the government and almost always as the party of the premier (the main exception was from 1981 to 1987, when first a Republican, Giovanni Spadolini, and then a Socialist, Bettino Craxi, held the office). In this sense the Christian Democratic regime has been one of the most stable in Europe. The major political change during this long era was the "opening to the left" in 1963, whose results before the fact were either much feared or much anticipated and whose results after the fact were quite minor. Indeed, the rapprochement with the Socialists in 1963 can be compared in its system-maintaining character with the opening to the Social Democrats in 1947.

As is usual with dominant parties in a parliamentary system, the Christian Democrats have been amorphous and faction-ridden. The coalition-building process within the party has been reminiscent of the trasformismo process within the Italian parliament from the 1870s to the 1910s. Since the fall of Alcide de Gasperi in 1953, however, there has been no one central figure as commanding as Depretis, Crispi, and Giolitti were then. If trasformismo has been present in contemporary Italian politics, one might also expect to find caciquism. Patron-client politics has been prevalent in some rural areas, and there have been cases of electoral fraud and coercion. It would not be accurate, however, to say that caciquism has been a dominant feature of contemporary Italian politics.[19]

Greek politics since the war has been far less stable than in Italy. The outcome of the Greek Civil War was a curious system of parallel hierarchies. One was a parliament composed of several personalist parties organized along patron-client lines and characterized by frequent cabinet turnovers. The second was the alliance between a conservative military and a politically active king. Once the communist rebellion was suppressed, the internal dynamics of Greek politics probably would have led to the familiar pattern: the military would have made their coup twenty years earlier, there would have been something of a restoration of the Metaxas regime, and Greece, like Spain and Portugal, would have acquired a corporatist-authoritarian regime.

It was the American government, with the influence that came with its military and economic aid, that prevented a Greek regression to the authoritarian mean. It was also the American government that disapproved of the continuation of cabinet instability, which resulted from the array of several small and weak parties. In 1952, it encouraged a

19. Guiseppe DiPalma, *Surviving without Governing: The Italian Parties in Parliament* (Berkeley, Calif., 1977); Raphael Zariski, *Italy: The Politics of Uneven Development* (Hinsdale, Ill., 1972).

change in the Greek electoral system, from proportional representation to single-member districts, in order to produce a majority for a single conservative party. This was the Greek Rally led by Field Marshal Alexander Papagos; its successor after Papagos' death in 1955 was the National Radical Union led by Konstantinos Karamanlis. From 1952 to 1963 Greece, like Italy, was governed by a dominant conservative party.

The National Radicals lost their dominance for a variety of reasons, one being that the very weakness of the extreme left meant that a large left-center party, the Center Union, could win a majority. In 1967 the prospect of a Center Union electoral victory, which would be followed by a purging of the military, provoked a coup.[20]

The new military government was at first reminiscent of the proroyalist Metaxas regime of 1936–41 and later of the antiroyalist military governments of 1922–24, and in 1973 it too culminated in the establishment of a republic. In fact, however, it was the longest and harshest authoritarian regime in Greece since independence a century and a half before. It was brought down finally in 1974 by its own recapitulation of the catastrophe of 1922. As then in Asia Minor, so in Cyprus in 1974, an adventurous Greek policy led to the total destruction by the Turks of Greek communities whose roots went back 2,500 years. In their time of distress, the Greeks turned again, not surprisingly, to Konstantinos Karamanlis, and he turned again to the construction of a new dominant party, New Democracy, which recapitulated his National Radicals of the 1950s.

Southern Europe (1980s): Postindustrial Economy and Patrimonial Socialism

The 1970s had seen a great transformation or at least a time of troubles in each of the four countries of Southern Europe (revolution and counter-revolution in Portugal, the collapse of an authoritarian regime in Greece and the dismantling of another in Spain, and political bombings and assassinations in Italy). By the end of the decade, however, this period of turmoil largely had come to an end; it turned out to have been merely another interregnum between phases, like the late 1940s in Italy and Greece and the early 1920s in all four countries. About the time the four countries entered the 1980s, they also entered into a new and sixth phase, as each established a stable liberal-democratic system.

The next four chapters of this volume present detailed discussions of the four countries during the 1980s, and those discussions will not be summarized here. This section will only present two developments that were common to these countries during this most recent phase: European integration and socialist governments.

20. Legg, *Politics in Modern Greece*; for a narrative of events, see Jane Perry, Clark Carey and Andrew Galbraith Perry, *The Web of Modern Greek Politics* (New York, 1968).

Each of the four underwent far greater integration into the rest of Europe than ever before. Italy had been a founding member of the European Economic Community in 1958, but it was only in the 1980s that it achieved full economic equality with its northern members. During the decade, the other three also became members of the (now renamed) European Community. At the same time, foreign investment from the north (especially West Germany and France) entered the southern countries in massive amounts and with major consequences.

Also, in each of the four countries, the socialist party achieved far greater power than ever before. In Spain and Greece, the socialists were the governing party for virtually the entire decade (led by Felipe González in Spain and by Andreas Papandreou in Greece). In Portugal they provided the premier from 1983 to 1986 and the president from 1986 to the end of the decade (Mário Soares in both offices). Even in an Italy still dominated by the Christian Democratic party the premier was from the Socialist party from 1983 to 1987 (Craxi). The 1980s were to some extent a "pink" decade in Southern Europe.

Together these two developments, European integration and socialist governments, appeared to have brought an end to the long history of that distinctive Southern European way of politics described in this chapter. At last, it seemed, Southern Europe had become joined to the European continent and entered the modern age.

As it turned out, and as the four country chapters that follow demonstrate, the achievement of Europeanism and socialism, of modernity and equality, has been problematic and paradoxical. As always in Southern Europe, things are not as they appear, and the "official" country differs from the "real" one.

European integration and investment have not brought a robust industrial economy, but, to most of Southern Europe, a postindustrial one. The major sectors of a classical industrial economy (steel, chemicals, electrical goods, automobiles) had never been robust enough in Southern Europe to be competitive in the international market but they had at least existed, and had provided both sizable employment in protected national markets and major leadership in national political classes. These national industries were devastated by foreign imports in the 1980s, especially in Spain and Portugal.

What economic activities have taken the place of the ruined industrial sectors? We can discern and distinguish four kinds: (1) high-technology, or flexible, production; (2) high-service, or financial, enterprises; (3) low-technology, or putting-out, production; and (4) low-service, or tourist, industry, i.e., service workers as servants.

The most productive and most famous sector of the Southern European economy is high-technology industry using flexible-production methods, located principally in northern Italy. This industry is truly efficient and competitive in the international market, and northern Italy is truly European and modern, but then northern Italy has been as European and as modern as Northern Europe ever since the beginning of our story in 1815.

The most active and most fashionable sector of the Southern European economy is what we have called high-service activities, i.e., financial enterprises. Many of these deal in real estate, and many are merely speculative rather than productive. This sector greatly expanded throughout Southern Europe in the 1980s and was especially prominent in Spain and Greece.

Most Southern Europeans, however, are not employed in these sectors of the high economy. They are employed in the low economy, e.g., engaged in low-technology industries using putting-out production methods or in low-service activities such as the tourism industry. From one perspective, these activities greatly expanded in the 1980s. From another perspective, however, they have been prominent in Southern Europe for many decades; the only real change is that now they are more so. It is as if much of Southern Europe skipped over the modern, industrial era and instead went directly from preindustrial to postindustrial.

The development of the postindustrial economy affected the development of socialist parties. A labor force composed of putting-out and tourist workers is not much of a base for a socialist party in the original Marxist sense. For that, there had to be an industrial working class. A postindustrial labor force, however, is a suitable base for a socialist party in the contemporary Mediterranean sense.

In Southern Europe, socialist parties historically had been based upon lower paid professionals (especially teachers), office workers, and other public employees. These sectors expanded in the 1980s and were joined by greater numbers of people in comparable low-technology and low-service jobs. Together, they comprise the electoral base for the socialist parties of Southern Europe, and their growth provides part of the explanation for the coming to power of socialist governments, especially in Spain and Greece.

The socialist governments, however, did not bring equitable social policies to Southern Europe, but rather preferential individual benefits. The benefits now went to different people than before and were more broadly distributed, but they were as much the result of political preferences and personal connections as they had been under earlier regimes. Indeed, as the chapters on Spain and Greece demonstrate, the socialist regime brought about a new version of the patrimonial state, which has characterized Southern Europe for many centuries. Just as much of Southern Europe seems to have gone directly from preindustrial to postindustrial economies, so a large part of the region seems to have skipped over the modern, "rational" – in the Weberian sense – era of rule-governed and due-process bureaucracy, going directly from "prerational" to "postrational" states.

II. PATRIMONIAL AUTHORITY AND SOUTHERN EUROPE

Are there some general analytical models or explanatory paradigms which can account for most of the distinctive and decisive features of Southern European politics, as we have described them in Section I? In this essay, we shall consider two possibilities. One, discussed in this section, is the model of patrimonial authority, derived from the work of Max Weber and Richard Morse, and the related concept of patron-client politics. The second, treated in Section III, is the model of delayed development, derived from the work of Alexander Gerschenkron and Albert Hirschman, with its kindred theory of dependent development.

The concept of patrimonial authority was originally developed by Weber as one of the ideal types of traditional authority.[21] Weber distinguished a number of different forms of traditional authority; the most important for our purposes are feudalism, patrimonialism, and sultanism, listed in order of increasing power of the ruler over lesser lords and over his staff. The characteristics of patrimonial authority were summed up well by Richard Morse, who applied the concept to the empire of the Spanish Habsburgs and to the states of Latin America since independence:

> The patrimonial ruler is ever alert to forestall the growth of an independent landed aristocracy enjoying inherited privileges. He awards benefices, or prebends, as a remuneration for services; income accruing from benefices is an attribute of the office, not of the incumbent as a person. Characteristic ways for maintaining the ruler's authority intact are: limiting the tenure of royal officials; forbidding officials to acquire family and economic ties in their jurisdictions; using inspectors and spies to supervise all levels of administration; defining only loosely the territorial and functional divisions of administration so that jurisdictions will be competitive and mutually supervisory. The authority of the ruler is oriented to tradition but allows him claim to full personal power. As he is reluctant to bind himself by "law," his rule takes the form of a series of directives, each subject to supersession. Thus problems of

21. Weber, *Theory of Social and Economic Organization*, and Bendix, *Max Weber*. Also see Guenther Roth, "Personal Rulership, Patrimonialism, and Empire-Building in the New States," *World Politics* 20, no. 1 (1968): pp. 194–206.

adjudication tend to become problems of administration, and the administrative and judicial functions are united in many different offices throughout the bureaucracy. Legal remedies are frequently regarded not as applications of "law," but as a gift of grace or a privilege awarded on the merits of a case and not binding as precedent.[22]

A corollary of patrimonial authority is patron-client politics. A patrimonial state can be seen as a great pyramid of patron-client chains, culminating in the top patron, the patrimonial ruler. The patron-client relationship has been much discussed in the literature of political science; a typical definition was given by James Scott, who applied the concept to Southeast Asia:

> The patron-client relationship – an exchange relationship between roles – may be defined as a special case of dyadic (two-person) ties involving a largely instrumental friendship in which an individual of higher socioeconomic status (patron) uses his own influence and resources to provide protection or benefits, or both, for a person of lower status (client) who, for his part, reciprocates by offering general support and assistance, including personal services, to the patron.[23]

Although it appears that all patrimonial states are composed of patron-client chains, not all systems with patron-client politics are patrimonial states. A political system may be composed of several sharply competing patron-client chains. Sometimes such a system may look like a multiparty democracy.

Although scholars have applied the concept of patrimonialism to many traditional societies around the world, a good case can be made that Southern Europe and Latin America were the areas where patrimonialism reached its purest expression. Louis Hartz and Richard Morse saw Latin America as a "fragment" of Latin Europe, especially the Iberian peninsula. In these two regions, Morse argued, the political structure of patrimonial authority was massively reinforced and legitimized by the intellectual structure of Catholic, especially Thomist, theology. Earlier, as Marc Bloch and others have observed, the political institutions of true feudalism never fully developed in Southern Europe. The closest equivalents were in a few regions of northern Spain (significantly Catalonia and Aragon), northern Italy, and, briefly, Norman Sicily.[24] Still earlier, as Fustel de Coulanges argued in a brilliant work a century and a quarter ago, the politics of patrons and clients was the fundamental pattern in

22. Morse, "Heritage of Latin America," 157.
23. James C. Scott, "Patron-Client Politics and Political Change in Southeast Asia," *American Political Science Review* 66, no. 1 (1972): p. 92.
24. Marc Bloch, *Feudal Society*, 2 vols. (Chicago, 1964), 1: pp. 186–88. (Originally published in 1940.)

JAMES KURTH

ancient Greece and Rome.[25] Conversely, the locus classicus of feudalism was France, the regions along the Rhine, and England. That of sultanism was the Middle East.

But patrimonial authority and patron-client politics are not only phenomena of traditional societies. They can also be common to modernizing societies, where they are reinforced by the increasing role of money and mobility in the economy, and to modern societies, where they are strengthened by the increasing role of government contracts and administrative discretion. Furthermore, just as for traditional societies patrimonial authority can be distinguished from a feudal system on the one hand, and from sultanist rule on the other, so in modernizing societies, patrimonial authority can be distinguished both from a parliamentary system or *démocratie censitaire*, with genuine electoral competition between autonomous parties of notables, and from personal government or caudillo rule. Similarly, in modern societies, patrimonial authority can be distinguished both from pluralist democracy, with genuine electoral competition between autonomous mass parties, and from totalitarian dictatorship, with a single, coercive, and ideological mass party.

Let us accept the assumption that the countries of Southern Europe were characterized by patrimonial authority on the eve of the Napoleonic Wars. Of course, by this time, under the impact of centralizing monarchies, the other countries of Europe had moved away from their feudal structures and also contained patrimonial elements. Nevertheless, in the northern countries the role of feudal remnants and of parliaments, *parlements*, and estates was greater than in the southern countries. Southern Europe was the purest case of patrimonial authority. Given this assumption about Southern Europe at the beginning of the nineteenth century, we may then be able to account for some of the major political events that have occurred since.

Many of these political events can be seen as the probable consequence or central tendency of economic development within the framework of a patrimonial state. Within a patrimonial state economic development produces large numbers of "masterless men," persons who have no connections to the established patron-client chains and channels. Some of these persons perform new economic tasks (e.g., an industrial bourgeoisie); some of them merely seek to perform old ones (e.g., official *clases medias*), but in a situation where the number of candidates greatly exceeds the number of available positions. These persons seek a readjustment in the distribution of patrimonial benefits, of patronage,

25. Numa Denis Fustel de Coulanges, *The Ancient City* (Garden City, N.Y., 1964). (Originally published in 1864.)

56

PARALLEL POLITICS IN SOUTHERN EUROPE

offices, and contracts, in their favor. In order to extract these benefits, they must create new patron-client channels and force their acceptance by the patrimonial ruler. Each group employs that political weapon with which it has a comparative advantage: "The wealthy bribe; students riot; workers strike; mobs demonstrate; and the military coups."[26] Economic development within a patrimonial state leads to praetorian politics.

In Southern Europe in the early nineteenth century, the new social groups were actually the old *clases medias*, which had expanded too rapidly to be fully coopted and incorporated into the old patron-client channels. Their political organizations were the Masonic society and the national army; their political weapon was the "middle-class military coup."[27] In a patrimonial state, the capacity for both cooptation and coercion decreased as the distance from the capital city increased. Thus many of these middle-class military coups took place in provincial commercial cities (e.g., Cádiz, Barcelona, Porto).

The new patrimonial benefits demanded by the middle class of course required new offices and new sources of money. Thus the middle classes pushed the patrimonial rulers toward centralization and secularization, particularly toward expansion of royal offices and taxes, and toward expropriation of church and communal lands. This in turn posed a threat to traditional and regional groups and provoked their rebellion against the patrimonial center. The most severe rebellions occurred in the most peripheral regions of the two largest states (the three Carlist wars in Catalonia, Aragon, Navarre, and the Basque lands; the Brigandage in southern Italy). The remoteness of the periphery from the center meant that patrimonial authority was especially weak and local immunities especially great. In addition, in Spain these northern peripheral regions were the ones where feudalism had been most developed. The Carlist wars were in part a feudal rebellion against a patrimonial regime.

Thus, given a patrimonial state, one would expect the early stages of economic development to result in pronunciamentos and civil wars. The pronunciamentos would be most frequent in those states with provincial commercial centers; the civil wars would be most severe in those states with peripheral feudal regions.

Another variable, monarchical legitimacy, worked in much the same direction as that of center versus periphery. In Spain and Portugal in the first half of the nineteenth century, the legitimacy of the patrimonial

26. Samuel P. Huntington, *Political Order in Changing Societies* (New Haven, Conn., 1968), p. 196.
27. See José Nun, "A Latin American Phenomenon: The Middle-Class Military Coup" in *Latin America: Reform or Revolution,* eds. James Petras and Maurice Zeitlin (Greenwich, Conn., 1968), pp. 145–85.

monarchies was unusually diminished. Its decline began with their dependence on and compromises with foreign powers during the Napoleonic Wars and the restoration, and was accentuated by the dynastic conflicts between the two branches of the Bourbons and Braganças. It was further exacerbated by the outcome of the First Carlist and Miguelist wars, which installed in each country a child-queen as monarch, hardly the ideal type for the top patron of the realm.

The situation in Italy and Greece at the time was rather different. In the Italian states, the patrimonial monarchies shared a dependence on foreign powers, but they were not touched by two added debilities of dynastic strife and minors as monarchs. Moreover, Piedmont soon developed a high degree of independence that enhanced the legitimacy of its king. In Greece, the patrimonial monarch was certainly dependent upon foreign powers, but his dependence also rendered him the conduit of foreign resources. The rebellion of 1843 redirected these resources away from the foreigners in the king's clientele and more to the Greeks themselves; the rebellion in 1862 came after the foreign powers had withdrawn their support from the king. Overall, the legitimacy of the patrimonial monarchies was greater in Italy and Greece than in Spain and Portugal. From the perspective of patrimonial authority, then, it is not surprising that pronunciamentos were more frequent in the latter two countries than in the former two.

Once the middle classes had forced the acceptance of new patron-client chains and indeed once they had become upper middle classes through the acquisition of redistributed church and communal lands, it was possible to reestablish a stable patrimonial state in a new political form. The widening of the circle of patrons required the widening of representative bodies, i.e., the institution of parliaments. These parliaments, however, operated through trasformismo, in which the new style of patrimonial ruler, the premier and on occasion the king, continued the old reality of patrimonial rule, the distribution of patronage, offices, and contracts. Caciquism, the companion of trasformismo, was itself the embodiment of patron-client politics and a miniature form of patrimonial rule.

The process of economic development continued, however, and began to undermine the new political equilibrium, The commercialization of agriculture created a new class, even a mass, of landless agricultural workers and proletarianized sharecroppers. Industrialization also created a new class, or mass, of propertyless industrial workers and proletarianized craftsmen.

A mass can be seen as a group of persons with no clientage ties to a patron and with virtually no expectation of obtaining them. A mass consists of permanently masterless men. Such persons can only achieve their political goals with collective efforts among equals, not selective efforts toward a superior. From a different perspective, a government can only approach such persons with collective benefits for all, not selective benefits for a few; the former obviously impose greater costs upon the established centers of power and property. A social mass created by a modernizing society is likely to find a patrimonial regime especially unresponsive, more so than either a parliamentary system, with genuine electoral competition between autonomous parties of notables, or personal government, which normally relies on some degree of populist support. Conversely, a patrimonial regime is especially likely to find a social mass threatening or incomprehensible.

Thus, in a patrimonial state, agricultural workers and proletarianized sharecroppers are especially likely to be radical, syndicalist, or even anarchistic. To them, the state is only a collection of patron-client channels that are closed to them. It is therefore not surprising that they would prefer no state at all. Their radicalism is reinforced by another characteristic of patrimonial states, the absentee landlord. In a state where personal connections are important even for commercial exchanges, landlords need to reside in the metropolis or at least in provincial centers in order to succeed as businessmen. Absent from his estate and his workers, the landlord performs few of the traditional functions of a patron.

Similarly, industrial workers and proletarianized craftsmen are also especially likely to seek radical political solutions in a patrimonial state. Again, the state is only a collection of patron-client channels which are closed to them. Their radicalism is reinforced by the radicalism of agricultural workers who migrate to the city and join the industrial work force. Given the model of patrimonial authority, then, one would expect Southern Europe to have been the modernizing area where syndicalist and anarchist movements were the strongest among the agricultural and industrial working classes, and this was in fact the case. (Left unexplained, by this model, however, is why some workers became syndicalists, others anarchists, and still others socialists.)

Patrimonial states might also be expected to be especially ineffective in containing radical movements, but as we have seen this did not prevent the patrimonial states of Southern Europe from accomplishing that task after the First World War. Nevertheless, frequent cabinet turnovers, with a new top patron every few months, could only impose a severe strain on a society used to one well-established and long-familiar patrimonial ruler, and this contributed to the ready acceptance of the new corporatist-authoritarian regimes.

The corporatist-authoritarian regimes themselves can be seen as the ideal type and normal form of patrimonial authority in an advanced modernizing or modern society. Morse's description of a traditional pat-rimonial ruler and Schmitter's description of a modern corporatist-authoritarian regime have much in common. It is not surprising that the Iberian peninsula should be the locus classicus for both, nor, given the resiliency and durability of the Habsburg monarchy in one era, that we should observe the resiliency and durability of the Franco regime at a later time.

For a country with a patrimonial tradition, the normal path to the modern world has led to a corporatist-authoritarian regime. There is a second, exceptional path, however, which has also led to a stable politi-cal system, a parliamentary system dominated by a conservative party. Here the purest case is the Christian Democratic party in Italy. As the permanent governing party, the Christian Democrats have been able to recapitulate the traditional stability of patrimonial monarchy, and as the anointed Catholic party, they have also been able to recapitulate the Catholic legitimacy of patrimonial monarchy. An inferior and less stable example of a conservative party was the National Radical Union of Greece, led by Karamanlis.

By itself, this model of patrimonial authority might lead one to expect that these two types of political systems – corporatist-authoritarian regime and dominant-party system, Habsburg Monarchy and Christian Democracy – would be the only stable political systems that Southern Europe could produce in the modern era. As it turned out, however, in the 1980s Southern Europe did indeed produce a new kind of political system, which was the socialist-party regime. As the chapters on Spain and Greece demonstrate, however, this was also the patrimonial state in a new and higher form.

III. Delayed Development and Southern Europe

A second analytical model or explanatory paradigm that we can apply to the politics of Southern Europe is based on the concept of delayed development and the associated theory of dependent development. Economists have long debated differences in the character of develop-ment between the countries that first industrialized and those that fol-lowed later. Some of these economic differences may have implications for differences in politics.

One of the most important analyses of economic differences resulting from delayed development is that of Alexander Gerschenkron. Ger-schenkron ranked the major countries of Europe along a continuum defined in terms of their economic backwardness as of the mid-nine-teenth century. The most advanced country was England, followed by

France, Germany, Austria, Italy, and Russia, in that order. Gerschenkron then argued:

> The main proposition we can then make with regard to countries so ranked is that, the more delayed the industrial development of a country, the more explosive was the great spurt of its industrialization, if and when it came. Moreover, the higher degree of backwardness was associated with a stronger tendency toward larger scale of plant and enterprise and greater readiness to enter into monopolistic compacts of various degrees of intensity. Finally, the more backward a country, the more likely its industrialization was to proceed under some organized direction; depending on the degree of backwardness, the seat of such direction could be found in investment banks, in investment banks acting under the aegis of the state, or in bureaucratic controls. So viewed, the industrial history of Europe appears not as a series of mere repetitions of the "first" industrialization but as an orderly system of graduated deviations from that industrialization.[28]

At a later point, he added some other propositions, among them:

> The more backward a country's economy, the greater was the stress upon producers' goods as against consumers' goods . . . [and] the heavier was the pressure upon the levels of consumption of the population.[29]

Italy was the only country in Southern Europe that Gerschenkron discussed. He argued that in general it fit his pattern of delayed development, including monopolistic compacts among industrial producers, organized direction by investment banks, and substantial government assistance with subsidies and tariffs. Gerschenkron also found, however, that Italy departed from the pattern in that "the great spurt" was less vigorous, the role of consumer goods (textiles) was more pronounced, and tariff protection was more retarding in its effects than in the other late industrializers.

These Italian variations on the late-industrializer theme suggest that there is another pattern of delayed development. And, in fact, Albert Hirschman considered another group of countries, which he designated the "late late industrializers," in particular the countries of Latin America. Hirschman argued that few of Gerschenkron's propositions about the late industrializers actually fit the late late industrializers:

> Almost the opposite can be said to hold for our late latecomers. Their industrialization started with relatively small plants administering "last touches" to a host of imported products, concentrated on consumer rather than producer goods, and often was specifically designed to improve the levels of consumption of populations who were suddenly cut off, as a result of war or balance of

28. Gerschenkron, *Economic Backwardness*, p. 44.
29. Ibid., p. 354.

61

payments crises, from imported consumer goods to which they have become accustomed. . . .

As a result, late late industrialization shows little of the inspiring, if convulsive elan that was characteristic of the late industrializers such as Germany, Russia, and Japan.[30]

In brief, Hirschman's late late industrializers seem to be distinguished from Gerschenkron's late industrializers in much the same way as Gerschenkron's Italy was distinguished from his other late industrializers. Italy and, *a fortiori*, Spain, Portugal, and Greece seem to fit the "late late" pattern. We should not forget, however, that in both the late and the late late industrializers, there have been monopolistic compacts among industrial producers, organized direction by investment banks, and substantial government assistance with subsidies and tariffs.

Can one explain certain political phenomena in terms of these economic patterns? It appears that such economic distinctions explain a good deal of the political outcomes in Europe during the period from the 1870s to the 1930s. In both the late and the late late industrializers of Europe, as compared to the early ones, the network of industrial cartels, investment banks, and government bureaucracies brought about close integration of industrial interests by the late 1870s and the smooth operation of the state on their behalf. Accordingly, the importance of parliamentary legislation and party competition in the policy process was less. In addition, in both these late and late late industrializers, as compared to the early ones, the need by the late 1870s of both the industrial and the agricultural elites for tariff protection made for the close integration of their interests. This also diminished the importance of party competition. (In contrast, in both Britain and the United States, there were long periods during the nineteenth century when disagreement over the tariff formed a basis for party competition and probably for the institutionalization of the two-party system.)[31]

However, there were also important political differences between the late and the late late industrializers. In the late late industrializers, as compared with the early and the late ones, the industrial elites lacked prestige; they were not so much a "conquering bourgeoisie" as a collaborating one. British industrialists first produced consumer goods for foreign markets (textiles), then capital goods for foreign markets (rails, merchant

30. Hirschman, *Bias for Hope*, p. 95.
31. The importance of the tariff in politics is discussed by Peter Gourevitch, *Politics in Hard Times: Comparative Responses to International Economic Crises* (Ithaca, N.Y., 1986), especially chapter 3. Also see Alexander Gerschenkron, *Bread and Democracy in Germany* (Berkeley, Calif., 1943). A more general analysis of coalitions between agricultural and industrial elites is Barrington Moore, Jr., *Social Origins of Dictatorship and Democracy: Lord and Peasant in the Making of the Modern World* (Boston, 1966).

vessels, and machinery), and finally capital goods for national defense (naval vessels). The French and German industrialists did the same, with more emphasis on the second and the third. In these three countries, the vital role of the industrialists in foreign exchange and national defense endowed them with much prestige, and the pioneer achievement of the British and "the great spurt" of the French and Germans infused them with a strong sense of confidence or, in Hirschman's term, élan.

The industrialists of Southern Europe, however, mainly produced consumer goods in a protected market, and they were not so much involved in a "great spurt" as in the adding of "last touches." Thus, they lacked the prestige and confidence of their northern predecessors. This made the Mediterranean industrial elites especially willing to maintain the power of the agricultural elites, to accept their demands, and to merge the economic interests and the political parties of the two. The result was caciquism in the countryside and trasformismo, el turno, and "rotativism" at the center. It also meant that when both industrial and agricultural elites were threatened by radical movements they could early and readily come to agreement upon the establishment of a corporatist-authoritarian regime, whose mentality has more in common with the agrarian world than the industrial one.[32]

The character of the industrial elites had implications for the character of other social groups in the largest Southern European countries, Italy and Spain. Weak industrial elites resulted in high agricultural tariffs, which in turn further strengthened agricultural elites. Furthermore, high agricultural tariffs contributed to the commercialization of agriculture, which in turn resulted in the proliferation of landless agricultural workers and the attendant strong anarchist and syndicalist movements in the countryside. Finally, to complete the cycle, anarchist and syndicalist migrants from the countryside increased the strength of anarchist and syndicalist movements in the city, threatening the industrial elites. [There may be a more direct connection between backward industrial elites and strong anarchist and syndicalist movements in the factories. It was often the case that workers in small plants (textiles) tended toward anarchism and syndicalism while workers in large plants (steel, machinery) tended toward socialism. The high tariffs on textiles resulted in the perpetuation of many small factories and perhaps in the strengthening of anarchist and syndicalist movements.]

The models of late industrialization and late late industrialization, then, can be used to explain some features of Southern European politics, in particular the prevalence of trasformismo and caciquism during

32. For a discussion of the concept of mentality, see Linz, "An Authoritarian Regime: Spain."

JAMES KURTH

the early period of industrialization and the establishment of corporatist-authoritarian regimes during a later one. However, the explanatory power of the concepts is time-bound, that is, largely limited to the era from the 1870s to the 1930s.

A geographically narrower but historically broader use of the concept of delayed development is also possible. In particular, in Spain and Italy, there seems to have been a connection between economic backwardness and ideological fragmentation. Here our starting point is the work of Louis Hartz.

Hartz argued that Western Europe spun off ideological fragments that landed in the empty lands of the New World and then developed in isolation. He identified three major European ideologies: feudalism, liberalism, and socialism. The United States, as a liberal fragment, developed in the absence of feudalism and therefore, by Hartz's dialectical reasoning, in the absence of socialism; the result for the American fragment society was a massive consensus on liberalism.[33]

As we shall see, a rather different pattern resulted when Western Europe spun off ideologies which landed in the ancient societies of the Mediterranean world and then, especially in Spain, developed in coexistence. If America was a fragment society with a massive consensus on one ideology, then Spain was the opposite, a fragmented society with perpetual conflict between many ideologies. And the list of West European ideologies does not stop with feudalism, liberalism, and socialism. In the four centuries between the discovery of America and the First World War, Western Europe developed not just three ideologies but six as each of the three split into at least two forms. Feudalism gave rise to two conceptions of monarchy, one traditionalist, the other absolutist (the Tudors and Stuarts in England, the Valois and Bourbons in France). Liberalism developed a more democratic offshoot known as radicalism. Socialism developed a less bureaucratic offshoot in anarchism.

Thus, by the beginning of the twentieth century, Western Europe had experienced six major ideologies. It had not experienced them all at the same time, however. In each country of Western Europe, the absolute monarchists had eliminated the traditional monarchists long before the rise of liberalism, to say nothing of socialism. In Britain and in France, although not in Germany, the liberals had also eliminated the absolute monarchists before the rise of socialism. At any one time, the countries of Western Europe retained only some of the ideologies that they had developed.

In Spain, the picture was different. Spain did not develop any of the five ideologies after traditional monarchy; rather, it imported them from

33. Louis Hartz, "A Theory of the Development of the New Societies," in *Founding of New Societies*, pp. 3–122; idem, *The Liberal Tradition in America* (New York, 1955).

64

Western Europe after they had been developed there to suit the needs of some rising social group. Because of Spain's economic backwardness, the Spanish social group that imported the ideology was not as developed as the West European counterpart that had created it; the "idea-bearing estate" in Spain was smaller and weaker than in Western Europe. As a result, in Spain the new ideology did not conquer an old one as it had in Western Europe; it merely coexisted with it. Delayed economic development meant premature ideological development.

Thus, in early eighteenth-century Spain, the social groups in favor of absolute monarchy were strong enough to clear a place for imported Bourbon conceptions; they were not strong enough, however, to permanently suppress the social groups in favor of traditional Habsburg monarchy. Thus the two conceptions coexisted uneasily in Spain throughout the eighteenth century, while in Western Europe the absolutists had destroyed the traditionalists long before.

Similarly, in the early nineteenth century, the liberals were strong enough to import a third conception, constitutional monarchy, while not being strong enough to eliminate the previous two. Before the upper bourgeoisie had constructed an English-style alliance around liberalism with the petty bourgeoisie, an alliance strong enough to eliminate the traditional and absolute monarchists and to establish a stable constitutional monarchy, the small bourgeoisie had imported radicalism (or republicanism) from Western Europe, an ideology for which they had a greater elective affinity and which was better adapted to their social condition.

Similarly, before the small bourgeoisie had constructed a French-style alliance around radicalism or republicanism with the skilled workers that would be strong enough to eliminate the "bourgeois monarchy" and to establish a stable democratic republic, the skilled workers had imported socialism, an ideology which was more suited to their interests. Finally, before the skilled workers had constructed a Scandinavian-style alliance around socialism with the unskilled workers strong enough to establish a strong and stable socialist party, the unskilled workers had imported anarchism, an ideology which was closer to their own understanding of their situation.

The simultaneous coexistence of several ideologies meant that at no time could one social group establish an ideological hegemony (in Gramsci's sense) and thus a political majority. No social group could become "the great simplifier" of the political system by permanently suppressing another group and excluding its ideology. Charles Anderson's observation that Latin American politics is a "living museum"[34] has

34. Charles W. Anderson, in *Politics and Economic Change in Latin America* (Princeton, N.J. 1967), p. 104.

been even more true of politics in Spain. By the early twentieth century Spain was not only a living museum but a broken mirror that reflected every ideology produced in Western Europe over the past four hundred years, in a way no country in Western Europe itself did. It is not surprising that two of the best books describing the period were entitled *Invertebrate Spain* and *The Spanish Labyrinth*.[35]

In Italy much the same dynamic was at work. During the Risorgimento, however, the Piedmont liberal monarchists were at least able to destroy the absolute monarchists of northern Italy and the traditional monarchists of the Two Sicilies. (In Italy the Austrian Habsburgs played the absolutist role of the Spanish Bourbons, while the Neapolitan Bourbons played the traditionalist role of the Spanish Habsburgs.) By the early twentieth century, however, Italy also was split into liberal, radical (republican), socialist, and anarchist camps.

And so, after Spain had disintegrated utterly into three years of civil war, it reached back across three centuries and five ideologies to pick up again the earliest and most Spanish ideology of all, that of the Spanish Habsburgs. So too, after Italy had been utterly defeated in the Second World War, it reached back even further to pick up not so much an ideology but a theology, that of the most ancient and most Roman of all Italian political institutions, the Catholic church. It was as if Spain and Italy, after three hundred years of importing the newest ideologies from Western Europe, only to distort them and to distort themselves, had decided instead to return to the most traditional and most Mediterranean political ideas.

In Spain, Italy, and also Portugal, the period from the 1940s to the 1970s – the fifth phase of political development described in this article – was a sort of Indian summer for distinctive Southern European political ideas. With the coming of the 1980s and the sixth phase, the countries of Southern Europe said good-bye to all that. Without looking back, they proclaimed that they were at last leaving behind the burdens of delayed development and traditional ideas and were finally entering the real Europe and the modern era. By the 1980s, however, to be up to date meant to be postindustrial, even postmodern, not industrial and modern in the way that Northern Europe had been throughout the twentieth century.[36] Thus Southern Europe became postindustrial and postmodern too, but in doing so, it merely entered delayed and dependent development at its highest stage.

---

35. José Ortega y Gasset, *Invertebrate Spain* (New York, 1937); Brenan, *Spanish Labyrinth*.
36. The distinctions between industrial and postindustrial and between modern and postmodern are discussed by James Kurth, "The Post-Modern State," *The National Interest*, no. 28 (1992): pp. 26–35.

3 THE RECENT BIRTH OF MODERN ITALY

Diarmuid Maguire

INTRODUCTION: SOCIAL TRANSFORMATION AND POLITICAL TRANSFORMATION, 1968–1993

In 1968, Italy was largely a traditional Catholic society with a strong agrarian sector, dominated economically by a few large industrial centers. In 1993, it has a dynamic, secular and advanced social structure, sustained by a myriad of small and medium-sized enterprises. In a quarter of a century, Italian society has been transformed through an economy that recently has produced some of the highest annual growth rates in Europe. "Europe's Japan" is one of the world's leading industrial powers and its wealth surpasses that of "the first industrial nation," Britain. Many of its citizens enjoy not only high standards of living but also considerable freedom from traditional social networks. The result is that a large number of Italians now experience a lifestyle that is very similar to that of their neighbors in Northern Europe.

One only has to walk around the streets of a city like Milan to observe this new secular Italy of affluence and conspicuous consumption. These streets are filled with people displaying their new clothes and cars; the shops are packed with an enormous variety of fashionable consumer goods. The fact that the *milanesi* have to work for these benefits is attested to by the recent proliferation of stand-up sandwich bars and the disappearance of the "long lunch." A Sunday morning visit to a Milanese church would demonstrate the attendant secularization of Italian society: there, a dwindling number of old people, mainly women, and young girls gather together for worship. An evening visit to a discotheque would provide a noisy illustration of the newfound freedoms of young people in a society increasingly free from family control.

If a Milanese Rip Van Winkle were awoken now after a twenty-five year slumber, he would recognize little of his old city's way of life. The continued existence of the cathedral and the monuments would not alleviate his confusion over his fellow citizens' strange behavior. Yet in his

67

disorientation he might find strange comfort in some familiar elements. A frustrating encounter with a post-office official would show that there are still some living state monuments to a bygone era. Similarly, an attempt to deal with a tax official over his failure to submit returns for the past twenty-five years, though Kafkaesque, might also be psychologically reassuring. A train journey to Naples with its late departure and unscheduled stops would further illustrate how the state refuses to bow to modernity. And Naples itself, with its continuing poverty and religiosity, would show that an entire way of life had not disappeared entirely.

This Italian Rip Van Winkle might even have asked a Neapolitan who the prime minister was and, as late as 1991, smile with great satisfaction at being told that it was Giulio Andreotti. He would probably conclude – like Tomasi di Lampedusa on the Risorgimento – that everything in Italy had been changed so that essentially things would remain the same.

This conclusion, however, would be false. Some features of Italian life have indeed changed and some things have indeed remained the same. Italy's social and economic transformation is real and important. At the same time, political stagnation and southern backwardness are continuing and producing severe problems for the system. Change itself, however, is increasingly rapid and profound, and the contradiction between the dynamic elements of change and the static elements of continuity has lately become more acute. The capacity of the Christian Democratic state to adapt to the consequences of this social transformation through political *trasformismo* has been weakened by the respective successes and failures of these two processes themselves.

In order to understand the current political impasse one first must analyze how Italy has been able to get as far as it has since the late 1960s. This helps explain why the gap between the polity and the economy has now become so large.

It will be argued in this chapter that Italy has recently experienced three successive waves of modernization which together have led to its development as an advanced industrial economy. Although the processes described in these three epochs are by no means chronologically discrete, it is nonetheless a useful simplification to examine the main features of each successive era.

After the "economic miracle" of the 1960s, modernization was pushed forward by mass movements at the base of Italian society. This era of movement pressure occurred roughly in the period 1968-75, and was followed by a phase of political co-optation (1976-79) when the working class through its workplace and political institutions (the trade unions and the Communist party) were recognized as legitimate actors by the state and partially incorporated into the polity.

But movement pressure from below and political incorporation from above was costly for Italian capitalism and it experienced a crisis of profitability. The period since 1979 has been characterized by the success of Italian capitalists in returning their enterprises to profitability and the emergence of a "second economic miracle." The ensuing attempts of the modern middle classes to establish the institutional reform of the state – in line with an advanced economy – have already begun and will shape the next phase of Italian modernization.

In the 1990s, modernizing Italians will try to turn their country – this time politically as well as economically – into an advanced country like any other. The modern middle classes and a revitalized bourgeoisie now represent the dynamic sectors of Italian society. They are demanding a political system that both meets their needs and reflects their power. And they are determined to escape the fate of trasformismo in this final phase of Italy's belated bourgeois revolution.

THE FIRST TWO PHASES, 1968–1979

Protest From Below, 1968–1975

In the 1960s, Italy became a predominantly industrial nation whose continued development seemed to rest on the successful mix of state intervention, cheap southern labor, and a strong export performance. Yet Italy's first economic miracle opened up a series of social contradictions in the process which the Christian Democrats (DC) tried to control through an alliance with the Socialist party (PSI). This "opening to the left" – excluding the Communist party (PCI) – only increased expectations of reform which state and industrial elites were either unable or unwilling to deliver. One of the results was an explosion of industrial militancy and social discontent which challenged one important element of the economic miracle's formula – cheap labor – as well as the framework of Christian Democratic power. At the end of the decade, Italy experienced a prolonged wave of popular protest which represented a profound challenge to the existing political and industrial order.[1]

The "Hot Autumn" of 1969 saw an explosion of strikes in northern factories which spread to other sectors of employment. This labor militancy, as Michele Salvati notes, was not blocked by Italy's weak trade unions. They wanted to institutionalize the movement through delegate councils without stifling its activist momentum. The unions were in the classic position in early full-scale industrialization of recruiting unskilled

---

1. See Sidney Tarrow, *Democracy and Disorder: Protest and Politics in Italy, 1965–1975* (New York, 1985).

and semiskilled industrial workers. Labor organization was also facilitated by the fact that striking workers were not subject to old-fashioned state repression. This was partly because the DC's coalition partner, the PSI, was opposed to this type of response.[2]

Thus industrial capitalists had to deal with widespread workplace disruption without the help of a compliant union bureaucracy or a repressive state. Furthermore, there was no middle-class counteroffensive against labor as happened later, under similar circumstances, in Britain. In fact, the middle class was pursuing its own political grievances at the same time through similar means of mass social protest.[3]

Socially and politically defenseless, industrial capitalists had no choice but to give in to workers' demands for higher wages and greater control over the production process. This led not only to a redistribution of wealth from capital to labor but also to a shift in power relations between the two.[4]

Italy's wage bill shot up and workers saw their pay approach, and in some cases exceed, that of their Northern European counterparts. Official and unofficial strikes, nonetheless, continued to disrupt the workplace and drive the wage spiral ever upward. In addition, the *statuto dei lavoratori* (Workers' Charter) of 1970 gave official recognition to some important workers' rights. The operations of the industrial shop floor were increasingly regulated and subject to negotiations with trade unions. Manufacturing workers enjoyed a shorter working week, were guaranteed time off for study and meetings, and exercised greater control over their daily working lives. As a consequence, the degree of unionization increased from 29 percent in 1968 to 49 percent by 1977.[5] Government benefits, known as the "social wage," also increased dramatically as the state met new societal demands and sought to offset some of the increasing costs for capitalists.[6]

Meanwhile, there was a tide of social protest that challenged other forms of power outside the workplace. The number of university stu-

2. Michele Salvati, "Muddling Through: Economics and Politics in Italy, 1969–1979," in *Italy in Transition: Conflict and Consensus*, ed. Peter Lange and Sidney Tarrow (London, 1980), p.36.

3. Sidney Tarrow, "The Crisis of the Late 1960s in Italy and France," in *Semiperipheral Development: The Politics of Southern Europe in the Twentieth Century*, ed. Giovanni Arrighi (Beverly Hills, Calif., 1985), p. 229.

4. Alfredo Gigliobianco and Michele Salvati, *Il maggio francese e l'autunno caldo italiano: la risposta di due borghesie* (Bologna, 1980).

5. Michael Kreile, "The Crisis of Italian Trade Unionism in the 1980s," *West European Politics* 11 (January 1988): 54–67.

6. Lange notes that by 1972 Italy's social expenditure was only 1 percent behind that of West Germany. Peter Lange, "Semiperiphery and Core in the European Context," in Arrighi, ed., *Semiperipheral Development,* 187.

dents had increased by 117 percent between 1961 and 1968 and this social constituency was key to the emergence of the New Left in the late 1960s.[7] New Left movements demanded not only a greater say in institutions of higher education but also called for a new society that would be democratic, secular, and socialist. The women's movement also became a pillar of general middle-class agitation for radical social change. The high point of this mobilization was the success of the referendum that legalized divorce in 1974. Although the content of this policy change was important, its symbolism was more important still. Catholic Italy was becoming secular Italy and the church was increasingly on the defensive.

In this period, the three main trade union confederations (CGIL, CISL and UIL) expanded their membership and power by harnessing industrial militancy. The Radical party (PR) and the PSI won some political prestige for pushing the prodivorce campaign. The 1975 and 1976 local and national elections made it clear, however, that it was the PCI that might become the major political beneficiary of these modernizing changes. Ironically, these were changes that the party had not initiated and in certain respects had opposed.

The Political Incorporation of Working-Class Institutions, 1976–1979

In 1976, the PCI obtained 34.4 percent of the vote and came within a few percentage points of the DC, which received 38.7 percent. The Communists had won the support of many young and progressive middle-class voters who wanted radical change. It also represented a more powerful working class that was demanding greater inclusion within the polity. The DC's "opening to the left," which had been limited to the PSI in the 1960s, was being widened to include the Communists in the 1970s. Some DC leaders reckoned that otherwise it would be impossible to slow down wage expansion and reestablish management control over the shop floor. Also, without the support of the PCI, it would have been extremely difficult for the DC to have entered into a reformist dialogue with a restless middle class.

The Christian Democrats' "opening to the PCI" began at the legislative level when the party obtained the chairs of important parliamentary committees and Pietro Ingrao was made president of the Chamber of Deputies. The concrete realization of the "historic compromise" strategy, formulated in 1973, would be PCI support for the DC in parliament, as well as wage discipline from its trade-union base. In exchange, the

7. Alexander De Grand, *The Italian Left in the Twentieth Century* (Bloomington, Ind., and Indianapolis, 1989), p.148.

PCI hoped to gain political legitimacy, social reforms, and eventually executive power.

Italian capitalism needed such an agreement to weather the economic storms of the mid-1970s. The 1973-74 recession, runaway wage costs, and inflation had led to a crisis of profitability for industry. The only way out, it seemed in the short term, was for management to establish wage discipline through negotiations. If that involved political costs, then some were prepared to pay. Christian Democratic politicians like Aldo Moro and Benigno Zaccagnini were the most prepared to bargain with the trade unions and the PCI in this way and they rose to the top of their party.[8]

The PCI delivered a trade-union movement prepared to accept austerity and a group of deputies ready to support the Christian Democrats in Parliament. The number of strikes declined and a large proportion of further wage rises were the result of the *scala mobile* (automatic wage indexation) that unions and employers had established in 1975.[9] The Communist party stood by the government as it was beset by leftist and rightist terrorist activity in this period, and proved to be a determined enemy of the Red Brigades during the Moro tragedy. The PCI believed that it was defending a fragile liberal democracy, which it had helped establish, from a series of profound and related crises.[10]

In this way, the PCI was co-opted by the ruling Christian Democrats and at quite a cheap price in the short term. The Communists obtained neither cabinet seats nor serious social reforms. What legitimacy the party may have gained from its responsible policies were not translated into executive power,[11] and the failure of the PCI to achieve radical reforms delegitimated it in the eyes of its social base. Indeed, it was only in 1989 that the party formally recognized the true nature of its 1975-76 vote which, as party secretary Achille Occhetto put it, was a vote for "a new society for a new government."[12] Unfortunately for the PCI, this recognition was more than a decade late.

In January 1979, the PCI withdrew its support for the government and in 1980 it abandoned the strategy of "historic compromise." Admittedly, the party had obtained some lasting gains by establishing greater

8. Sidney Tarrow, "Historic Compromise or Bourgeois Majority? Eurocommunism in Italy, 1976–1979," in *National Communism in Western Europe: A Third Way For Socialism?*, ed. Howard Machin (London and New York, 1983), p. 130.

9. OECD Economic Surveys, *Italy* (Paris, 1980), p. 19.

10. See Tarrow, "Historic Compromise," 140–41.

11. For the American role in setting these limits see Zbigniew Brzezinski, *Power and Principle: Memoirs of the National Security Advisor* (London, 1983).

12. Cited by Sergio Fabbrini, "Le strategie istituzionale del PCI," *Il Mulino* 39, no. 331 (September–October 1990): 770.

control over the legislature, but without direct access to the executive, as Judith Chubb has pointed out, it bore the costs of exercising responsibility without power.[13] Trade union and grass-roots opposition had forced the leadership to cast off this burden.

The PCI's conscious decision to defend capitalist democracy rather than risk authoritarian backlash meant that a crucial opportunity for radical (though certainly not revolutionary) transformation was lost. Industrial capital and the DC were able to come off the defensive having tamed the workplace and political wings of labor. To paraphrase Hobsbawm's description of nineteenth-century British labor, the new Italian working class had "learned the rules of the game."[14] It was a game in which it would have a limited, though important, share and whose basic rules it would have to accept.

THE THIRD PHASE: ITALIAN POLITICAL ECONOMY, 1980–1993

Economic Growth and Industrial Restructuring: The State

Insurgency from below paved the way for incorporation from above and both had an effect on the political management of the economy. Future bargaining with labor might mean that salaries would increase at a rate lower than prices but in key industrial sectors Italy was now a permanent high-wage economy. A return to profitability and international competitiveness would have to be based on methods other than the simple reliance on cheap labor to cut costs and increase productivity.

At the same time, the state's tremendous efforts at maintaining "legitimation and accumulation" during more than a decade of upheaval had led to enormous budget deficits. Throughout the 1980s, Italy had the highest deficits in Europe and at the end of the decade the total debt was over 100 percent of Gross Domestic Product (GDP).[15] The central questions for economic and state elites in the 1980s was whether and how it could reduce these costs of maintaining social peace and keeping the Christian Democrats in power.

The questions of labor and social costs, though separate, were clearly linked. The incorporation of labor into the polity had exacted a heavy price from capital and the state, and it was one that they could not afford to pay indefinitely. Competition from Japan, the newly industrialized countries (NICs) in Asia, and from an increasingly integrated market in Europe, put Italian capitalism under considerable international pressure. The replacement of labor by capital, subcontracting to small and medium-

13. Judith Chubb, *Patronage, Power, and Poverty in Southern Italy* (New York, 1982).
14. Eric Hobsbawm, *Primitive Rebels* (New York and London, 1959).
15. OECD Economic Surveys, *Italy* (Paris, 1989).

sized enterprises, and negotiating greater labor market flexibility became the main means by which leading industrial sectors sought to meet the challenges of domestic labor and international competition. Many of Italy's political and economic elites also wondered if a vastly reduced state sector, pursuing neoliberal policies, might assist in this process.

The Italian state has played a heavy role in four areas targeted by neoliberals for reform throughout the 1980s: that is, in investment management; industrial planning and production; social welfare; and wages. State investment and planning – particularly through public enterprises and holding companies – had helped industrialize the economy in the 1950s and 1960s, but Italy's first economic miracle was also based on low market and social wages.

As we have seen, the miracle did not last and the state was forced to help regulate market wages and expand social wages. Welfare-state expenditure doubled from 1954 to 1980 (as a percentage of GDP), and expenditure on state enterprises increased fivefold in the same period.[16] During economic recessions, governments also engaged in countercyclical policies, taking ailing firms into the public sector and engaging in the highest deficit spending in the Organization for Economic Cooperation and Development (OECD). In the 1980s, the Italian state gave more direct aid to industry (3 percent of GDP in the middle of the decade) than any other major European country.[17] In short, after a period of mass militancy and political incorporation, Italy had an expanding Keynesian welfare state. This expansion occurred when Keynesian spending was contracting elsewhere.

In 1981, Italy's deficit stood at 11.8 percent of GDP compared to an OECD average for major countries of 2.2 percent. Furthermore, from 1973 to 1981, the public sector on average consumed about half of the country's domestic credit.[18] This led to concerns, analyzed in successive OECD reports, that the public sector would "crowd out" private investment. The proposed solutions offered by neoliberals were for the state to deregulate the financial sector, privatize some of its holdings, and reduce expenditure on welfare. Not only would this help reduce a chronic budget deficit but also would provide the private sector with more autonomous sources of capital.

It is important to note, though, that the state was not just some enor-

16. Vincent Della Salla, "The Italian Budgetary Process: Political and Institutional Constraints," *West European Politics* 11 (July 1988): 110–25.

17. OECD Economic Surveys, *Italy* (Paris, 1989).

18. Gerald Epstein and Juliet Schor, "The Divorce of the Banca d'Italia and the Italian Treasury: A Case Study of Central Bank Independence," in *State, Market and Social Regulation: New Perspectives on Italy,* eds. Peter Lange and Marino Regini (New York, 1989), p. 155.

mous parasite feeding off a weak private sector, or, if it were, it certainly kept its host very much alive. This is because, as the OECD notes, "the public sector has also played a role in redistributing income, to the productive sector in particular."[19] For example, it has been estimated that in 1979 one-third of private investment funds came from government transfers.[20] Add to this the role that the state plays in reducing market wages through social wages, as well as its generous investment incentives, and the image of the greedy state parasite would have to be modified.

Nonetheless, there were concerted attempts in the 1980s to introduce neoliberal reform and "bring the market back in." Italy's financial system was deregulated through successive legislative acts. The Bank of Italy was granted its independence from the Treasury in July 1981. In December 1984, the rules for financial investment abroad were liberalized, as, less than a year later, were regulations for foreign borrowing. In February 1987, the banks were deregulated and exchange controls were liberalized in May that year. By the end of the decade, as Epstein and Schor put it, "Italy's financial sector has been 'Anglo-Saxonized'."[21]

Yet this did not lead to the type of "casino economy" that helped reduce British and American productivity in the same period. The main route to wealth in Italy was still through control of the production of goods and services. Due to continuous high interest rates and stringent rent controls, real-estate speculation did not provide a tremendously profitable outlet for capital. Also, the Italian stock market, as the *Economist* put it, was "paper-thin," and was dominated by big tycoons.[22] Domestic savings, which are extremely high, have helped finance the deficit rather than the private sector directly. This is due partly to the incentives offered by the state to hold its paper and partly to popular suspicion of the stock market itself. Thus, despite financial liberalization, the state still plays a major role as the "nation's banker" and, therefore, the private sector's political dependence on the state has not been broken.

The deregulation of the financial system has also been accompanied by the privatization of state holdings. Between 1983 and 1989, the Institute for Industrial Reconstruction (IRI) sold seventeen large enterprises.[23] In the same period, IRI liquidated a number of minority shareholdings. The most important privatization was the sale of Alfa Romeo to Fiat in 1986. At the time, some saw this as a signal of future full-scale denation-

19. OECD Economic Surveys, *Italy* (Paris, 1989), 17.
20. Epstein and Schor, "The Divorce of the Banca d'Italia," 157.
21. Ibid., 147.
22. "A Survey of Italy," *Economist*, 26 May 1990.
23. See "Survey of Italy." Also, Patrizio Bianchi, Sabino Cassese and Vincent Della Salla, "Privatisation in Italy: Aims and Constraints," *West European Politics* 11 (October 1988): 87–100,

alization, but Italian privatization turned out to be a very modest affair, only a fifth to a quarter the rate in Britain or France.[24] It turned out that Mrs. Thatcher and Monsieur Chirac were much more consistent neoliberals than Signor Craxi and his colleagues.

The Italian government's footdragging over supporting Enimont – a joint venture between the National Hydrocarbons Corporation (ENI) and Montedison – revealed one major reason for its inconsistent approach to reform. There was a deep resistance on the part of state managers to accept the political consequences of radical privatization. Since it would be the large tycoons of Italian capitalism who would benefit most from privatization, the state was reluctant to strengthen this alternative source of political power. Large-scale privatization in the absence of a "popular" stock market would see private power even more concentrated rather than dispersed. This was something that the Christian Democrats and some of their allies could not tolerate.

In addition, the state did not leave the arena of industrial planning and coordination to the market. While its actions may not provide a great model of Keynesian efficiency, it continued to occupy this space, which had an important effect on economic life. The state has tried to give industry a leg up in the product cycle through funding research and development (R&D) and the purchase of high-tech equipment. Public funds for R&D tripled between 1981 and 1986, and a law granting cheap loans to small industry for advanced machinery was passed in 1982.[25] With initiatives like these, it was clear that the state – more by political circumstance than design – was pursuing Anglo-Saxon (financial liberalism) and Japanese (managed capitalism) strategies simultaneously.

On the Anglo-Saxon side, neoliberal welfare reforms were introduced with the declared aims of increasing efficiency and reducing costs. Policies reflected the typical neoliberal solutions of having the user pay (particularly in health), strengthening private welfare through incentives, and weeding out recipients through new regulations.[26]

Again, by British or American standards the results were very modest. This was partly because the Christian Democrats' welfare and, more importantly, patronage constituencies were a crucial obstacle to change. The strength of the PCI in Parliament also gave it the power to block or amend radical reform of this kind. Also, the trade-union movement, though weaker since the 1970s, was still able throughout the 1980s to mount impressive campaigns in defense of the social wage.

24. Bianchi, Cassese and Della Salla,"Privatisation in Italy," 88.
25. OECD Economic Surveys, *Italy* (Paris, 1989).
26. Massimo Paci, "Public and Private in the Italian Welfare System," in Lange and Regini, eds., *State, Market and Social Regulation*, 217–34.

Meanwhile, the market wage was still regulated by automatic increases fixed by the *scala mobile*. As far as employers were concerned this was a major obstacle to profitability and reducing the country's high level of inflation. In January 1983, Italy experienced its "neocorporatist moment" when government, employers, and unions made a deal in which promises of social reform, reduction in working hours, and wage discipline were exchanged among the negotiating partners.

However, the problem of the *scala mobile* remained and was not resolved through neocorporatist bargaining. Instead, wage indexation was reformed through the exercise of executive power by the prime minister, who decreed a reduction in its scope in February 1984. The PCI's subsequent attempt to reverse this decision through a popular referendum was defeated in June 1985.

The referendum represented an important milestone in the political development of the new Italian working class. During the campaign, a politically divided trade-union movement with a declining membership could not agree on a common policy. The result of the vote, to some extent, represented a popular affirmation of political and executive authority. The referendum was a defeat for the trade unions – even if some had opposed the PCI's position – because it demonstrated how divided and unrepresentative their movement had become.

So in the spheres of finance, planning, welfare, and wages, important elements of neoliberalism crept into state policy-making. All the reforms, however, became enmeshed within the structures of the Keynesian welfare and patronage state. Financial liberalization did not dislodge the state from its role as an important "national banker" for the private sector. Privatization did not lead to the state being removed from the arena of industrial planning; if anything, it sought to increase its role in this area of activity. Moderate welfare reforms failed to reduce the government's enormous budget deficit, and wage deregulation and work-rules flexibility were promoted by a government that was determined to effect change but lacked the killer instincts of the Thatcher and Reagan regimes.

Italy's Keynesian, patronage, and now neoliberal state was not up to radical Thatcherite reform in the 1980s. As a result, Italy's political economy, as Romano Prodi aptly describes it, now occupies an awkward position between the Anglo-Saxon and German-Japanese models.[27]

Economic Growth and Industrial Restructuring: the Market

Government reforms and services, however tepid and inadequate, did help industrial capitalists recover after the upheavals and profit squeeze of

27. Romano Prodi, "C'e un posto per l'Italia fra i due capitalismi?" *Il Mulino* 40, no. 389 (January-February 1991): 23–33.

the 1970s. The state's Wage Supplementation Fund (*Cassa Integrazione Guadagni*), for example, financed the costs of redundancies. This allowed employers to shed labor. Early state retirement schemes also served the same purpose. Direct subsidies, investment incentives, and protectionism were other means by which the state helped industrialists survive and ultimately prosper. But these mechanisms only had a limited effect in assisting firms that were under domestic pressure to pay higher wages and international pressure to compete.

A direct capitalist offensive against labor in the British or American style was out of the question for a number of reasons. First of all, business itself was divided in its approach to labor, with "relatively capital-intensive firms . . . [pursuing] a strategy aimed at reducing the trade unions' power," and labor-intensive firms being more conciliatory.[28] Second, as has been pointed out before, employers could not rely on state repression or popular support in undertaking such a project.

Employers, therefore, were forced to negotiate with a relatively strong trade-union movement. They also followed, however, a strategy of changing their production systems, bypassing labor's centers of organized power, and finding new ways to increase productivity and cut costs. Utilizing these sorts of approaches, large industrialists in particular hoped to become more competitive domestically and internationally.

Following the broader global pattern, Italian enterprises introduced computer and robotic technology directly into industrial production; Fiat's Mirafiori plant in Turin was in the vanguard of this process. Another major industrial innovation in the 1970s and 1980s was the subcontracting of work by larger enterprises to small and medium-sized firms. This form of decentralization was particularly strong in the northwestern industrial triangle of Lombardy, Liguria, and Piedmont. In this way, employers were able to bypass the traditional centers of labor's industrial power and thus reduce their costs. In the process, they also weakened organized labor's hold on production by dispersing it throughout the economy.

It has been estimated that unit labor costs in Italy's large enterprises are 40 percent higher than in small and medium-sized firms. The hourly earnings of manufacturing workers in large firms are also 50 percent higher.[29] Thus, subcontracting to weakly unionized smaller firms has not only allowed the giants to reduce their wage bills indirectly but also to avoid less flexible work practices on their large factory floors.

This new division of labor in industrial production has produced what

---

28. A. Martinelli, "Organized Business and Italian Politics: Confindustria and the Christian Democrats in the Postwar Period," in Lange and Tarrow, eds., *Italy in Transition*, 81.
29. OECD Economic Surveys, *Italy* (Paris, 1989), 39.

Bruno Grancelli has called "areas of proletarianization" and "areas of nonproletarianization" in the Italian economy.[30] In the areas of proletarianization, contracted labor works in large urban enterprises and enjoys some protection from direct management control. In areas of nonproletarianization, nonunion and autonomous labor operates in small firms and is subject to greater demands from owners. An estimated 20 to 33 percent of dependent workers hold second jobs in small enterprises of this kind.[31]

But the growth of the small and medium-sized firms is not just a function of the large enterprises resolving their internal problems with labor. There has also been an "organic" growth of these companies. This has been due partly to the expansion of the service sector, but it also represents an economic response to world demand for specialized products that can be transformed quickly in response to market tastes.

These latter sorts of enterprises mirror the type of production being carried out by the Asian NICs. In global markets the Italians specialize in producing high-quality but traditional goods. According to Bagnasco, these sorts of firms tend to be concentrated in the central and northeastern regions of the peninsula.[32] Employees in these enterprises – which, like a lot of small firms, are family managed – operate in a working environment that stresses commitment and flexibility rather than conflict and rigidity.

The final area of nonproletarianization can be located in Italy's enormous informal economy. Estimates of the size of this sector vary tremendously. The state's statistical bureau, ISTAT, reckoned in 1987 that the size of the underground economy was about 18 percent of GDP.[33] Estimates of earnings from clandestine employment have also been put at anywhere between 20 and 33 percent of Gross National Product (GNP).[34] Whatever its true size may be, the informal sector exerts considerable power over economic life. Its freedom from union and state regulation presents a great challenge to organized labor in particular.

Not surprisingly, the growth of these new forms of production has

30. Bruno Grancelli, "Political Trade-Offs, Collective Bargaining, Individual Tradings: Some Remarks on Industrial Relations in Italy," in *The Unofficial Economy: Consequences and Perspectives in Different Economic Systems,* ed. Sergio Alessandrini and Bruno Dallago (Aldershot, U.K. 1987), pp. 257–70.

31. Ibid., 260.

32. Arnaldo Bagnasco, *Tre Italie: la problematica territoriale dello sviluppo italiano* (Bologna, 1977). See also B. Cattero, "Industrial Relations in Small and Medium-Sized Enterprises in Italy," in Industrial Relations in Small and Medium-Sized Enterprises, (Luxembourg, 1989), pp. 175–210.

33. "A Survey of Italy."

34. L. Weiss, "Explaining the Underground Economy: State and Social Structure," *British Journal of Sociology* 38, no. 2 (June 1987): 219.

had a tremendous impact on the conduct of class and political conflict. With decentralization and subcontracting, trade unions now have to cope with a crisis of control over the mechanisms of industrial production. More importantly, with such a segmented work force, they also have to deal with a crisis of representation that affects not only them but also, as we shall see, class-based political parties. Some workers who have been locked outside of unionized sectors of employment have found ways into the labor market through nonunion work. In addition, a high percentage of unionized employees themselves – the "double workers" – have discovered new ways to increase their incomes without resorting to industrial and political struggle.

Under such pressures, trade union presence in the workplace began to decline in the 1980s. Union membership, which comprised 49 percent of the workforce in 1977, had dropped to 42 percent by 1985.[35] A considerable proportion of those that remained were pensioners. This last category of unionist represents the human residue of a previous form of production that was much kinder to movement organization. By the 1980s, by contrast, a weaker trade-union movement had been forced onto the defensive in its dealings with employers. It had accepted the reintroduction of short-term and part-time work and ceded greater control to management over the hiring process.[36]

This transformation of Italian methods of production has been the product of previous class and political struggles. Worker pressure for both higher wages and greater control over production has helped force the Italian bourgeoisie to innovate. It has also contributed to an increase in the size of the bourgeoisie by indirectly encouraging the growth of small and medium-sized enterprises. The result is that Italy now has a social and class structure which is not so far removed from that of a typical advanced industrial economy.

If one examines the number of those employed in agriculture, for example, it is apparent that there has been a tremendous decline over thirty years, from 32.6 percent of the workforce in 1960 to 9.8 percent in 1988. The 1960 figure was 11.5 percent higher than the European Community average; by 1988 the difference had fallen to 2.4 percent. Thus Italy's "peasant dynamite" has been defused through economic erosion, and labor organizers can no longer rely on newly arrived southern peasants to help fuel militancy in the north as they did in the late 1960s.

The percentages of workers employed in manufacturing (24.3 percent) and services (57.7 percent) are also in line with OECD and EC

35. Kreile, "The Crisis of Italian Trade Unionism," 63.
36. See E. Reyneri, "The Italian Labor Market: Between State Control and Social Regulation," in Lange and Regini, eds., *State, Market and Social Regulation,* 129–46.

averages.[37] This growing number of service workers, particularly in the private sector, are less willing to join trade unions, and indeed a large proportion are self-employed. The service sector also tends to facilitate the growth of the small-enterprise economy.

This new configuration of class forces reflects Italy's recent entry into the world of advanced capitalist nations. The rapid decline in agricultural employment and the expansion of the service sector demonstrate the short period it took for full-scale industrialization to be transformed into advanced capitalism. Italy's weak trade-union movement and its domesticated social-democratic party (the ex-PCI) also illustrate how the political processes associated with this type of transition have followed a typical political logic.

CHRISTIAN DEMOCRACY VERSUS CAPITALIST DEMOCRACY, 1980-1993

The Christian Democrats and the Patronage State

Through all these momentous changes, however, the persistence of the Christian Democratic state sticks out like a sore thumb. To put it crudely though accurately, there is now a very stark contradiction in Italian society between its economic base, which is dynamic, productive, and secular, and elements of its political superstructure, which are stagnant, parasitic, and Christian Democrat. As a consequence, it seems as if the Italian bourgeoisie, with broader popular support since the 1980s, has begun a belated struggle to effect a modern political revolution.

The Italian Keynesian welfare state expanded in the 1960s and the 1970s as a result of the Christian Democrats' opening first to the Socialist and then the Communist left. As we have seen, neoliberal attempts to strip back this area of state activity have met with modest success. In the meantime, the patronage state has continued to distribute benefits to the clients of the Christian Democratic party and its allies.

The process of *lotizzazione* (allotment) results in jobs being parceled out in the state sector according to party political affiliation. The Christian Democrats control IRI and the Socialists run ENI. In the state-controlled television system, the Christian Democrats operate Channel One and the Socialists, Channel Two. As a result, His Holiness John Paul II and *onerevole* Bettino Craxi have each received a lot of air time on one of these channels.

Patronage benefits are also distributed to the electoral clients of the

37. These and preceding figures from OECD Economic Outlook, *Historical Statistics, 1960–1988* (Paris, 1990).

81

DC in particular. For example, the clientelistic distribution of disability pensions is an enormous enterprise that has thoroughly corrupted the welfare system. In some areas of southern Italy, for example, more than 20 percent of the population obtains disability allowances. In the polite words of a 1985 OECD report, the Italian state has "fairly flexible qualification criteria for disability pensions."[38] To put it more bluntly, these criteria tend to center around providing political support for the ruling DC.

Using these sorts of methods, the Christian Democrats and their allies have managed to create a patronage class that is heavily reliant on the state for its economic existence. Security rather than prosperity is the primary goal of this social stratum and it has fought, tooth and nail, all attempts to subject it to the control of the free market or an efficient state. Meanwhile, its allies in the commanding heights of government have worked to protect it in order to hold on to power. Italy's transition to an advanced capitalist democracy has reduced other sectors of traditional DC support and forced the party to rely much more heavily on this part of its social base.

For example, the decline of the Catholic subculture has resulted in the DC being less "Christian" at its grass roots. Regular church attendance has dropped from almost 70 percent of the population in 1956 to about 25 percent in 1985. As a further sign of secularization, Italy's birthrate is among the lowest in all of Europe. Furthermore, the relationship between what remains of the Catholic subculture and the politicians in the DC is no longer based on automatic reciprocity. This political gap has been an undercurrent in Catholic-DC relations for quite some time. For example, Catholic mobilization against Italian participation in the Gulf War demonstrated an increased political autonomy on the part of the faithful.[39]

The change in the class structure has also undermined other traditional social bases of Christian Democracy. Gianfranco Pasquino noted in 1980 how the decline in agriculture weakened the Federation of Small Farmers (*coldiretti*) which had traditionally supported the party.[40] This change reflected Italy's transition from a predominantly agrarian to a predominantly industrial economy. The transformation brought about by the move from an industrial to an advanced industrial economy has led to social change that is even more challenging to the DC.

38. OECD Economic Surveys, *Italy* (Paris, 1985), pp. 14–15.

39. See Franco Garelli, "La religione in Italia: verso una nuova egemonia culturale?," *Il Mulino* 40, no. 389 (January-February 1991): 148–59.

40. Gianfranco Pasquino, "Italian Christian Democracy: A Party for All Seasons?," in Lange and Tarrow, eds., *Italy in Transition*, 88–109.

With the expansion of the modern middle classes and the emergence of a vast number of small-scale entrepreneurs, the DC has been forced to deal with a much larger bourgeoisie. The ensuing development of autonomous forms of wealth creation and mechanisms of social control has made the Christian Democrats' patronage state seem increasingly redundant. We have noted before how the change in class structure produced simultaneous crises of control and representation for organized labor. Similar crises have now begun to envelop the ruling Christian Democrats.

It has long been accepted in studies of Italian politics, from Gramsci to the present, that the nation's political exceptionalism has been due to "the relative weakness and cultural backwardness of the Italian bourgeoisie."[41] Thus, in the postwar period, Italy's failed bourgeois revolution allowed a nonbourgeois party to construct a state structure that supported its catchall electoral needs. From 1945 onward, this division of economic and political labor allowed Italian capital and the state to survive much social instability.

However, Italy's two economic miracles and the successful incorporation and division of the working class have shifted the power balance between capital and the DC. As M. Follini puts it, the DC now lacks the internal capacity to represent properly its external environment.[42] At the end of the twentieth century, it is no longer the Italian bourgeoisie that seems "relatively weak and culturally backward" but rather the Christian Democratic state.

As an important theoretical note in passing, these changing power relations between the Italian bourgeoisie and the state should be of considerable interest to students of late industrialization. If the equation "small and cartel bourgeoisie equals weak democracy" is correct, then the recent expansion of the small-industry and service bourgeoisie should have an impact on Italy's one-party democracy. Whether it will come crashing down – like its dictatorial counterparts in the East – or simply wither away remains to be seen.

It is certainly now the case that the DC is politically weak and socially exposed. Most accounts of continued DC dominance tend to stress its great capacity to wear down its opponents. However, not enough attention has been given to the internal costs to the party of swallowing its allies. The first opening to the PSI in the 1960s, the opening to the

41. Martinelli, "Organized Business and Italian Politics," 67. See also Sidney Tarrow, "The Crisis of the Late 1960s in Italy and France," in Arrighi, ed., *Semiperipheral Development*, 223.

42. M. Follini, "Divisioni democristiane," *Il Mulino* 39, no. 331 (September-October 1990): 804.

Communists in the 1970s; and the second opening to the PSI in the 1980s, have left the DC internally divided. Some party members and factions have often been unable to "stomach" their latest political victims. As a consequence, they work to destabilize any new governments that might emerge out of their own party's alliances.

In the 1970s, the DC had to grant key parliamentary positions to PCI worthies. In the 1980s, it had to cede the post of prime minister to Giovanni Spadolini of the Republican party and then to the Socialists' Bettino Craxi. Furthermore, the Socialist party also won the presidency of the republic and Sandro Pertini enjoyed seven years of very popular stewardship. This distribution of legislative and executive positions represents the DC deciding to cede governmental power in order to hold on to state power, but it also demonstrates that both can be exercised quite well without them. The worry for party leaders now, with the decline of their social and electoral base, is that their opponents – that is, their "allies" – may have already begun a successful "long march" through the institutions of power.

Past and Future Heroes of the New Bourgeois Revolution

The PCI

Could a reformed and revitalized PCI have played the role of modernizing the Italian state and dislodged the Christian Democrats from power? Can the ex-PCI (the Party of the Democratic Left) play such a role in the future?

The PCI entered the strategic wilderness when it left the "government of national unity" in 1979 and abandoned the "historic compromise" a year later. It called for a "left alternative" to Christian Democratic rule but because the Socialists refused to play along, the strategy was futile. The party also became internally divided when its unofficial leftist, centrist, and rightist factions struggled to gain control in a period of political and ideological confusion.

The PCI's internal political problems were exacerbated by the crisis of organized labor and the decline of its electoral base. The June 1979 national election saw the party lose the support of 4 percent of the electorate (from 34.4 to 30.4) and it faced the possibility of dropping below the psychological threshold of 30 percent. In 1983, it did just that, but by only the smallest of margins (29.9 percent). In 1987, the PCI lost a further 3 percent, receiving 26.6 percent of the vote. Finally, in the local elections of May 1990, the party experienced its worst electoral result since 1958 when it received 24 percent of the vote, down from 30 percent in the 1985 local elections.

The drop in membership was equally precipitous, the most significant indicator of which was the collapse of its youth federation, the FGCI. Its enrollment plummeted to a low of fifty-thousand from a peak of ten times that figure. It also became an internal source of rebellion – from pacifist, feminist, and environmentalist movements – against the party's concentration on traditional industrial and political issues.

The ideological transformation of the PCI in the 1980s was long and painful. It ended with the party's decision on political liquidation, changing its name and program. This process began in the early 1980s when the PCI declared – with considerable prescience – that the historic phase initiated by the October Revolution had come to an end. In the 1970s, the party had sought to distance itself from the Soviet government. In the 1980s, it began to eradicate its own Bolshevik roots.

The collapse of communist party regimes in Eastern Europe in the autumn of 1989 speeded this process up. Party leaders saw the political writing on the Berlin Wall and realized that if they did not effect immediate change then the PCI would be only one of a handful of communist parties in Europe, most of which would be in the West.

On 3 February 1991 the PCI was formally dissolved by 1,500 delegates attending a special congress in Rimini. The decision came after intense internal debate among the party membership at large. The new Party of the Democratic Left (PDS) adopted the symbol of an oak tree, which now overshadowed a much smaller hammer and sickle. The PSI had engaged in a similar symbolic exercise in the 1970s when its old hammer and sickle were dwarfed by a new red carnation.

These decisions to be represented by the products of nature rather than instruments of production in some ways signified these parties' adaptation to an advanced industrial class system. Neither can rely on the alliance of a declining traditional working class and a disappearing peasantry to achieve political power.

However, a divided political party cannot obtain power either. The PCI was factionalized and split throughout the decade because of dramatic internal and external changes. With the "alternative left" strategy, the PCI did not know how to deal with a DC that was occasionally flirtatious when it was not getting on with the PSI. The possibility of a renewed "historic compromise" was tantalizing for some PCI leaders but, in reality, the offer was simply a DC cudgel to threaten the Socialists and keep them in line. Also, the PCI was somewhat bewildered by its ambiguous relationship with Craxi's highly aggressive and ambitious Socialists. The Communist party often found itself in the awkward situation of heavily criticizing the only major ally its strategy permitted.

With all its internal and strategic problems, the PCI/PDS could not be a dynamic agent for political reform in the 1980s and early 1990s. Whether it can play this role in the future depends on whether it can overcome its tendency to be locked into the internal dynamics of the PCI/PDS transition and become an outward-looking PDS. Party leader Achille Occhetto, who has presided over Italian communism's death and its social-democratic rebirth, is certainly anxious to achieve this goal. He has set up a British-style shadow cabinet in Parliament and has encouraged party members to think programmatically rather than ideologically. Whether this pragmatic approach can unite a party that has recently abandoned democratic centralism is not yet very clear.

It may well be that the PCI/PDS has already played its heroic part in Italy's new bourgeois revolution. It missed out in "the moment of 1976" by making a conscious choice to defend capitalist democracy rather than seize the opportunity to effect its radical reform. This choice cost the PCI the support of modern middle-class allies. Also, by helping incorporate a new industrial working class into the polity, the PCI eased the way for its eventual social reconstitution into separate islands of production. This has helped undermine the working-class base of the party itself. Thus the party that was neither the architect nor the beneficiary of Italy's recent transition to advanced capitalism, may turn out, in the end, to be its biggest victim.

The PSI

The fact that the political future of the PDS had been so tied to that of the PSI was testimony to the weakness of the former and the increased strength of the latter. The nightmare of the PDS was that Craxi's aggressive Socialists could succeed in implementing a "Mitterand solution" for Italy's divided left. By overtaking the PDS electorally, the PSI would become Italy's most powerful left-wing party and might then send its "old-new" rival off to the museum of antiquities. On the other hand, the two parties might be forced to cooperate if they were provided with the opportunity – under mutually favorable circumstances – to remove the DC from power. In the meantime, they eye each other suspiciously, realizing that ultimately their fate may be linked.

Bettino Craxi was one of the few Italian politicians to read the political tea leaves correctly during the 1970s. He understood that Italian society was being transformed by the new middle classes and he soon sought to establish "a dialogue with the modernizing sectors."[43] Craxi had

43. Spencer Di Scala, *Renewing Italian Socialism: Nenni to Craxi* (New York, 1988), p. 195.

become party general secretary as the result of a "young Socialist" putsch in 1976. Two years later, in March 1978, Craxi led the PSI to its own Bad Godesberg when, like the German Social Democrats in 1958, it abandoned the ideology of proletarian socialism and made itself presentable for a middle-class electorate. In keeping with his later leadership style, Craxi also strengthened executive authority within the party and reduced the power of its grass roots. A convinced anticommunist, he was determined to suppress pro-PCI elements in his own party.

Yet during the government of national unity, Craxi called on the PCI to abandon the historic compromise with the DC and support a left alternative with the PSI. This was clearly a tactical maneuver designed to embarrass the Communists. The call for a left alternative allowed the Socialist party to exploit popular dissatisfaction at PCI tepidness during a period of radical discontent. At the same time, the PSI cooperated politically with the Radical party which had become one of the more eccentric voices of progressive middle-class politics. Craxi's Socialists were determined to detach and then represent the modern middle-class electorate. They believed that this was the future social base of political power in the nation.

When the PCI did abandon the historic compromise and advocated the left alternative, the PSI promptly took up the PCI's vacated position and allied with the DC. This return to a center-left government seemed to indicate that nothing really had changed politically in over two decades. But the Socialists were determined not to repeat the errors of their predecessors in the 1960s and of their rivals, the Communists, in the 1970s.

For a start, they forced the Christian Democrats, who had been weakened by scandal and electoral decline, to pay more for alliance support. Craxi wanted to be prime minister and break the DC's stranglehold on high office. Instead, in 1981, the DC chose Republican leader Giovanni Spadolini as the first non-Christian Democrat to hold this position. Spadolini was supposed to be a barrier but ended up being the stepping stone on Craxi's path to the premiership. Craxi was sworn in as prime minister in August 1983.

The new Socialist government sought to carve an image out for itself and a set of policies that would smack of strong government, Keynesian efficiency, and neoliberal reform. Craxi set up an inner cabinet made up of the most important ministers in the five-party (*pentapartito*) coalition. He also relied more often on rule by decree to get around a parliamentary system that gave considerable power to the opposition PCI. In short, Craxi wanted to cultivate the impression among a middle-class electorate that he could make modern Italy governable through strong executive control.

87

With the support of Republicans, Liberals, and business elements in the DC, the PSI became the driving force in promoting neoliberal reforms. Adopting the reduction of inflation and the budget deficit as its main economic goals, the Socialists limited the *scala mobile*, supported privatization, reformed elements of the health and welfare systems, and liberalized financial and other markets. As has been pointed out before, the impact of these reforms was modest due to internal and external opposition.

Craxi's government was successful, however, on two fronts which posed problems for the DC when they reassumed the premiership in 1987. First of all, Craxi's period in office had provided the longest and most stable period of government since the national unity government of 1976-79. Second, the Craxi era was associated with the Italian economy's return to profitability and the second economic miracle. The government's fight against inflation was successful and the rate dropped to levels much closer to Italy's OECD partners.

Yet despite these achievements, the basic parameters of the patronage state remained intact. Political institutions had been subject only to minimal reform. Furthermore, the budget deficit remained shockingly high and threatened the stability of Italy's new dynamic economy. Perhaps the greatest indictment of the PSI's failure to transform the political system in the 1980s is that ultimately they were replaced by Italy's great Christian Democratic patron and political manipulation, Giulio Andreotti.

Was this political failure of the PSI due, once again, to the success of the DC in co-opting an ally and adversary? In some ways yes, but in others one also has to take into account the objective circumstances of the PSI itself. For example, the PSI did achieve electoral successes throughout the 1980s and climbed from 9.8 percent of the vote in 1979 to 14.3 percent in 1987, and in the local elections of May 1990 the party received over 15 percent. However, even with the DC's share of the electorate having dropped to a third and the PCI's to a quarter, the PSI, despite its increased support, was still subject to the logic of a system dominated by two major parties.

Wolfgang Merkel analyzes this logic very well when he depicts the PSI as having simultaneously to compete with the PCI for the "modern" vote in the north and with the DC for the "client" vote in the south.[44] In this manner, the PSI's clientelistic pursuits undermine its claims to modernism. In fact, the PSI's "dialogue" with the modern middle classes has not moved much beyond mere talk. The party has failed to harness

44. Wolfgang Merkel, *Prima e Dopo Craxi: le trasformazioni del PSI* (Padua, 1987), 197.

the mass support of the new middle strata, thus "creating a contradiction between the socialist leadership's reformist elaboration and its social base."[45]

In the 1980s, the Socialist party had to deal with a southern clientele that it had inherited from the old center-left. By increasing its political power, it also experienced renewed "southernization" as client strata identified a new "saint in heaven" sitting alongside the DC. This phenomenon, which is by no means confined to the PSI, nonetheless helped delegitimate it in the eyes of middle-class progressives. Only greater electoral advance, and the decline of the PDS in particular, will allow the PSI greater room to reduce the political role of its client constituency.

In the meantime, the PSI is locked into an alliance with the DC which it eventually hopes to replace. Craxi continues to call for radical reform of the political system and the introduction of a French-style presidency. The PSI's solution to Italy's ungovernability is the establishment of strong executive authority. Without mass electoral support, it will be unable to push this reform through.

A Revolution without an Agent?

At present, the DC, the PDS, and the PSI are incapable of transforming Italy's state structures to meet the demands of an advanced capitalist economy. A politically weak and socially isolated DC is too bound up with patronage politics to institute serious reforms. The new PDS is too concerned with its old PCI past to be a genuine innovator, at least in the short term. The PSI lacks the social and electoral base to combat deeply embedded structures of traditional political power. So if the three major parties are unable to effect real change, which political agent can provide a concrete alternative?

One possibility is that a reformist coalition might emerge simultaneously from within and across all the political parties. A modernizing neoliberal coalition could involve the Republicans, the Liberals, the PSI, neoliberal DC politicians like Guido Carli, and even some elements within the PDS. Christian Democratic leader Ciriaco De Mita attempted unsuccessfully to turn the DC into a modern bourgeois party in the 1980s. With this sort of alliance, he, or someone like him, could have a greater impact next time.

Such a coalition has already worked together over reforms in the financial system and the establishment of Italy's independent central bank. With a favorable political conjuncture, it might develop more clearly in the future and attempt to institute radical political change.

45. G. Martinotti, cited indirectly in Di Scala, *Renewing Italian Socialism*, 212.

Also, the European Community has often attempted to force the Italian state to behave in accordance with the community's neoliberal norms and regulations. Increasing pressure of this kind would give a domestic neoliberal alliance important transnational support.

But this "Anglo-Saxon" coalition would encounter severe obstacles within Italy's state structures. Disentangling the welfare and patronage states – in order to make sure reforms were correctly targeted – would be almost impossible. Part of the coalition, say the PDS or the DC left, might agree with the dismantling of patronage systems but would want to defend welfare. Propatronage elements in the state could then hide behind the latter in order to defend the maintenance of the former.

Similarly, the "Japanese" elements of state life – that is, the structures in place for managed capitalism – have strong support across the party system and would blunt the reforming efforts of radical marketeers. The fact that the patronage state is also enmeshed in this arena provides it with yet another hostage to threaten its divided adversaries.

Thus a neoliberal coalition, even if it were gradually to emerge, would be unlikely to have much success in radically reforming the system. The internal obstacles established in state structures are simply too formidable.

The external barriers to such a reform effort are also very strong. Client strata would suffer great immediate hardship if their patron networks were broken and it is likely that they would engage in widespread disruption. Even if the market could be shown to be in their long-term interests, the short-term costs would be too great.[46] Supported by their "saints in heaven" – in Rome and elsewhere – one could imagine clients rioting throughout the south and producing the sort of disorder that gripped Reggio Calabria in 1970.

Even among the upper echelons of Italian society there would be resistance to full-scale reform. We have already examined how the state recycles money for capitalists to invest and provides generous subsidies and incentives for all sectors of industry. Agnelli's Fiat, for example, receives state protection from Japanese competition in the form of so-called "voluntary" quotas. Thus a freer Italian market would also inflict costs on sections of the well-to-do. And if a modernizing coalition reformed the tax system so that the middle classes actually had to pay

46. Judith Chubb provides a wonderful account of how the PCI faced the problem of convincing Neapolitans to accept the short-term costs of breaking patronage ties in order to receive long-term benefits. See Chubb, *Patronage, Power and Poverty*, 219–44. There is a dynamic at work here similar to that identified by Adam Przeworski in any possible transition to socialism. In this scenario, the immediate pains inflicted by a strike by capitalists (e.g., capital flight) undermines a socialist party's mass base. See Adam Przeworski, *Capitalism and Social Democracy* (Cambridge, 1985).

their fair share, the ensuing revolt would probably result in its political collapse.[47]

The Dynamic Forces for Change

So with all these barriers to change, will everything remain the same at the political level while Italy's economy and society continue to be transformed? Three factors militate against such an outcome: (1) severe social problems brought about by the north-south divide, organized crime, and illegal mass immigration from the Third World (mainly) and Eastern Europe; (2) northern revolts against existing state structures and populist demands for radical and even revolutionary political change; (3) the continued expansion and rise to social power of dynamic bourgeois and modern middle strata.

The problem of the south's relative backwardness has, if anything, increased in recent years. While the economic picture is not uniform, the south nonetheless continues to eat up a large proportion of the state's resources without developing economically. Southern productivity is lower than that of the north and it provides a key social base for the DC's patronage system. The south is also associated with organized crime – the Camorra, Mafia, and 'Ndrangheta. The power base of the criminal classes seems to have increased in recent years not only as a result of their share of the international drug trade but also because of the region's continued underdevelopment.

The social problems of the south have plagued the Italian nation since its inception, but the influx of well over a million immigrants from abroad is new. Both factors have helped fuel populist revolts in the north which have been led by new radical political movements, or leagues. The northern leagues have come to represent the frustration and resentment of modern Italians with backward social sectors and the state. Some leagues have called for the reversal of the Risorgimento and the breakup of the nation-state into regional units. Others have called for the repatriation of Italian migrants from the south and non-Italian migrants from the Third World. They see the unified state in Rome as the political force that maintains southern backwardness, gives covert support to organized crime, and allows illegal immigration because of its inherent inefficiency. From the leagues' perspective, the only solution to these problems is northern secession. Recently, they have emerged as the fourth large electoral force in Italian politics, and the Piedmont League has obtained 20 percent of the vote in its region.

47. In 1984, for example, it was estimated that 40 percent of the value-added tax, which would have paid a quarter of the deficit that year, was not collected. "A Survey of Italy."

The leagues may well be a passing phenomenon and Italy will probably avoid a war between its states, but northern populist revolts are symptomatic of the fact that the gap between the dynamic elements of the socioeconomic system and those sectors of the state that sustain underdevelopment cannot continue. If the political system cannot reform itself, an all-out "revolt of the haves" could be the result.

These three related elements – severe social problems, northern populism, and rising modern strata – continue to press on the political power of the Christian Democrats. They cannot deal with these issues and cling onto power simply by virtue of habit and patronage. When the DC chose Andreotti as the new prime minister, it showed, in the words of La Malfa, that "it was scraping the bottom of the barrel." As a tactical genius of "ad-hockery," Andreotti represented a party that can only live its political life on a daily basis. As Follini puts it, the DC cannot "play the game and change the rules of the political game" at the same time.[48] Furthermore, there is no longer any excuse for not changing the rules because Italy no longer has a communist party.[49]

Conclusion: Three Possible Outcomes

It is possible that the DC will continue to hang on to power well into the next century, but if it manages to do so it is likely that we shall witness the slow transformation of this remarkable political institution in the direction of "ordinary" bourgeois conservatism. This would be a gentler process of political transition than that offered by a neoliberal coalition which would contribute to widespread social disruption.

A second possible outcome might be the establishment of an alternative government led by the PDS and the PSI that would exclude the DC from the executive and attempt to wedge it out of the state. If such a government agreed to maintain the welfare state and a coordinated industrial policy, it might avoid the political problems associated with radical neoliberalism. Measures to ease clients into the labor market or onto a more rational welfare system would alleviate some of the problems described above.

Probably the worst scenario would be a populist coalition of neoliber-

48. Follini, "Divisioni democristiane," 803.
49. Students of Christian Democracy in the past have argued that anticommunism has been crucial for the DC staying in power. For example, in 1980 Gianfranco Pasquino wrote that anticommunism was "the most appealing" aspect of the DC's ideological positions for "many voters." Pasquino, "Italian Christian Democracy," 96. Leonardi and Wertman noted in 1989 that "vital to the DC's electoral and political success is the fact that the major opposition party – and second largest party – in Italy has been the Communist party." Robert Leonardi and Douglas Wertman, *Italian Christian Democracy: The Politics of Dominance* (London, 1989), p. 246.

als, antisoutherners, and racists coming to power. This would be a more virulent and probably violent version of the Thatcherite coalition that was successful in Britain's 1979 election. In this regard, the most disturbing thing about the northern leagues is that they have emerged during a period of plenty, but what will happen if the Italian economy begins to suffer a downturn in the future? This could be stimulated by global recession, the budget deficit, or competition from the NICs in traditional high-quality goods. In these circumstances, it would be possible that affluent but threatened northerners could become even more aggressive toward southerners, immigrants, and the unified nation-state.

Let us hope that such a nasty transition is never set in motion. Better a continuance of the Italy that "muddles through" celebrated so eloquently by Joseph La Palombara.[50] Much has been achieved in the past quarter of a century even though Italy has lost a lot of its anarchy and color. Democratic participation has been expanded, living standards have been improved, and Italians have never experienced such levels of personal freedom.

Most of the actors involved in this transition have something of which they can be proud. Even the DC, in some respects, has played an honorable role. It kept the middle classes democratic through the largest social upheavals since the 1920s. The Italian state's humane performance during the terrorist challenge of the 1970s compares favorably with that of Britain or West Germany in the same period. Certainly, one of the DC's main failings has been their incapacity to obey the commandment, "Thou shalt not steal," but the Christian Democrats have contributed to a civic culture committed to teaching the authoritarian state they inherited that "thou shalt not kill." The recent accusations of Christian Democrat complicity with bombings and assassinations, whether by the Mafia or rogue elements in the security forces, are therefore all the more shocking. Outwardly the party has advanced the civic education of the middle classes toward principles of due process and non-violence.

The left, and the PCI/PDS in particular, must also be judged in terms of the objectives it set itself. Togliatti realized in 1944 that his party and the working class had to win a place in the new republican polity. The extent to which the PCI has been politically incorporated in the process is a measurement of its failure. The extent to which it has been politically included without an authoritarian backlash is an indicator of its success.

One would like to end this analysis with an optimistic, though schematic, political program arguing that it holds the key to the future of

50. Joseph La Palombara, *Democracy Italian Style* (New Haven, Conn., and London, 1987).

the Italian left. Such a program might argue that under advanced capitalism, the Italian left must unite the segmented working class, reach out to the new social movements, and establish transnational alliances with similar forces elsewhere.

But what is so striking about the predicaments – and possible prescriptions – for the Italian left is that they are not so different from those of any other left living under advanced capitalism. The only peculiarly Italian dimension to the left's continuing struggles is that it must now try to reform the nation's exceptional state structures. It would certainly be unwise to leave this task to unfriendly political forces. At the very minimum, the Italian left should attempt to participate in the nation's long-delayed bourgeois revolution. At the very most, it should try to subvert it in a radical direction.

4 SPANISH SOCIALISM: THE POLITICS OF NEOLIBERALISM

James Petras

INTRODUCTION: THE RISE OF THE NEW CLASS

The most lasting impression one receives after living in Spain is the striking contrast between the promise of the Socialist regime and its practice. The contradictions of Spanish Socialism are numerous; a party that contested for power from a strong working-class base (after all, it is officially the Spanish Socialist Workers Party – PSOE) and that upon assuming power pursued a business orientation with a single-mindedness that would impress the most earnest Thatcherite; a party that promised comprehensive social changes and realized a capitalist transformation; a party that ascended to power on the back of rising working-class militancy and presided over a policy aimed at weakening working-class organization; a party whose ideologues and publicists subscribed to and promoted an ideology promising to extend the power of civil society against the state and that in power witnessed the extension of state power over civil society; a party that attracted a substantial number of antibureaucratic intellectuals and transformed them into functionaries of the state.

The contradictions of Spanish Socialism can best be understood by analyzing the class character and aspirations of its leaders and cadres. The drives and motivations, the shifts in policy and the divisions between the government and its working-class base can best be understood by locating interests specific to their class aspirations.

The exercising of power by the Spanish Socialist party has had little or nothing to do with the working class, even less with the elimination or amelioration of class differences. Specifically, the Socialist party was the vehicle for the coming to power of a new class of upwardly mobile professionals whose only recourse to rapid ascent was politics, and it was through politics and specifically government office they gained access to private wealth and social status. The Socialist party elite has followed a typical three-stage pattern: early militancy involving popular mobilization, leading to election victories and public office, followed by the conversion of public office into entrée into elite circles, investments, and high incomes.

Among the new rich Socialist and Socialist-connected bankers and business figures are multi-millionaires Mario Conde and his partner, Juan Abello, who have made their fortune in banking and speculation in less than three years of Socialist government. Alberto Cortina and Alberto Alcocer have gained a fortune through public contracts and concessions granted for municipal services. Rafael Escuredo, Socialist ex-president of the Andalusian junta, Julio Feo, ex-secretary of the office of president, and José Maria Calvino, former director-general of public television, run a very lucrative business in consulting firms, matching their contacts in government with their business clients. Probably the most notorious case is Miguel Boyer, formerly Prime Minister Felipe González's minister of the economy and finance, who became one of the country's highest-paid bankers, drawing an annual salary of over $500,000, plus perks. The list of newly rich socialists is interminable. The rampant growth of speculative capital provoked one Socialist ex-minister of transport, Enrique Baron, to describe the Spanish economy as a "casino," in which there is a frenzy for easy profits.

It is telling that the leading economic figures under the Socialist regime have all risen through nonproductive, speculative, and financial dealings.[1]

The Spanish Socialist upwardly mobile professionals professed an anti-oligarchical ideology aimed at the Francoist elite: bankers, industrialists, generals, and party-state leaders. The core of this opposition, however, was class resentment at being excluded. Once power was shared and the upwardly mobile professionals were included, the Socialists dropped their antioligarchical rhetoric and rebaptized their new coalition partners as "modernizers" and "democrats." Henceforth, to attack the "oligarchy" was to be against "modernity" or in the European integration phase, un-European, both capital offenses according to the propaganda of the Socialist-controlled mass media.

The essential point is that Socialist class resentment did not translate into opposition to class domination, but was only expressed in the desire to rule, to escape from the dominated class and became part of the dominant class.

From 1982 to the present, the Socialist regime has led to the substitution of one exclusive ruling political class for another. The "new class"

1. Gonzalo San Segundo, "El dinero, la nueva furia de los españoles," *Cambio 16,* no. 872, 15 August 1988, pp. 14–19; *El Periódico* (Barcelona), 30 November 1988, p. 41. *Epoca* suggested that the acronym for the Socialist party should read the Spanish Socialist Entrepreneurial Party (instead of Workers Party). *Epoca,* 12 September 1988.

that dominates Spanish politics is held together in part by family ties, nepotism being one of the major characteristics of the regime's leading representatives. Four well-known "Socialist families" – the Solano, Fernández Ordoñez, Yañez-Barrionuevo, and Rodríguez de la Borbolla families – occupied twenty-one high positions in the Gonzélez administration. Promotions and senior appointments have included spouses, brothers, brothers-in-law, cousins, and other relatives.[2]

In the economic sphere, the Socialist regime has presided over the fusion of old and new members of the dominant class. Most evident is the large number of newly rich Socialist bankers, real-estate speculators, and building contractors. What has clearly not appeared among the nouveau riche Socialist elite is an industrial class with a vocation for creating a technologically advanced national industrial complex capable of competing in the European Community. For high-tech industries, the Socialists have provided generous concessions to outside capital, which has for the most part only set up assembly plants that demand very low skill levels.

Despite all the rhetoric about high technology and industrial reconversion, the Socialist government has not formulated or executed a comprehensive industrial policy. Its policies of industrial reconversion have led to the massive closing of industrial firms with no commensurate development of new industries; its entry into the common market has not been accompanied by the growth of new competitive Spanish industries, but has led to the displacement of Spanish products by European ones. In the agricultural and fisheries sectors, Spanish producers have similarly been hard hit by EC reductions, quotas, and competition, its strong areas restricted and its weak ones overwhelmed by the competition. The upwardly mobile professionals have brushed off these failures as part of the costs of becoming "modern" and "European;" but with a double-digit unemployment rate and a dependence on cheap, nonunionized labor and tourist earnings, Spain resembles more those countries described as "developing."

The new class in Spain is deeply conformist in the substance and style of its politics. In the mass circulation weeklies and public pronouncements, the ideology of the new class is nothing more than a celebration of the success of the upwardly mobile; a celebration of the political system that has opened the door to their success; a celebration of the economic and social structures that provide the markets for the big real estate deals and the summer homes and vacations on the beaches of Marbella and Menorca. In the ordering of political priorities, the Gonzélez regime prizes political stability over change, the management of the

2. *El País*, 17 October 1988, pp. 20–21.

economy over structural reforms, and law and the existing order against all struggles from below.

It is as if these lower-middle-class politicos have been trying to outdo their socioeconomic betters in demonstrating their capacity to run up bigger profits and exert greater restraint on labor and wages. The excesses of the González regime are public knowledge, such as its arrogant disregard of labor and the parliamentary opposition in setting income targets and its ramming legislation through parliament with only perfunctory debate, and the crass and unquestioning submission of the party faithful to the "infallible helmsman," Comrade Felipe. The ritual declarations of success by the economic ministers have echoed throughout the state-controlled media (and repeated with an occasional critical nuance in the privately owned press) based on growth rates increasingly dependent on temporary workers (temporary workers comprise almost a quarter of the labor force, up from less than 15 percent a few years earlier).

This political showmanship and self-celebration without industrial or technological depth is the hallmark of political entrepreneurs; their skills are found not in the creation of stable and remunerative employment, but in manipulating mass media. Their trajectory as marginal outsiders – in the double sense of being outside the Franco order and outside the main anti-Franco resistance – allowed them to approach the populace with populist rhetoric and then, once political power had been achieved, to monopolize the levers of state power.

Vertical mobility followed by horizontal integration is another way of describing the Socialist elite's obsession with affluence, respectability, and social status. The crass consumerism that has become emblematic of the Socialist nouveau riche is evident in the massive growth of luxury imports: the number of imported autos sold grew by 60 percent in the first quarter of 1988 over the previous year; sales of imported French champagne rose by 40 percent. Similar figures for luxury furs and perfumes increased at a 20 percent yearly average, while the consumption of expensive jewelry increased by nearly half.[3] The elite's reference group was the already wealthy and powerful not only in Spain, but even more their European counterparts. The establishment of responsible credentials in the eyes of the local and foreign bankers and investors was presented as an economic strategy.

High profit growth was a sign that the economy was doing well. The success of the new class was converted into the success of the whole society.

The new class and its academic "post-modern" ideologues proclaimed the end of class politics and denied the relevance of class consciousness in the day-to-day life of the working class. In reality, these upwardly

3. San Segundo, "El dinero" 17.

98

mobile professionals were themselves so deeply embedded in their new class roles, interacting with their new investor colleagues, that they "understood" only one class – the ruling class, its power, and its prerogatives. While they denied the relevance of class politics to the workers, their policies and life-style were defined in clear class terms – imitations of the dominant classes.

What the late Franco and Suarez regimes could not or would not dare to do – reduce living standards, introduce permanent insecurity in the labor force, subsidize employers to hire nonunion workers – the Socialist government pursued with doctrinaire zeal in the name of the working class.

The Socialist party of Spain is totally alien to the traditions and practices of the left, alien even to the least reformist, "welfarist" social democracy. It has ruptured all relations to its own past, the tradition of Largo Caballero and militant workerist reformism. It is not a party of technocrats and industrialists either – it is a party of propertyless professionals on the make, hooking into "where the action is": massive real estate deals on the Costa Brava (and in the major cities where land prices have quadrupled between 1985-1991) and laundering massive amounts of illicit funds. Spain under the Socialists has the dubious reputation among narcocapitalists of being the easiest site to launder money, hence the massive inflow of investment, mostly from drugs.

The Socialist party is the New Right today in Spain. Populist in style, plebeian in appearance, conservative and elitist in policy, it practices the politics of great entertainment spectaculars and mass diversions to convert the critical public into Ortega's passive masses. It is the regime of international conferences, of prominent intellectuals (including left-wingers) at five-star hotels discussing world ecology problems, perestroika, and socialism for the year 2000, while water in Tarragona is so polluted it cannot even be used in auto radiators. Socialist trade unionists who dare to criticize the party are abused by the party apparatus and the majority of sons of workers under twenty-five years of age have never held a job. However, visiting European and North American intellectuals forget to mention the discrepancies between the grandiose thematics at the international conferences and the mundane problems of the Spanish working class, so as not to upset their generous host.

SPANISH SOCIALISM: THE EMERGING CLASS SYSTEM

Under the González regime, a clearly identifiable class system is emerging, one in which sharp socioeconomic cleavages define social opportunities and political access to governing circles. It is a three-tiered class structure, in which there is considerable movement at the boundaries and within the boundaries, and occasionally "social jumps," as when key political actors shift toward the private sector.

At the top of the hierarchy are banking, real-estate, and speculative groups, combining old wealth and the upwardly mobile nouveau riche socialists. They are joined by the corporate executives and lawyers who are the auxiliaries of the multinational corporations that have become more and more visible in the industrial landscape. Finally, there are the highly placed state technocrats and executives who manage the state enterprises and financial institutions as well as control the allocation of state contracts. Together, this corporate-political elite makes the key decisions affecting the distribution of national income, deciding which shares go to wages and salaries, profits, and interest. They make the big decisions regarding the role Spain will play in the European division of labor. They shape the fiscal and state investments and budgetary allocations that provide the basis for private accumulation.

In the middle are the professional classes – the lawyers, civil servants, the parliamentarians and other elected officials who react to the policies and decisions made at the top. It is here that the noisy debates on the effects and costs of elite policies are discussed and ritually debated and legitimated, providing a democratic gloss on the highly centralized power structure. Neither the governing party nor, for the most part, the parliamentary opposition challenge the power or prerogatives of the nonelected officials and their corporate associates. And, in most cases, the middle fails to link the public to the big decisions.

The primary role of the government party is as a transmission belt for González and his inner circles: theirs is not to debate and decide, but to do his bidding exactly as they have been told. The former secretary-general of the Socialist party in Vizcaya, Ricardo García Damborenea, reflecting on the monolithic centralized personalized power structure in the party, called on Gonzalez to "demonstrate that within the Socialist party there could exist conceptions distinct from his and that coexistence of different viewpoints was possible." He went on to call for an end to "errors by unanimity in the PSOE."[4] With all of the public freedoms, it is curious the degree to which centralized executive power still dominates the legislative process, how little intraparty dissent is tolerated, and how the Socialist ministers presume their infallibility, rejecting inputs from any subaltern classes or their representatives. And, more generally, it is striking how much the Socialist party is in fact a party of state bureaucrats. In fact, it is hard to conceive of the very existence of the "party" outside of the state machinery.

4. *El País,* 9 December 1988, p. 14.

It is this close identity of party and state that marks a further instance of the similarities and continuities of the post-Franco Socialist regime with its corporatist predecessor.[5] Even more to the point is the use to which the centralized command structure is put in a continual effort to subordinate the trade unions to the state. The affirmation by the UGT (General Workers' Union-Socialist Confederation) of its autonomy of action and its decision to criticize and engage in strikes against the party state are considered a breach of party discipline, and serious thought is given to taking administrative and disciplinary action.[6] The party-state elite realizes that its middle-level functionaries are unable to retain organizational control and lack credibility among rank-and-file union activists to restrain labor action and therefore avoid taking draconian measures that would reflect upon their impotence, at least on labor negotiations.[7] These middle levels have then become internally polarized as the political elite has moved so far and so fast toward an exclusive corporate-investor direction that they leave little margin to co-opt the trade unions. Hence the emergence of the "double impotence" of the middle-sector political class, subservient to the top and impotent to control the bottom.

At the bottom of the political-economic hierarchy is the alienated populace, subject to incessant propaganda from regime-controlled mass media, distracted by state-sponsored spectacles, and increasingly divorced from the state-manipulated organizations of civil society. The populace is increasingly disenchanted by widespread greed and corruption that characterize the upwardly mobile functionaries. They deeply resent the ostentatious life-styles of the top echelons of the new classes – their Mercedes Benzes, their partying at fashionable resorts, the photos on the covers of the glossy weeklies, the toothy smiles with the bankers, corporate executives, celebrities, and aristocratic jet-set riffraff. They are indignant and cynical about the political scandals and the multimillion peseta incomes of the personages that surround "Felipe," the ministers that use state funds for concert pianos and fashionable wardrobes, and so on.

This obscene behavior takes place while the employers engage in an assault on the most elementary conditions of labor, their employment security. By the late 1980s, 20 percent of the labor force was out of work and the temporary work force had increased from 16 percent to 24 percent. Nearly 30 percent of the Spanish population, some 11.5 million, have incomes below 500,000 pesetas a year (approximately U.S. $4,000),

5. For a comparison, see J.I. Gonzáles Faus, "Carta a Felipe González," *El País,* 24 September 1988, p. 16.

6. *El País,* 3 December 1988, p. 18; 11 Dec. 1988, p. 14.

7. "El PSOE escoge la prudencia para frenar la huelga general," *El Periódico,* 15 November 1988, p. 3.

putting them below the poverty line.[8] While corporate profits doubled between 1986 and 1987, the regime refused to allow salaries to be raised by two percentage points to compensate for the increase in inflation, claiming the need for restraint to hold down inflation.[9] These gratuitous insults finally transformed the general malaise of the labor force into open revolt. On 14 December 1988, between 85 and 90 percent of the labor force closed down the entire country; the regime had gone too far.[10] Despite the initial hopes of labor militancy, in the subsequent period the two major labor federations returned to the bargaining table, securing few concessions but demobilizing labor.

SOCIOECONOMIC POLARIZATION AND THE MERGER OF THE OLD AND NEW RIGHT

During the period of Socialist rule, Spain has experienced a dual process of social convergence and polarization in which traditional cleavages between the pro-Franco economic elite and the post-Franco Socialist regime have virtually disappeared, even as the socioeconomic class divisions between labor and capital continue and even deepen.[11] What has become obvious to the Francoist right (the *Alianza Popular*), bankers, and the business sectors in general is that the Socialists have provided a

8. *El País*, 30 August 1988, p. 35.

9. A study of 4,200 firms by the Bank of Spain showed that aggregate profits increased from 423 billion pesetas in 1986 to 856 billion pesetas in 1987. At the same time, Spain continued to have the second lowest social expenditures as a percentage of gross domestic product of EC countries. On profits, *El País*, 16 November 1988, p. 49; 11 December 1988, business section, p. 2. On social expenditures, *El País*, 3 December 1988, 59. On pensions and salary adjustments, see *El País*, 28 October 1988, p. 61. The González regime's social expenditures as percent of GNP is less than Thatcher's, 18 percent compared to 22.8 percent and far behind Holland's 32.1 percent, West Germany's 26.4 percent, France's 28.4 percent, and even below Italy's 26.4 percent and Greece's 20.2 percent.

10. Figures for the general strike show that 89.5 percent of workers went on strike, 75.4 percent farmers, 91.1 percent of the commercial sector and 82.7 percent of administrative employees. *El Periódico*, 16 December 1988, p. 8. An indication of how out of touch the Socialist leadership has been with reality was its estimate of the number of participants in the Madrid demonstration following the general strike. Most newspapers estimated it at hundreds of thousands, "a monstrous demonstration" according to *El Periódico*; one million attended according to the organizers. The González-controlled media gave a figure of forty thousand. *El Periódico*, 17 December 1988, p. 3.

11. The wage and salary share of national income has declined substantially during the González years, from 52.2 percent in 1982 to 49.9 percent in 1986, while the share going to nonsalaried income increased from 45.8 percent to 50.1 percent. See Joan Martínez-Alier and Jordi Roca Jusmet, "Economía política del corporativismo en el estado español: del franquismo al posfranquismo," *Revista española de investigaciones sociológicas*, no. 41, (January-March 1988):54. Unemployment insurance, which covered 46.7 percent of the unemployed in 1978, reached only 28.9 percent in 1987. Instituto Sindical de Estudios, *Evolución social en España 1977–1987* (1988), p. 27.

better business and investment climate – while holding down wages – with less conflict than any rightist regime could have accomplished. The Socialists have stolen the old right's economic program while continuing to sell itself to a substantial sector of the electorate as some sort of liberal, progressive alternative. To be sure, there were far fewer true believers at the beginning of the 1990s than a decade earlier, and crude efforts to evoke the old "worker-peasant" rhetoric could provoke derisive laughter.[12] Still the belief that the Socialist party is still a reformist party that has been led astray, and that Felipe can be convinced or pressured to take a "social turn" (*giro social*) is fairly pervasive, at least in certain Socialist trade-union circles.[13]

The Socialist regime's historic shift to the right, its firm advocacy of free-market policies, and its close ties with the recognized spokespersons for financial-corporate elite have significant consequences for Spanish politics. In the first instance, it has produced a huge political gap in the center-left. The mass of reformist working class and petty bourgeois voters who are, for whatever reason, not likely to support the Communist party, do not have a political vehicle, at least in the electoral arena, hence one reason for the success of the general strike and the successful role of the trade unions in providing political leadership in the absence of a political party with the authority to lead the struggle.

It is clear, however, that the general strike did not signal a new phase of syndicalist-led extraparliamentary struggle but rather a return to conventional bargaining and electoral politics. What is also clear is that the parliamentary majority does not represent or reflect the basic needs of a very significant sector of the electorate and a substantial majority of the working class. The evidence is in the increasing number of voters who abstain – 40 percent in the municipal elections of May 1991.

The second point is that the Socialist party's appropriation of the center-right political space crowds out the traditional right. Since big business far prefers to have a probusiness party in power to one out of power, the right flounders in a deep identity crisis.[14] Its effort to change its image

12. The most boisterous outburst of laughter heard during the summer courses at the Universidad Complutence occurred when Vice President Alfonso Guerra affirmed with his usual aplomb that the PSOE "is the party of the workers and peasants in Spain."

13. Both Nicolás Redondo, the secretary-general of the UGT, and its organizational secretary, Anton Saracibar, were hoping that the González regime would see the light and implement the social turn after the general strike. Their hopes were dashed in a first set meeting where González simply reiterated his basic position on the need for keeping inflation down and wages and pensions within his guidelines. See the interviews with Redondo in *El País*, 20 November 1988, Sunday supplement pp. 1–4, and with Saracibar in *El Periódico*, 5 December 1988, p. 10.

14. "La Crisis de la derecha," in *El País*, 3 November 1988, supplement, "Temas de nuestra época," pp. 1–8.

toward that of a modern conservative democratic party has had little impact in changing its electoral fortune. Its feeble efforts to demagogically adopt populist positions against some of the government's more outrageous income measures have not had much credibility. Essentially, the old right is discovering that Spanish politics does not have room for two major electoral parties contending for business and banking support. Paradoxically, only if a party to the left of the Socialists emerges, capable of drawing significant support from González, can the old right hope to make a comeback. In the meantime, the old right is condemned to a minoritarian ghetto unable to compete with the Socialists in providing business with lucrative contracts and low wage scales.

The policies for the Socialists have contributed to socioeconomic polarization, essentially through their so-called industrial reconversion schemes, which have doubled the unemployment rate, increased the temporary labor force, and undermined collective bargaining. The institutional underpinnings of these changes have been underwritten through the subordination of the Socialist trade unions to the party state and the bureaucratization of civic and community organizations.[15]

An army of ex-leftist intellectuals has provided the ideological mystification of this process of social regression.[16] Their job has been to sell the proinvestment, antilabor programs of the Socialists as the only possible, realistic route open to Spain, given its constitutional system, the need to integrate into Europe, Spain's underdevelopment, the threat of a military backlash, and so on. In their presentation and analysis of the Spanish power structure, the ex-leftist ideologues of the new right focus on the middle levels of power: they delve into the everyday decisions, the electoral process, the parties, the personalities, the voters – all the noisy

15. See Martínez-Alier and Roca, "Economía política," 47 and *passim*. According to the authors' data, labor conflict declined from 18.9 million labor days lost in 1979 to 2.7 million in 1982 and 3.2 million in 1985. The decline is one indication of the Socialist capacity to subordinate labor to their economic project without any commensurate payoff as wage increases consistently lagged behind the consumer price index: 12 percent and 14.4 percent respectively in 1982, 11.4 percent to 12.2 percent in 1983, 10 percent and 11.3 percent in 1984. Ibid., 50.

16. It is said that the biggest party in Catalonia is the party of ex-Communists. In 1988, Gonzalez's cabinet contained two: Minister of Culture Jorge Semprun and Minister of Justice Enrique Mugica. Typical of the motivations of many ex-Communists were the comments of the former general-secretary in Extremadura, Eugenio Triana: "Being a Communist I could never get to be a minister," *El Independiente,* 19 August 1988, p. 7. Many of the ex-leftists turned-Socialists have landed in institutes such as the Fundación Pablo Iglesias or regularly receive consultantships and subventions for their defense of supply-side economics, antilabor employment schemes, and support of NATO. A sample of the style of these organic apologists of the PSOE apparatus can be found in an interview with Ludolfo Paramio, chief of the Fundación Pablo Iglesias, in ibid., 8. For a critical view, see Julia Varela, "Revolteo de sociólogos," *El País,* 28 October 1988, 15.

events that fill the pages of the opinion columns of the dailies – while the impersonal institutions (the boards of directors of the leading banks and corporations, the technocrats, and economic advisors) which make the crucial decisions affecting the class structure remain in obscurity. The new right's imagery of a society of free elections, competitive markets, social opportunities, and consumer affluence masks the politics of elite decision-making and abysmal inequalities.

SOCIALISM FOR THE RICH AND OPENINGS FOR THE LEFT

In the Boqueria in Barcelona, an old Socialist militant, overhearing a discussion I was having with a friend, respectfully interrupted and told us, "That's not the Socialist party I joined in 1947. . . . They have kidnapped the party. They practice socialism for the rich." It is politics that provides upward mobility for the well-connected and ambitious 10 percent: it is the socialism of ideological mystification, of private accumulation, and state clientelism. The party has harnessed a tradition of struggle to private appropriation. In the practice of real, existing Spanish socialism, corporate fusions have replaced worker unity, corporate competition replaces class solidarity, and supply-side economics takes the place of class struggle. The inversion of socialist values, their transformation into their opposites, defines González's version of a neo-Orwellian world in which the wealth of the rich is for the benefit of the poor. According to Carlos Solchaga, minister of the economy and finance, "Spain is the country in all of Europe and perhaps in the whole world where you can make the most money in the shortest time."[17] This is a country with 15 percent unemployment, with 30 percent of the population below the poverty line – obviously the profits need time to trickle down. It is no wonder that the PSOE has employed an army of academics to work on a project entitled "Socialism for the Year 2000."

In one area, the Spanish Socialist party has been successful: it has devalued socialism, emptied it of meaning, and transformed it into a state ideology legitimating the new privileged ruling class, that fusion of upwardly mobile professionals and newly rich bankers.

The Socialists' move to the right, however, provides an objective basis for the revival of left politics in the political gap between the bureaucratic party state and increasingly alienated populace, in the social gap provoked by increasingly concentrated capital and an increasingly insecure and vulnerable labor force, and in the economic gap in which the econ-

17. Quoted in Augustín Moreno García, "El Gobierno en el país de las maravillas," *El País,* 11 August 1988, p. 26.

omy offers everything to the new upwardly mobile political class and little or nothing to the mass of unemployed youth.

The challenge for the Spanish left is to recreate a critical public, to demonstrate that the alienated populace possesses a collective power and is capable of isolating and confronting a Socialist party that has become a party of functionaries. A revived left would recapture the tradition of class solidarity as a condition for, as well as a consequence of, collective struggle. Above all, the left must displace the dead hand of the state bureaucracy in civil society and reconstruct the autonomous movements of the 1970s. There is no way that the industrial or farm workers, intellectuals or academics can effectively fight the state–party machinery while depending on it for subsidies and handouts. There is no automatic conversion of objective economic deprivation to subjective political radicalism. The decay of the old does not necessarily create something new. Only sustained action by consequential militants can fill that enormous vacant space and create a popular socialist movement that can represent the hopes and aspirations that have been frustrated in the past decade.

So far, the left has failed to fill the political vacuum. The United Left, which includes the Communist party, has been largely an electoral coalition that has on occasion shared municipal power with the Socialists, trading posts for minor reforms. The leftist trade unions, the Workers' Commissions, have engaged in joint actions with dissident Socialist unions but have focused on narrow economic issues.

THE ELECTORAL REGIME AND THE DECLINE OF CIVIL SOCIETY

The consolidation of the electoral regime, particularly the ascent of the Socialist party, has been accompanied by the decline of civil society. More specifically, the electoral regime has been deeply involved in centralizing political power and subordinating the organizations of civil society to the state apparatus.

During the last stages of the Franco dictatorship and in the period of transition to the electoral regime, a rich array of social movements emerged that engaged vast numbers of Spaniards, particularly workers, neighborhood activists, students, and intellectuals, in active struggles, public debates, and critical discussions. Membership in secondary associations flourished, trade-union membership skyrocketed and intellectual journals and pamphlets proliferated.[18] Civil society grew as the state

18. Numerous interviews with trade-union, neighborhood and university leaders in Catalonia, Valencia, Andalusia, the Basque country, and Galicia all confirm the view that public activity peaked before the electoral pacts and before the political class consolidated itself.

apparatus retreated. Particularly with the Socialist takeover of government, the process was reversed: the central thrust of policy was toward
the incorporation of social movements in the state bureaucracy. The
electoral party apparatus transformed movement activists into functionaries; and ex-activists-turned-bureaucrats demobilized autonomous
organizations or turned them into appendages of the state, atomizing
their supporters and rendering them claimants for state favors.[19]

The collective struggles, street parliaments, and popular assemblies that
characterized the period prior to the consolidation of the electoral regime
were replaced by the centralized state-directed electoral process, reducing
the populace into passive individuals voting sporadically in highly struc-
tured contexts. The Socialists in particular, with their personality cult
around González and their vacuous slogan of change (cambio), debased
socialist values and narrowed political discourse dramatically.

Playing on the populace's genuine fear and hostility toward the Francoist right, González and his entourage posed the issue of politics as one
of placing public trust in the power of the central state. The Socialists
contributed to the decline of public debate, substituting the central state
and the mass media for the autonomous collectivities based on personal
exchange, meeting on a daily basis, acting in solidarity.

The reassertion of the state over civil society through the electoral
regime and the reassertion of control over social organizations led to concerted efforts to subordinate working-class demands to the capitalist state
in the name of "consolidating democracy." Every wage demand, strike,
mass mobilization was declared to be "endangering democracy," threatening to provoke a military reaction, and so on. The whole burden of
renewing capitalism and strengthening of the state apparatus was placed
on the backs of the working-class with the active support of the Communist party. The Moncloa Pact (October 1977) formalized the process by
which the upwardly mobile political class and the subordinate trade-
union functionaries were able to gain access to public office, perquisites,
budgets, legality, and respectability at the price of demobilizing the working class and strengthening the state's control over civil society.

What was (and is) described as "consolidating democracy" obscured a
more complex and basic process: the consolidation of capital and the
strengthening of capital's control over the state. By strengthening the
state, the regime was able to implement regressive income policies,
attack trade-union rights, and close major industries which were strong-

19. On the co-optation of the trade unions through the "social pacts," see the thorough
analysis in Joan Martínez-Alier and Jordi Roca Jusmet, "Economía política del corporativismo en el estado español del franquismo al posfranquismo," Desarrollo económico, 28, no.
109 (April-June 1988): 3–37.

holds of worker militancy. The consequences of the consolidation of capitalist power that accompanied the consolidation of the electoral regime included a steep increase in the percentage of national income to owners of capital, increases in productivity, greater insecurity of employment for labor and, conversely, an increase in the power of capital to hire and fire workers, contract temporary workers, or subcontract work to home production. This shift in class power, engineered by the Socialist regime, manifested itself in a precipitous decline in trade-union membership and the weakening of collective bargaining and the capacity to strike.[20]

By understanding the process through which the electoral regime concentrated power in the capitalist state, we can explain the apparent paradox that wage and salaried workers had a greater capacity to increase wages beyond increases in inflation and productivity in the latter phase of the Fascist regime and during the transition to the electoral regime than under the Socialist government. The existence or nonexistence of an electoral regime does not indicate the degree of state control over civil society. In the Spanish case, it is clear that there was less effective de facto control over civil society during the late Franco and transitional periods than during the González regime.

The electoral regime's consolidation coincided with the establishment of bourgeois hegemony,[21] and the Socialist party, by constantly pointing to "dangers" for democracy, highlighted the nonelectoral forces that had to be accommodated both before and during the process of electoral consolidation. If the consolidation and promotion of bourgeois hegemony was a necessary condition for the consolidation of the electoral regime, the latter had to demonstrate its superiority to other types of regimes as a mechanism for legitimation. This demonstration took the form of not only providing guarantees to the propertied and investment classes, but of decreeing and legislating positive measures regarding labor, investment, and income policy. By dismantling existing state regulations and providing generous state financing, and by promoting the privatization and denationalization of industry, the Socialists ensured the continued strategic support of capital for the electoral regime.

The Socialists were able to identify bourgeois hegemony with the electoral regime and, in an even more extreme departure from tradition, identify economic policies directed toward promoting capital at the expense of labor as necessary for consolidating democracy. Efforts by

20. Interview with Simón Rosado, member of the executive board of the metalworkers union in Catalonia, 14 November 1988.
21. For a discussion of some of these issues from the angle of particularistic associations, see Salvador Aguilar et al., *Interest Associations in the Spanish Transition* (Barcelona, 1988).

labor to improve living standards were in the early years of the Socialist regime condemned as destabilizing democracy.

As the gap between the gains of corporate enterprises and wage earners widened, labor's challenge to some of the macroeconomic supply-side economic policies were treated as tantamount to challenging democracy. As the Socialist regime proceeded to consolidate political power and it became obvious that bourgeois hegemony was secure, the Socialist regime shifted the axis of its arguments for supply-side economics: the labor movement was then told that the "restructuring of the economy," the implantation of the new "modern" economy, and the creation of competitive conditions for entry into the EC required that worker incomes continue to stagnate or regress and that returns to capital keep growing. Most Socialist trade-union officials accepted these arguments, at least until 14 December 1988.[22]

By the late 1980s, the majority of the labor movement recognized that the probusiness attitude of the Socialist party was neither a clever tactic clearing the way for a social democracy which would provide welfare reforms nor a temporary measure to deal with a cyclical crisis of capital, but a strategic commitment based on interlocking interests raised to the level of state power. The discovery of this historic relationship was gradual and uneven. Socialist trade-union leaders have continued hoping that González will rectify his course or that as a result of strike pressure the regime would take a "social turn." The references to vague and limited "social reforms" indicate the degree to which the relentless move to the right by the Socialist regime has moved the axis of political debate in the same direction, removing socialism and welfare from the front burner.

The demands of the opposition trade unions are very moderate by any standards. Even during the general strike, the trade unions sought to recover two percentage points in living standards lost when inflation exceeded government guidelines, the rescinding of a youth-employment scheme in which the state subsidized 80 percent of the private employers' wage bills for young nonunionized, temporary workers paid below the minimum wage with no social benefits (a project which would have

22. Tensions between the regime and the UGT date back at least to 1985 over incomes and pension policy, but the UGT refused to back the general strike called by Comisiones Obera in 1986. From this period on, relations deteriorated rapidly, and the UGT divided between a rump of state loyalists, increasingly isolated from the membership and the Redondo faction, increasingly criticized by González, which began to increase its membership, claiming a growth of 150,000 in dues-paying members between 1986 and 1988. *El País*, 1 November 1988, p. 48. On the conflict between the PSOE and the UGT, see the interviews with González, *El País*, 4 December 1988, Sunday supplement, pp. 1–4, and Redondo, *El País*, 20 November 1988, Sunday supplement, pp. 1–3. The best background on the "*ruptura*" appears in *El País*, 18 December 1988, special supplement, pp. 1–4.

undercut the very existence of union organizations and collective bargaining), and an increase in the percentage of the unemployed covered by unemployment insurance.[23]

In a sense, the unions and opposition have been struggling to conserve the shrinking political space and living standards against the extremist neoliberal onslaught. Even if the regime conceded every point, it still would not represent a turn toward reformist social democratic welfare politics; it would merely slow the rush toward a completely neoliberal economy. The party regime responded by threatening harsh punitive disciplinary actions against the dissident Socialist unionists, offering malleable union officials economic rewards, as well as discussing the prospect of forming a rival union confederation. The latter idea has been dropped, but the scope of state patronage to subvert autonomous unionism is substantial.[24]

Increasingly, labor strikes have become a common form for expressing citizen disenchantment with the socialist regime and an electoral system which has failed to provide a forum for representing majoritarian interests. The absence of a parliamentary alternative to the Socialists does not mean the Socialist electoral majority represents the populace. It means that the electoral system itself has failed to provide a basis for articulating majoritarian grievances, thus finding expression in growing abstentions, private life, and multiple employment.

The critical theoretical issue is the false equation of an electoral regime with representative democracy. Democracies require elections, but not all electoral regimes are democratic, subject to a sovereign popular will. The electoral regime in Spain had been explicitly conditioned and predicated on the political class following rules dictated by the permanent state apparatus and dependent on creating the conditions for capitalist reproduction. Whatever external pressures may have been initially exerted on the Socialists were subsequently internalized. The Socialists for-

23. On the workers' demands leading up to the general strike, see *El País,* 1 December 1988, p. 32, for a critique and alternative to the regime's so-called youth employment scheme. The seven key demands of the trade unions were: (1) the replacement of the government's temporary job employment scheme with one providing stable employment with the same social benefits as other workers; (2) the recovery of the two points lost to inflation; (3) an increase in the percentage of unemployed covered by unemployment insurance to 48 percent; (4) an increase in pensions to equal the minimum wage; (5) the right of collective bargaining for public employees; (6) an increase in the minimum wage; and (7) collective agreements for groups whose salary is fixed by the budget. *El Periódico,* 13 December 1988, p. 11.

24. On efforts by the PSOE to destabilize the unions, see *El País,* 11 December 1988, 14, 3 December 1988, 18. On PSOE threats, see *El País,* 6 December 1988, p. 13. On the internal party discussions to deepen the break with the trade unions, see *El País,* 25 September 1988, p. 15.

mulated a development program which took over and embodied the positions of their historical adversaries, absorbing and integrating their economic program with the upward-climbing social aspirations of their leadership groups.

In the first and most fundamental sense, the political transition to an electoral regime in Spain was determined by the political class's acceptance of the basic rules set by nondemocratic, nonelected officials and socioeconomic actors. The authoritarian nature of the process of establishing political rules and the parameters of political action is obscured by the focus on the political processes (parties, elections, policy decisions) operating within these boundaries. The authoritarian foundations and boundaries were internalized by the political class and its publicists, and conveniently forgotten when it came time to discuss or theorize Spanish politics. As a consequence, a consensus emerged among political analysts and political actors equating the electoral regime with democracy.

The authoritarian and elitist foundation of the electoral rules of the game help us to explain another feature of Spanish politics: the electoral regime's reproduction of the same style of politics as its Francoist predecessor. The Socialists practice the same centralization and concentration of legislative and executive power. They have encouraged the emergence of personal power (the caudillo), ministerial disdain and arrogance toward parliamentary interpellators, the strong drive to bureaucratize civil society, the continual effort to transform the trade unions into appendages of the state, and state dictation of wage and salary increases.[25] There is even a significant carryover of economic policy advisors and foreign-policy makers from the Franco era into significant sectors of the Socialist regime. There are, of course, many and significant differences between the Franco and electoral regimes, for example, far greater individual rights in the latter and greater job security and economic protectionism in the former.

The coincidence of styles and forms of politics reflects the continuities in the underlying substantive structures. The electoral regime's horizontal integration with the economic elites generates pressure for the vertical integration of social organization in civil society. The foundations of electoral politics guarantee the continuities in institutional power which, in turn, propel the electoral regime to reproduce the political practices of its predecessor. It is, therefore, nonsense to trace the "centralism,"

25. An article headline just prior to the general strike captures the arrogant style of the regime: "The government will unilaterally set the minimum services that will apply in the general strike," El País, 10 December 1988, p. 15. Capturing the new spirit of the labor movement, the headline the following day read, "The unions refuse to comply with the minimum services dictated by the government." El País, 11 December 1988, 18. Indeed, it was the unions who decided the issue for a change.

"caudillismo" and "corporatism" of contemporary Spain to vague psychological notions of Spanish character or to residual atavistic features of the past; the deepening and single-minded pursuit and practices of centralist executive rule by the current regime can most parsimoniously be explained by examining the state institutions and interests it defends.

In Spain and elsewhere, left-wing writers have criticized the negative effects of the subordination of class politics to the "consolidation of democracy," but they have done so from a narrowly focused, empiricist perspective.[26] The critics have identified the problems generated by "neocorporatist" policies: co-optation of the political opposition and trade-union leaders and state absorption of civil society leads to the deterioration of the trade-union influence and membership, declining wage-earner income, greater employment instability, and rising unemployment. In empiricist fashion, these critics attribute these problems to neoliberal policies or ideologies.

However, the ascendancy of neoliberal political economy must be located deeper in the very structure of the state, more specifically in the relationship between the electoral regime and the state. The very foundation of the political transition, the securing of bourgeois hegemony as a necessary condition for the emergence of electoral politics, was the basic determinant of the neoliberal socioeconomic policies.

This puts the critics of these policies in an ambiguous position, for while they attack the socioeconomic policies of the regime, they defend the process and underlying structures that gave birth to them (what they call the "democratic transition," the electoral regime, and the like).

As a result, the critics of neoliberalism are also in an ambiguous position vis-á-vis the regime, particularly when faced with a real or imagined regime crisis; they are susceptible to being blackmailed by the regime into accepting all sorts of arguments concerning political restrictions and regressive economic policies in the name of consolidating democracy. In a word, the critics become hostages of the government because they share the latter's premises about the classless nature of the electoral regime.

In summary, the critics of neoliberalism subordinate their socioeconomic or class criticism of regime policies to the sacred cow of the electoral regime ("consolidating democracy"), thus contributing to the disorientation of the labor movement and reinforcing the basic premises of their ostensible adversaries. Only by opposing the electoral regime embedded in its reactionary foundation and postulating an alternative basis for electoral politics rooted in the autonomous organization of civil

---

26. See Martínez-Alier and Roca, "Economía politica." These criticisms are not meant to detract from an otherwise brilliant critique of the PSOE regime.

society can leftist critics develop an unambiguous, consequential, and consistent critique of Socialist neoliberal policies.

In many ways, the Socialist electoral regime has gone beyond the decaying dictatorial regime in pursuit of its control over civil society. During its latter stages, the dictatorship, in disarray and decay, concentrated its strength on state control, conceding to the opposition a substantial margin of autonomous space in civil society. In contrast to the dictatorship retreating from civil society, the electoral regime, particularly the Socialist regime, has expanded from the state into civil society, absorbing autonomous groups into their electoral apparatus and instrumentalizing them. In the process, they have atomized political society, transforming an active critical public into a passive private consumer of the mass media.

Ironically, the socialist ideologues, indeed the entire electoral political class, have projected a discourse that emphasizes the importance of civil society and its autonomy as essential ingredients in the growth of a democratic polity, even as their practice has diminished its importance.

The paramount feature of Socialist politics has been the shrinking of civil society, with the decline of political participation, the bureaucratization of neighborhood associations, and the erosion of trade-union membership. Likewise, political debate over principles has been turned into a technocratic monologue: a shift from public debates over the big question of class and state power, of equity and self-management, of planning and democracy, and of national industrial policy, to ministerial consultations on the appropriate techniques for increasing investment, the most appropriate incentives for attracting foreign capital, and the kind of index that will allow wages to trail inflation. Important issues to be sure, but always set in contexts and premises defined by the ideology of neoliberalism.

The decline of politics and the bureaucratization of the language of politics defines the practice of the real, existing Socialist electoral regime, under which electoral rituals contested by well-financed political elites displace public debate with mass spectacles, and caudillo-managed media events replace citizen participation.

THE TIES THAT BIND: THE INTERNATIONAL CIRCUITS

The neoliberal economic policies pursued by the Socialist regime have primarily been directed toward strengthening the international circuits of capital. A new set of institutions and policies organized around newly privatized enterprises provide the services – e.g., transport, communications, education – that facilitate the reproduction of the privileged financiers, entrepreneurs, and public functionaries connected with these circuits. The state's role is to subsidize, promote, and protect these circuits and their participants.[27]

The circuits based in the internal market (including public services for wage and salaried employees and local business and industries) and linked to older productive sectors have been squeezed by the state.[28] As a consequence, these sectors are deteriorating as the neoliberal elite reallocates major resources toward the private international, financial, real estate, and speculative circuit. The regime's trade-off with the national productive sector is to provide them with a flexible labor market in exchange for lowering protective barriers and opening the economy to foreign investment and imports. In operational terms, the regime has allowed factory owners greater leeway in firing workers and subcontracting production to small shops and home industries, thus lowering their labor costs.[29] In effect, the costs of competition in the "open economy" have been shifted from local capital to labor, thus allowing capital to retain a high profit margin while international capital expands its links to the Spanish economy.

The costs to labor have been extremely high. Home workers lack any social protection, legislation, or health protection: the fumes from chemicals such as glues in the making of shoes, for example, have led to numerous reports of toxic illnesses. Contract workers are nonunionized and essentially temporary workers lacking any collective bargaining rights.[30] The multinationals, in turn, draw their work force from a huge, unemployed labor pool which weakens existing union organizing and limits for a time the propensity to strike.

Moreover, this shift from protected national industrial growth to the internationalization of the economy has stimulated a massive shift of

27. On the regime policies promoting the international circuits see the business pages of *El País*.

28. *El País*, 25 September 1988, business section, p. 15. On the transfer of capital from industry to real estate, see *El País*, 6 November 1988, business section, p. 3; on foreign takeovers of key Spanish-owned food corporations, see *El País*, 30 October 1988, business section. p. 12.

29. On regime labor policy, the most detailed critique is to be found in Instituto Sindical de Estudios, *Evolución social*, especially chapter 3, "Derecho individual de trabajo;" part II, "La Situación de los trabajadores - Economia sumergida," pp. 83–98; and volume II on the growth of temporary labor and the decline of health, pp. 99–178.

30. Less than 2 percent of the labor force contracted as temporary workers under state subsidies became permanent workers. See *El Periódico*, 16 November 1988, p. 33. A study by the Workers' Commission trade union found more than three million workers suffering from stress, with suicides increasing 37 percent in the areas of industrial restructuring; *El Periódico*, 18 August 1988, p. 27. On the issue of social security, see *El País*, 5 December 1988, p. 48. On "labor flexibility" in the construction industry, see Víctor Santos Valenzuela, "Flexibilidad laboral y empleo en la construcción," *El País*, 15 October 1984, p. 52.

Spanish capital from productive to real-estate speculation and to the financial sector.[31] Nonproductive investment has been the fastest growing sector over the past several years and its growth has outstripped the productive base, creating a false sense of prosperity with high growth and high unemployment. Spain has become one of the major poles of attraction for all sorts of "hot money," i.e., illicit funds, as its banking and investment laws ask the least questions, exercise the weakest regulation and provide the easiest opportunities for laundering money. Hence, as noted earlier, Spain has become one of the favorite investment sites for Latin American and European narcocapitalists.[32] Socialist labor policies have also attracted the attention of Northern European and Japanese capital eager to invest in assembly and export platforms into the unified European market.

The Socialist regime's conception of Spain's role in the international division of labor is thus as a major labor reserve for foreign-controlled labor-intensive industry, as a magnet for the attraction of speculative and real-estate capital, and as the site of the continued expansion of an already overdeveloped tourist industry. This is accompanied by a dual policy toward industry of promoting high technology in specified industries and of promoting low-paid labor-intensive industries ostensibly to absorb redundant labor displaced by the high-tech industries. In some cases, the steel mills in Bilbao, for example, both processes are combined: small groups of highly skilled workers operate the computer controls, a second group of permanent workers feed the furnaces, and a third and growing group of nonunion temporary workers who are subcontracted do the dirtiest and most hazardous work. The state's efforts to promote the integration of Spanish capital into the international circuits are matched by its efforts to fragment labor at the its basic level, the plant.

The growth and prosperity of the international service circuit is matched by the deterioration of the national circuit of production and consumption. The state has launched several attacks ("efficiency campaigns") on public education, postal, and transport workers, all of whom are subject to cuts in employment and salaries but who have, in some cases, successfully resisted the state through strikes and collective action. The entire notion of the public sphere has been under attack by the Socialist regime. Its strategy has been to induce reductions in funding,

31. The real estate speculative boom can be seen in the prices for apartments: a 100-square-meter flat in Barcelona rose in value from 6.7 million pesetas in 1986 to 14.6 million in 1988. The prototype of new capital is the kidnapped entrepreneur, Emiliano Revilla, who went from being a sausage maker to billionaire real estate speculator in less than two years.
32. On the ties of Socialist municipal officials with narcocapitalists in Galicia, see *El País,* 19 November 1988, p. 15.

resulting in deteriorating services, which provoke user discontent, and then to use public discontent and declining services as the basis for an ideological attack on public ownership ("inefficiency") as a weapon to promote further privatization or simply the abandonment of public services.

Just as the Socialist regime's policy of state encroachments empties civil society of its active citizens and critical public, its neoliberal economic policies undermine collective welfare and foster a society of private wealth and public poverty, of elegant seashore villas along contaminated shores,[33] and of accident-prone public transport amidst large-scale imports of private autos, airplanes, and yachts and massive investments in costly new highways, luxury marinas, and airports. The exception to this is the high-speed railroad linking Seville to Madrid and from there to Europe, another link to the EC market.

The dynamic growth of the sectors linked to the private international circuit come into conflict with the crisis-ridden public internal circuits, generating a dual vision of Spanish society, in which visions of triumphant personal success are juxtaposed with images of large-scale, long-term collective marginality.

Socialist ideologues have invented a discourse to legitimate the subordination of the working class to Spain's new role in the international division of labor. *Modernism, modernity* and *modernization* purport to describe (and justify) the massive displacement of workers from established national industries and the transfer of capital to nonproductive sectors. The transition from factories to banks, from machinery to hotels, from factory to home production, all are subsumed under the vacuous phrase, "modernization."

Regime ideologues sense the desire among many Spaniards to escape from the traditional constraints of the past, repressive personal constraints as well as those imposed by authoritarian institutions. Modernity connotes the promise of alternative, freer life-styles, greater opportunity from class rigidities, and access to a larger variety of consumer goods. In fact, the Socialist socioeconomic policies promote the demise of the older constraints and the construction of newer ones, in some cases equally or even more confining: unemployment (40 percent) for young people, insecurity of factory employment (26 percent of the labor force), and marginality in home industry.[34] The freedom and mobility associated with modernity is

33. The regime announced that the beaches of Marbella, vacation playground for both the new and old rich, contained fifteen times the level of contaminants allowable. The announcement was made after the tourist season had ended. *El País*, 1 September 1988, p. 15.
34. On unemployment, temporary work and home industry, see Instituto Sindical de Estudios, *Evolución social*. One estimate is that 43 percent of those working in the underground economy are under twenty-three years old, and that women account for 38 percent of those employed. Over one-third of employment is service or irregular.

116

confined to the 20 percent who are well ensconced in the new networks and circuits. Modernity is the ideology of the upwardly mobile professionals, as well as it is their ideological justification. They generalize as a universal good what is in effect a class-based phenomenon.

Likewise, the Socialist regime's ideologues have taken advantage of the desire for Spaniards to partake of Northern European living standards and, during the Franco period, to obtain the same political freedoms, to introduce an Europeanist ideology that promotes the subordination of the Spanish economy to the needs of European capital. The subtle and not so subtle depreciation of things Spanish, both by the state and the private commercial sector, involves positive references to imported clothes and durable goods through invidious comparisons. This allows the regime to promote foreign-capital takeovers, foreign colonization of resort regions, the displacement of Spanish producers through foreign imports, as well as restricting Spanish producer-exporters to the EC. Becoming European means accepting multinational control of the vital transportation industry. Becoming European means restricting the Galician fishing industry's catch to accommodate the EC. Becoming European means undermining the Catalan dairy industry through EC imports. Trading on consumer preferences, the Socialists undermine the national productive sector and promote the international circuit, that is, the links between European and Spanish banks, real estate developers, the tourist-resort builders, and speculators. These are the groups for whom becoming European has substance and meaning.

The military has become an important component of the "international strategy" of the Socialist party. The integration of the Spanish economy into the international circuits requires a military capable of fulfilling Spain's new role as junior partner in policing European interests, hence the Socialist proposal to create a rapid deployment force to intervene in regional conflicts.[35] Secondly, the military is an important element in the Socialist centralist development strategy, particularly as regional inequalities increase and national claims intensify.[36] Thirdly, the

35. On Spain's integration into NATO and development of an interventionary force, see *El Periódico,* 15 November 1988, p. 16. For González's compromises on nuclear weapons in Spain, ibid., 17. On the Socialists' sale of arms to Pinochet and South Africa, *El Periódico,* 18 November 1988, p. 80, and *El País,* 29 November 1988, p. 16. Two out of three Spaniards believed that González conceded much more to the U.S. than was received in the new base treaty, particularly on the issue of nuclear arms. *El País,* 2 October 1988, p. 13.

36. Regional inequalities have deepened, and Spain under González remains the most centralist regime in Western Europe. On regional inequalities see *El País,* 24 August 1988. Regarding the continued concentration of powers in the central government, only France exceeds Spain in terms of budgetary centralization. The Spanish state controls 76.2 percent of budgetary expenditures, compared with 55.8 percent in the six federal states and 65 percent in the six unitary states. *El País,* 7 December 1988, special supplement, p. 14.

Socialist party as a mass party in the northern European (or even Italian-Greek) sense does not exist – outside of the state apparatus and electoral campaigns, it has few, if any, activists with the capacity to organize and mobilize support. The army stands as a necessary back-up support for any substantial challenges to neo-liberal policies.[37] This is not as far-fetched as it seems, as a growing malaise and restiveness in the Spanish labor force became apparent in the early 1990s.

As the Socialists have moved to consolidate their ties and interdependence with the military, they have increasingly identified the "threat to democracy" with social forces challenging capitalist institutions. In Spain, the Socialists have not only fought for the restoration of bourgeois hegemony but perceive the Francoist military as strategic allies in the maintenance of bourgeois hegemony and the electoral regime against the challenges from national, regional, and social movements. The de facto alliance between the González regime, international corporate and local financial capital, and the military can only be sustained through the Socialists' successful demobilization of civil society and its subordination to the electoral apparatus.

In the new political order that the Socialists hope to consolidate, the state is subordinated to bourgeois hegemony, the political class to the state, and civil associations and social organization to the political class. The model for the Socialist party is the Institutional Revolutionary Party (PRI) in Mexico, not the constituency-influenced social democratic parties of Northern Europe.

THE IDEOLOGY OF ECONOMIC RESTRUCTURING AND THE CONCENTRATION OF CLASS POWER

In the economic order, the parameters of economic policy are delineated by the political bureaucracy. The rhetoric of "social contracts" (*concertacion social*) between labor, capital, and the state is evoked to give a veneer of legitimacy to policies already decided and implemented by the economics ministry. The first order of business for the Socialist regime upon coming to power was the necessity of promoting the conditions for the reproduction of capital. This involved several areas of policy: an income policy designed to favor capital over labor; a policy to restructure

37. A survey of military officials found that while 56 percent preferred a democracy, 36 percent favored an authoritarian regime under certain circumstances. When asked under what conditions the military could take over the government, they cited "political chaos and serious disorder." About 44 percent opposed military intervention under any circumstances. Comparing the Franco period to the González era, 44 percent believed they were better off under the latter, against 33 percent who thought it was better under Franco and 23 percent who did not know or did not say.

capital facilitating the transfer of investment from low-profit competitive to high-profit oligopolistic sectors; a policy to restructure the labor force through new rules for employment and high levels of unemployment to increase the prerogatives, power, and profits of capital.

The emergence of this new accumulation regime based on neoliberal commitments is the consequence of the consensus between the Socialists, capital, and the military component of the state. The terms of the agreement – the trade-off between capitalist hegemony and electoral politics – is guaranteed by the military as long as the political class retains control over civil society. This consensus explains the Socialists' single-minded obsession with elite legitimacy, their efforts to create an open ruling class, and their drive to extend their political prerogatives. The result has been a political system stable in the short-run but based on strategic social polarities that could, over time, produce a very volatile political situation.

Just as it is a misconception to consider the Socialist party within the reformist workers' party tradition, it is equally erroneous to consider what the González economic team described as "economic restructuring" or "reconversion" part of an effort to technologically upgrade the economy. A survey of the application of state policies associated with "restructuring" reveals that it had little or nothing to do with developing the means of production or introducing high technology, except in isolated pockets, and a great deal to do with transforming the social relations of production. The regime's policy has been largely oriented toward an electoral strategy – short-term impact spending – and to opening the country to speculative and foreign investment. For the fiscal year 1989, the regime allocated eight billion pesetas to "current operations" and only one billion to real investment in productive activity.[38] In effect, the regime utilized an economic modernization discourse to transform the relations of power, both at the factory and on the regional and societal levels.

While scores of factories were closed and hundreds of thousands of workers were made redundant, there has not been a coherent operational industrial plan to substitute new industries or new investments in research and development to upgrade industry. Instead, centers of worker mobilization in the steel, auto, shoe, textile, and other industries witnessed the decimation of factory-based leadership, the dispersal of shop-floor militants, and, in many cases the reorganization of production on the basis of a more primitive technology (home industries) which were subject to total control by capital. Industrial restructuring from the per-

38. *El País*, 1 October 1988, p. 49.

spective of long-term, large-scale change was in the first instance a political and social process.

The Socialist party and regime was well suited to engineer this transformation because of its working-class credentials and the confidence deposited in it by the working class. When it began the process of shifting power under the restructuring process, broad sectors of the working class placed their faith in the regime's promise that indeed new jobs awaited them at the end of the tunnel, that only a few sectors would be affected, probably not theirs. Through its carrot-and-stick policies of substantial severance pay and early retirement for older, malleable workers, and forced expulsion for others, the Socialist regime succeeded in closing down firms and allowing employers to decisively shift the composition of their labor force from permanent to temporary workers.

During the early phases, the Socialist trade unionists, many transformed into state functionaries, ministers, and parliamentarians, played an active role in promoting "economic restructuring,"[39] but over time the adverse impact began to affect not only militants on the left but also Socialist trade unionists. A perceptible gap developed between Socialist trade unionists whose loyalty was primarily to the party-state apparatus and those who, in one form or another, felt obligated to respond to the rank and file as their membership shrank and they began to lose elections in larger firms. By the middle of 1988 even Socialist trade-union officials were publicly acknowledging that the whole program of economic sacrifice was not conjunctural or equitably distributed between capital and labor, but strategic and unequal, and they shifted their alliances from the party state to their left-wing counterparts in the workers' commissions.[40]

Essentially what the Socialist regime meant by restructuring involved changes at two levels: changes between the state and society and changes at the point of production.

The restructuring of relations of production at the factory level has taken various forms: (1) dispersion of the labor force from large plants to numerous smaller firms, usually through a system of subcontracting; (2) destabilization of work tenure, through the increased use of temporary workers; (3) revival of cottage industry, the transfer of production from the factory to the household; and (4) the conversion of unprofitable firms into "workers' coops."

39. The role of the Socialist trade unionists as transmission belts of regime economic policy was bluntly stated by the former economics minister (now bank president) Boyer, when he told Redondo that "the norm in democracies is that the government takes decisions and afterwards informs the social agents." Such, are the joys of social contracting. *El País*, 18 December 1988, special supplement, "La Ruptura," p. 3.
40. For a detailed account of the rupture, see ibid.

At the national level, restructuring has involved a shift in the relation-ship between state and society – the subordination of civil society to the bureaucratic apparatuses of the state. Co-optive mechanisms have been widely and successfully used to convert social activists and intellectuals into state functionaries.

The basic purpose of Socialist-sponsored restructuring has been to shift the balance of power decisively from labor to capital in the post-Franco period. From the other side, the trade unions have ineffectively struggled to shift the axis of power toward a new equilibrium, reversing the trend initiated by the González regime.

Essentially, there are three areas that are affected by restructuring: trade-union organization, the rates of profit, and the composition of the ruling class. The restructuring process was directly aimed at marginaliz-ing the trade unions by breaking up working-class solidarity. The policy of supply-side economics and increased labor-market flexibility was directed at expanding management prerogatives and the rates of profit. The new liberal economic policies were designed to channel resources toward facilitating the entry of Socialist-connected entrepreneurs and bankers into the upper echelons of the ruling class.

Even more important, restructuring was aimed at fitting Spain into the international division of labor as (1) a banking and financial center; (2) a low-cost resort center; (3) a supplier of docile labor for the subsidiaries of multinational capital; (4) a center for real estate and speculative capital; and (5) a means of deepening Spain's participation in such European and American military alliances as NATO.

What is absent from this list of concerns is the transformation of Spain into an industrial and agricultural center. Spain under the Socialists is a classical example of growth without development.

The relatively high growth of the Spanish economy in the late 1980s, celebrated in the mass media both at home and abroad,[41] is largely based on imports, foreign borrowing, the entry of "hot money," the expansion of financial and real estate services, and consumer spending. In great part, Spain's growth is based on a fragile and shrinking productive base and is increasingly dependent on external financial, investment, and technolog-ical sources. Growth has been unevenly spread, located in specific enclaves identified with financial and real-estate capital, largely the Cos-tra Brava, Madrid, and Barcelona. Growth enclaves and assembly-plant sites, which have been built by foreign subsidiaries, predominate in these "growth" poles. Growth under Gonzalez has not meant the creation of

41. Predictably, a *New York Times* front-page headline read: "With Spain in Common Market New Prosperity and Employment," *New York Times,* 15 January 1989, p. 1, 12.

local autonomous sources of design, research, and development, nor has overseas borrowing of technology led to adaptation and innovation; rather it perpetuates dependence, vulnerability, and large-scale profit and royalty remittances. In summary, Socialist party policy, despite the technocratic jargon of its economic team, is not developing the means of production or generating new technology with positive spread effects throughout industry and agriculture, among all classes and regions.

There is a profound absence of a truly national technocratic group in control of Spanish economic policy. Those in command of this policy are basically politicians who have been concerned with consolidating control and who have been more effective in managing power than in developing productive forces. Spain's policies of opening to the European Community demonstrate a greater perception of possible political benefits than the adverse effects on producer groups in Spain. The Socialists have demonstrated a greater capacity to create opportunities for enrichment for its upwardly mobile professionals than in developing a coherent industrial policy. The major contribution of the Socialist government has been its capacity to open up the ruling class to new entrants from its own ranks and entourage at the cost of developing a socially responsible employment and income program for the army of young, unemployed workers.

By the end of 1992 the Spanish Socialists had little to celebrate. Opinion polls in September of 1992 indicated that voters intending to vote for the PSOE had dropped to 37 percent (from nearly 50 percent earlier), compared to 31 percent for the right-wing Popular Party and 12 percent for the United Left. In 1992, Spain had the largest trade imbalance in the OECD after the U.S., an estimated $34 billion, up 11 percent over 1991.[42] Inflation was increasing, pegged at seven percent for 1992. The public deficit for 1991 was three billion dollars, but during the first six months of 1992 it rose by 40 percent. Unemployment rose steadily in the early 1990s, reaching 17 percent by late 1992, double the rate of the EC, despite the billions spent on a high speed railroad linking Madrid and Seville and billions more on the World Exposition in Seville and the Olympics in Barcelona. The huge accumulated debt in non-productive investments and the declining economic prospects (one-third of the firms interviewed in late 1992 planned reductions in the work force) are setting the stage for difficult times – as González confessed in an interview in the *Wall Street Journal* in the fall of 1992.

The boom of the late 1980s and early 1990s was largely built on for-

42. José Manuel Martín Medem, "Te llaman porvenir porque no vienes nunca," *Brecha*, 18 September 1992, p. 28.

eign investment and loans, covering trade and budgetary deficits. In large part, this was at best an unreliable and fragile basis for sustaining growth: on the one hand, much of this capital was invested in speculative ventures, on the other, when the investments began to mature, the profits and interests remitted out of the country soon began to outweigh new investments, as the Spanish market began to shrink. Spanish GNP for 1992 is estimated to grow only two percent and to continue stagnating into the mid-1990's, meaning rising unemployment. González continues to promote Spanish participation in a European fighter plane project at a cost of five billion dollars, while proposing to reduce budgetary expenses by six billion dollars, particularly unemployment and health expenditures.

The Socialist regime's wage and salary policy continues to exacerbate socioeconomic inequalities. While government policy tries to limit wages to predicted inflation rates, five percent in 1991, salaries of chief executive officers rose by 13 percent.[43] The public health system is in danger of collapse: accumulated debt by the spring of 1992 had reached 600,000 million pesetas and was growing.[44] Over the years, the debt was disguised by rolling over payment to suppliers and transferring costs to the regions. In this sense, the health sector is emblematic of the false sense of prosperity generated by the González regime: short-term socioeconomic prosperity was bought on the basis of medium-term debt. Under the glittering facade of late 1980s growth was an industrially and technologically weak economy dependent on foreign capital and borrowing and with little or no capacity to meet its future debt payments.

The positive programs of the PSOE, its national pension plan for all senior citizens, its construction of cultural centers for retirees and civic associations, its generous holiday schedule (thirty-one days out of the year) were not accompanied by a sustained effort at long-term, large-scale productive investments. While the social programs secured a steady electoral base (especially among the elderly), the lack of productive investments is now undermining the very social programs that sustained the regime, leading to growing political discontent. Meanwhile, the "de-regulated economy" has spawned corruption in the highest offices. The Vice President, Alfonso Guerra, was forced to resign because his office was used by his brother to secure lucrative contracts; the President of the Bank of Spain, Mariano Rubio, was implicated in "insider trade" dealing.[45]

In order to compensate for wasteful spending, massive public corruption, and unproductive investments leading to the fiscal crisis, the PSOE

43. *El País*, 27 October 1992, business section, p. 3 .
44. *El País*, 20 March 1992, p. 20.
45. Ignacio Sotelo, "Crisis de credibilidad," *El País*, 20 March 1992, p. 18. See also *El País*, 23 March 1992, p. 17.

123

regime has moved to drastically cut social expenditures, namely health and unemployment payments. Under legislation passed in the spring of 1992, unemployment payments would commence after one year instead of the previous six months of work, largely excluding the growing army of temporary employees.[46]

Temporary workers increased as a percentage of the total labor force (1987 = 15.6 percent; 1991 = 32.18 percent).[47] The decline in unemployment from 20 percent to 15 percent in the mid to late 1980s was absorbed by the temporary work category who earn 43 percent less than permanent workers. Hence the social cuts will largely affect this sector of the economy, mostly young workers and women.[48] Despite recent gains, Spain is next to last (Portugal is last) in social expenditures among the EC countries, 18.8 percent of GNP compared to 25.7 percent for the community.[49]

Meanwhile, the "postindustrial" strategy is falling on its face. In Valencia tourism declined 40 percent between 1988 and 1992 and shows no signs of recovery.[50] The construction industry closely linked to tourism is in crisis – with over 20,000 vacancies in Alicante alone. With industrial production growing at 0.4 percent in 1991, and construction declining from 10 percent to 3.7 percent in 1991, social tensions are inevitably accumulating.[51]

On 28 May 1992, a nationwide general strike was successful in convoking 80 percent of the labor force, despite government claims to the contrary. The regime's attempt to mobilize a counter-demonstration in Seville a few days prior to the strike was an abysmal failure; less than 15,000 loyalists turned out (less than one third of those expected) to hear President González and ex-Vice President Guerra, despite free bus transport and free tickets to attend Expo 1992.[52]

As the economic crisis deepens, the Socialists are determined to shift the burden of the austerity measures onto the backs of labor. The ambiguities in the elitist neoliberal economic policies and the "populist" consumer imports and budgetary policies are disappearing. The capacity of the González regime to retain electoral support for the corporate-oriented economic policies by piling up budget and trade deficits and securing overseas loans is declining. The populist consumerist "party" is over,

46. El País, 21 March 1992, p. 27.
47. El País, 27 March 1992, p. 50.
48. El País, 27 October 1991, p. 54, 55; El Mundo, 25 March 1992, p. 9; Diario 16, 28 March 1992, p. 51.
49. El País, 29 March 1992, business section, p. 12.
50. El País, 5 April 1992, p. 3
51. El País, 15 March 1992, business section, p. 12.
52. El Mundo, 24 May 1992, p. 11.

now the "broken dishes" of neoliberal deregulation have to be paid for.

The conversion of the PSOE to neoliberalism has only superficially "modernized" Spain – and that gloss is increasingly wearing thin as Third-World-style debt and unemployment begin to define the emerging reality of the Spanish political-economy.

CONCLUSION

The emergence and trajectory of the Socialist regime is intimately related to the accumulation process in Spain. Historically, accumulation models run a cycle of implantation, expansion, crisis, and restructuring, followed by a new cycle. The relevant point in our discussion is the moment of crisis. The crisis of the Francoist "national-protectionist-industrializing" model contained within it the socioeconomic forces for the transition to the new neoliberal model. The crisis in the old model of accumulation represented a threat to the very process of accumulation. To overcome the crisis required the restructuring of the capital accumulation model to ensure the functioning of the accumulation process. Restructurings of capital do not happen through the invisible hand or impersonal forces of the market; they occur because of the actions of class forces, for in reality models of accumulation reflect configurations of class power, and restructuring of accumulation models involves the reordering of the ruling class.

The González regime came to power in the midst of the crisis of the national-industrializing model, a time of increasing class struggle – massive strike waves, urban and rural protests, and military unrest – and economic stagnation. Within the older model of accumulation, his regime has formed a new power bloc of bankers, multinationals, importers, and speculators in tourist real estate, and has begun to restructure class, state, and economic relations to accommodate the new international neoliberal model of accumulation.

To overcome the crisis and implant the new model necessitated subsidies and financing from industrial capital to cushion the shocks, while the working class was divided between older workers who received lump sums of severance pay and younger workers who were marginalized. Once implanted, by the mid-1980s, the new model with its newly restructured dominant class proceeded to expand on the basis of foreign investment, technology, and financing, the growth of financial and real estate capital, and pockets of high-tech industries. Profits have increased, capital has been invested, but the new model operates on the basis of a large surplus labor force and an increasingly temporary labor force.

These features are not products of a conjunctural crisis of the neolib-

125

eral model but inherent features of its expansion. While the original growth of unemployment and temporary workers may have, in part, originated during the crisis period, their extension and perpetuation is linked to the new neoliberal model. The model depends on cheap and docile labor to attract foreign export-oriented industries, while the financial-real estate-construction-tourist industry requires seasonal labor. Left-wing analysts who have continued to write about the crisis of Spanish capitalism confuse these products (unemployment and temporary labor) of the earlier crisis and fail to see the integral role they have played in capital's emergence from the crisis. They have been referring to a crisis for the working class, not of the system, unless the working class acts on its crisis and through massive class action affects the accumulation process. The normal functioning of the new model is based on this class-centered crisis.

The deepening contradictions between the growth of fictitious capital and the deterioration of conditions of employment for workers looms on the horizon. A deeper structural conflict emerges on several levels: between the state's commitment to real estate, finance, and tourism and its inability to develop the productive forces; between the opening to international capital and the development of the internal market; between integration through subordination to European capital and the development of internal class solidarity; and between a ruling class tied to dynamic European circuits and a local economy in deepening crisis vegetating on the margins of state policy. The cumulating social forces – workers, youth, small business, fishermen, miners, displaced factory workers, temporary laborers, salaried employees in the public sector – are increasingly conscious that the neoliberal politics and the economic classes that the Socialists represent do not include them. The logic of Socialist policy and the needs of the Spanish working class are on a collision course.

Working-class struggles have twice broken with the corporatist and neocorporatist projects of the ruling classes: the first wave of militancy from 1976-79 broke the back of the vertical organization imposed by the Franco dictatorship. The rise of the Socialist party and particularly the ascendancy of its neocorporatist liberal wing, however, once again led to efforts to encapsulate the labor movement in vertically controlled trade unions through elite social-contract pacts (1982-86). The deterioration of socioeconomic conditions, the rupture of the trade-union-state pacts, and the organization of autonomous class action may auger a new post-corporatist phase, of class politics.

It is too early to predict the end of the corporatist cycle as the Socialist state party is still intact and the Socialist unions still retain important collaborationist elements from the recent past. The iron chain linking the trade unions to the party, the party to Parliament, Parliament to the executive, and the executive to the caudillo can be broken at its weakest link, its ties with the working people. That is the beginning of hope for the renewal and recovery of the Spanish traditions of class solidarity and struggle and a vision of society based not on self-centered claims of the upwardly mobile professionals but on the great mass of Spanish working people. Neither the Francoist old right nor the neoliberal González new right offers any meaningful programs to meet these needs.

5 Portugal: From Popular Power to Bourgeois Democracy

Ronald H. Chilcote

An interpretative analysis of the Portuguese political economy necessarily must begin with the military coup of 25 April 1974. This event brought an abrupt end to nearly half a century of dictatorship and began a volatile revolutionary process and struggle for power in which a broad consensus emerged around a future transition to socialism.[1]

The coup was the outcome of occasional moments of protest dating to the 1958 presidential elections in which the opposition unexpectedly ran a strong campaign and received a quarter of the votes. During March of the following year, the Salazar regime uncovered a clandestine movement of dissident military officers, including Vasco Gonçalves, who later emerged as a leader of the Armed Forces Movement (*Movimento das Forças Armadas* or MFA) and of several provisional governments during 1974 to 1975. By early 1961 Africans had risen against Portuguese colonial rule in Angola, and soon thereafter similar liberation struggles appeared in Portuguese Guinea (now Guinea-Bissau) and Mozambique.

The colonial wars and their draining impact on the Portuguese economy led to fragmentation within the major institutions supportive of the dictatorship, especially the military. Midway through 1973, some thir-

1. Among the many useful recent scholarly sources on the 1974 coup and ensuing revolutionary period are Nancy Gina Bermeo, *The Revolution within the Revolution: Worker's Control in Rural Portugal* (Princeton, N.J., 1986); Charles Downs, *Revolution at the Grassroots: Community Organizations in the Portuguese Revolution* (Albany, N.Y., 1989); and John J. Hammond, *Building Popular Power: Workers' and Neighborhood Movements in the Portuguese Revolution* (New York, 1988). A useful account, close to the revolutionary events and including documentation, is Phil Mailer, *Portugal: The Impossible Revolution!* (New York, 1977). A very general but helpful introduction to contemporary Portugal is Walter C. Opello, Jr., *Portugal: From Monarchy to Pluralist Democracy* (Boulder, Colo., 1991). The best account of fascism and opposition to the dictatorship is D.L. Raby, *Fascism and Resistance in Portugal: Communists, Liberals and Military Dissidents in the Opposition to Salazar, 1941–1974* (Manchester, 1988). For an annotated guide to two thousand sources on the period, see Ronald H. Chilcote, ed., *The Portuguese Revolution of 25 April 1974: Annotated Bibliography on the Antecedents and Aftermath* (Coimbra, 1987).

teen hundred captains and majors petitioned the government to resolve pay grievances and working conditions. During October two hundred officers met in Evora to seek a political rather than military solution to the colonial wars. They were alarmed at the loss of life, suffering of the wounded, and defeat in battle. Many even sympathized with the ideals of the African liberation movements and their criticisms of colonialism and imperialism, and they recognized that those benefiting from the war were the same financial groups that exploited people in Portugal itself. The burden of the colonial wars also had produced a fissure within the bureaucracy, between colonial-oriented interests on one hand and technocrats who were interested in organizing the domestic economy and integration with Europe on the other. A similar split also appeared in the bourgeoisie itself.

The April coup thus reflected a crisis of legitimacy and hegemony. It was a crisis of legitimacy because the old political system had failed to assimilate new social and political interests, and of hegemony because the bourgeoisie, its industrial and financial fractions in particular, were unable to prevail in a power bloc with the landed bourgeoisie whose hegemony had depended on the colonies. In addition, the bourgeoisie could not find a political program that would guide the subordinated strata. A counter-coup on 25 November 1975 led to the resolution of the legitimacy crisis, but the hegemony crisis would continue well into the 1980s.

There was some question whether a coup or revolution had occurred. Pezarat Correia, one of the participants, characterized it as a coup with peculiar characteristics because the MFA produced a progressive program and had led the military into a revolution aimed at democracy, decolonization, and development. The revolution, he believed, did not evolve correctly due to a power struggle within the MFA. The constitution incorporated the revolutionary thrust and even accepted the premise of an eventual transition to socialism, but it also resolved the question of democracy in favor of a formal, representative, and bourgeois parliament, and all ensuing governments sought to roll back the gains of 1974 until all traces of the revolution had disappeared.[2] Once the colonies had been granted their independence, the revolutionary fervor lessened, the development drive was aimed at an evolutionary and reformist course toward European integration, and ties to the Third World were all but severed.

It is this context, with the coup and its aftermath as backdrop, which has guided me in suggesting three propositions that are examined in the

---

2. From the transcript of an interview with Pezarat Correia, in Hugo Gil Fereira and Michael W. Marshall, *Portugal's Revolution: Ten Years On* (Cambridge, 1986), p. 77.

present chapter. First, despite the abrupt shift in regime from dictatorship to democracy and the apparent radical changes accompanying this process, the legacy of past traditions ensured a remarkable continuity in the economic structures and policies of the state. Further, although the revolution decimated the old family-controlled economic groups that had prospered through association with the state, control by new economic groups evolved in a familiar pattern after 1975. The economy remained relatively weak compared to advanced European countries despite modest economic growth and neoliberal reform administered by a stable center-right government that consolidated its political hegemony in the mid-1980s.

Second, although the dominant classes were weakened and the popular classes strengthened during the 1974–1975 period, this relationship was reversed in the wake of the revolution. Some capital, both domestic and international, continued to penetrate the economy, while organized labor in urban centers succumbed to the pressures and influences of the major political parties and rural workers suffered from the rollback of the agrarian reform and government inattention. This configuration of class forces and their incorporation in politics is also essential to my analysis.

Third, bourgeois rule has persisted, despite the active participation of other social classes. Neoliberal and social democratic parties have formed a pact, enabling a center-right regime to come to power and to marginalize extreme right and left, including the Communist party.

The State's Economic Structures and Policies

The first proposition suggests that a continuity has prevailed in the economic structures and policies of the state despite shifts in regime through various historical periods dating to the early twentieth century. The Portuguese state evolved through mercantilism, first under monarchical rule until 1910 and then under a republic to 1926; this continued through private financial and industrial investment associated with the fascist corporate regime led by António de Oliveira Salazar until his incapacitation in 1968, and the reformist corporate regime of his successor, Marcello Caetano, which survived until 25 April 1974. The April coup brought a progressive wing of the military to power, initially aligned with the Portuguese Communist party (PCP), facilitating the formation of political parties and leading to the consolidation of a bourgeois parliamentary period from 1976 until the present.

Political scientists such as José Durão Barroso believe that after 1974 the state had changed "in the sense of political culture of democracy and participation in society."[3] It is indeed true that the political form of the state changed from monarchical state to republican state to fascist corporate state to progressive authoritarian state and ultimately to the bourgeois democratic state of today. The drive toward a democratic socialist state, manifested in the turmoil of 1974 and 1975 and even projected in the constitution of 1976, was never consummated, however.

Despite these changes the political structures of the state have remained constant, for the state has tended to be decisive in the polity through its administration of government agencies, in law through its regulation of production, finance, and distribution, and in ideology through its influence in education and the mass media. Names of government institutions and agencies may have changed in the transitional period of 1974-1975, but many regulations, rules, and practices carried on as in the past. The democratic opening permitted political space, including the manifestation of demands from the population at large, but even this space was to become constrained by the similar or transformed apparatuses of the state. According to a political observer, "the state structures were essentially untouched by the revolution although democratic processes were implemented. The apparatuses of administration and police remained in place for the most part."[4]

There has also been stability in the economic structures of the state, for it has been state initiatives, concessions, and protection that have shaped capitalist development in Portugal, initially through a strong mercantilism during monarchical and early republican rule. This continued through private financial and industrial capital closely associated with public expenditure and planning in the corporate state, and finally through integration with Western Europe and the bourgeois democratic form that evolved after the collapse of socialist aspirations during 1974 and 1975.

Under the fascist corporate state, the administrative machinery ensured order, stability, and the implementation of policies in the interests of the dominant classes, specifically the large landowners and financial, industrial, and commercial bourgeoisie. Although Salazarism may have been "a fascism without a fascist movement,"[5] it is clear that ideologically it owed as much to conservative Christian Democracy as it did to the integralism that evolved through a disaffected monarchist movement during the First Republic. The ideological underpinnings of the authoritarian state were linked to Catholic interests at the University of Coimbra.[6]

---

3. Interview, José Durão Barroso, Lisbon, 13 and 15 November 1990.
4. Interview, Francisco Martins Rodrigues, Lisbon, 14 November 1990.
5. Manuel de Lucena, *A evolução do sistem corporativo português*, vol. 1, *O Salazarismo* (Lisbon, 1976), p. 98.
6. Manuel Braga da Cruz, *As origens da democracia cristã e o salazarismo* (Lisbon, 1980).

Theoretically, this "New State" would unify diverse social classes into a corporate whole, organized horizontally rather than vertically to ensure the harmony of divergent interests, such as those of employer and worker. In reality, however, control was exercised at the top in a presidential-style system in which power in the office of the prime minister prevailed through a hierarchical set of controls institutionalized through a single complex staff or superministry of reliable civilian and military officials accountable to Salazar himself. The legislature was subservient to the executive and consisted of a national assembly elected by popular vote but with a limited franchise in a corporate chamber of twenty-four sections, each representing a major social activity. An elaborate repressive apparatus was made up of a secret police and other police corps that served the regime and sheltered a national security state designed to control all elements of society and institutionalize collaboration in place of class conflict between capital and labor. Although military dissidence in the form of small revolts was evident from 1926 until the demise of the regime, the period was exceedingly stable.

Caetano attempted to move from fascism to political pluralism while clinging to the principle that the collaboration of social classes was essential to state and society. He desired the continuity of corporatism and a strong state. The executive remained as strong as that under his predecessor, the corporate structure was left intact, and the dominant classes continued to rely on the state. There were some changes, however, in particular the movement toward integration with Europe and the expansion of markets. Political liberalization allowed for a small opposition to appear within the parliament, while a left opposition outside legislative circles exploded into a multitude of political parties and organizations, some mobilized around young militants in the PCP and others with revolutionaries outside the party who favored a strategy of armed struggle. Others pursued more sectarian stances, following the precepts of Lenin, Stalin, and Trotsky.

The progressive MFA dominated six provisional governments from April 1974 to November 1975. Military authority at the top mediated various political and economic groups vying for influence during this period. The old state structures remained largely intact during the revolutionary period, despite changes in agency names and some personnel. Ideological division in society at large, however, was reflected within the MFA and its competing factions. The basic question was whether authority should be decentralized at the grass roots or devolve in the direction of a multiparty parliamentary system. This latter line was affirmed in the April 1975 elections for a constituent assembly, the victory of the Socialist party in the April 1976 elections, and the promulgation of the new constitution. The countercoup of 25 November 1975, led by moderate elements within the MFA, undermined the position of the Communist party within the government and isolated the radical parties of the far left, the unions, workers' commissions, neighborhood associations, and other popular organizations.

The period after November 1975 to the present was dominated by the bourgeois democratic state. In theory this implied the structuring of state power along pluralistic lines to ensure participation by all political parties and to undermine the authority of the military, so that no single party, including the Communists, could establish hegemony over the political economy. In practice, it also granted discredited rightist groups an opportunity to enter politics, and steered Portugal along the political path of neoliberalism and social democracy.

These historical periods, the changing political form of the state, and linkage to the emerging and consolidating capitalism are delineated in Figure 1.

Figure 1
Formations of the Portuguese State

Dates	Political	Economic
Until 1910	Monarchical	Mercantile capitalist
1910–1926	Republican	Mercantile capitalist
1926–1968	Fascist corporate	Commercial, financial, and industrial capitalists in conjunction with state capital
1968–1974	Progressive authoritarian	Socialized sectors in domestic industry and banking mixed with international and domestic private capital in commerce, industry, and finance
1974–1975	Democratic socialist	Trend toward socialization of private means of production with direct popular participation of workers and consumers
1975–	Bourgeois democratic	Trend toward privatization of state enterprise, concessions for international capital, stimulation of new economic groups of mixed foreign and domestic capital

THE STATE AND THE ECONOMIC GROUPS

This analysis turns briefly to the monopolization of capital under Salazar and Caetano and the fostering of national industries by the state, some of them in conjunction with national and international capital. Consequently, monopolistic and oligopolistic groups influenced public policy, and the state in turn shielded Portuguese industry.[7]

The postwar period from 1946 to 1974 was decisive for monopoly capital in Portugal, resulting in the consolidation of monopoly groups, some of which had been evolving since their establishment in the 1920s, a period in which some small and medium-sized firms began to concentrate capital in certain sectors of the economy. Each group had a specific commercial-financial-industrial cluster of companies under the aegis of a leading capitalist, family, or conglomeration of capitalist and family interests. Some, like the Companhia União Fabril (CUF), had grown rapidly through exploitation of vegetable oils from the colonies. During the 1950s these groups intensified their growth through integration of corporate and bank capital. At the same time the Salazar regime limited foreign investment, not, in the view of one observer, in defense of "an authentic nationalism," but with the intent "of preserving its economic and political influence in the most archaic sectors of the bourgeoisie and impeding the appearance of a concentrated proletariat."[8]

Within the limits of its dependence on advanced capitalism Portugal moved slowly in the direction of an opening toward Europe as one means of facilitating the expanding commercial and technological needs of the monopoly groups while allowing some modernization of its backward capitalism. Foreign capital also would serve to bolster and prolong the Portuguese colonial wars and possibly stimulate exploitation of untapped natural resources in Africa. Portugal initially joined the European Free Trade Association (EFTA) and by 1963 international capital began to have a domestic impact. This process was interrupted only by the revolutionary interlude of 1974–76, but was restored thereafter, and progressed until Portugal formally joined the European Community (EC) in 1986.

7. Fernando Medeiros argues that capitalism was given an impetus with the consolidation of the Salazar regime; see his *A sociedade e a economia portuguesas nas origens do Salazarismo* (Lisbon, 1978). Bruneau argues that Salazar was not controlled by any particular class although the bourgeoisie clearly benefited from his rule. Whereas Salazar exercised power on a personalist basis, Caetano, in contrast, did not rule effectively and lacked control of the regime; in his memoirs, he complained of lack of power and party to back him, the uncooperative attitude of the liberals, and the passivity of the capitalists. Thomas C. Bruneau, *Politics and Nationhood: Post-Revolutionary Portugal* (New York, 1984).

8. Ronaldo Guedes da Fonseca, *A questão do estado na revolução portuguesa (do 25 de Abril de 1974 ao golpe de Tancos* (Lisbon, 1983), p. 29.

The Caetano years represented a further effort at liberalization of the economy and a partial modification of the state apparatuses. This implementation of a "technocratic fascism" reflected the interests of the more dynamic sector of the bourgeoisie.[9] Through nationalization of the banking system in 1975 these interests generally were assimilated into an expanding state. Although the old groups were unable fully to recuperate their interests, by 1990 under increasingly conservative governments the state enterprises were being liquidated or sold to private interests; simultaneously new groups in the private sector were becoming prominent in the economy. The composition of these groups reveals the structure of the Portuguese dominant classes since financial, industrial, commercial, and sometimes landowning interests have been coalescing within each group.

Americó Ramos dos Santos has argued that with the rise to power of Caetano the industrial bourgeoisie and technocracy believed the moment opportune for transcending the colonial question by opening the economy to foreign, particularly European, capital and to modernization. They rapidly expanded and consolidated monopoly control over the economy through ownership of key firms, holding companies, and banks. This was a period in which small firms began to disappear in the face of monopoly and multinational capital. Technocrats would have a decisive role in the political apparatus and the large monopoly groups.

Objective conditions at the time included: political isolation from the outside world though with a perceived need to open the economy; the contradiction of both integrating the colonies into the national economy and reorganizing the economy in order to integrate with Europe; a tendency to rely on existing but obsolete industry and a low level of technological innovation; permanently stagnant agricultural production, based on traditional subsidy policies; a corrupt state apparatus; substantial emigrant labor; deterioration in monetary stability due to the colonial wars; and a crisis in trade only offset by a positive balance of trade with the colonies.[10]

By the end of 1973 seven large traditional groups constituted the monopolistic nucleus in Portugal: CUF, Espírito Santo, Champalimaud, Português do Atlântico, Borges e Irmão, Nacional Ultramarino, and Fonsecas e Burnay. The first four dominated as major financial groups because of the convergence of their control of large industry and leading position in commercial banking. Interspersed among them and other groups were fourteen traditional and powerful families. A secondary

---

9. Ibid., 32.
10. Américo Ramos dos Santos, "Desenvolvimento monopolista em Portugal (fase 1968–73): estruturas fundamentais," *Análise Social* 13 (1977): 70–71.

level, dependent on this nucleus but benefiting from the speculative Caetano period, comprised a bloc of some thirty families, with interests in real estate, tourism, insurance, and some industrial projects.[11]

One way of classifying the large traditional groups and families would be to divide them according to those closely linked with foreign capital, such as Espírito Santo, Burnay, and, after 1968–69, the CUF group; those oriented toward colonial exploitation, such as the Banco Nacional Ultramarino, Espírito Santo, and Champalimaud; and those groups protected economically within Portugal, such as CUF and Borges e Irmão.[12]

Since the 1930s the state had associated with private national and international industrial capital, particularly in the field of energy, in order to achieve self-sufficiency. The state envisaged joint ventures with private capital to build infrastructure and heavy industry.[13]

11. The fourteen traditional families were: Melo, Espírito Santo, Champalimaud, Quina, Mendes de Almeida, Queirós Pereira, Figueiredo, Feteira, Bordalo, Vinhas, Albano de Magalhães, Domingos Barreiro, Pinto de Magalhães, and Brandão Miranda. The secondary-level bloc of some thirty families included: Silveira Machado, Abecassis, Lagos, Cocco, Medeiros de Almeida, Pinto Basto, Sebastião Alves, and Manuel Bulhosa.

Beyond the pioneering study by Maria Belmira Martins, *Sociedades e grupos em Portugal* (Lisbon, 1975), my analysis draws upon the important article by Américo Ramos dos Santos, "Monopólios, capital financeiro e especulação – cinco anos de Marcelismo," *Economia e Socialismo* 17 (August 1977): 3–26, which concentrates on the 1968–73 period.

12. Maria Filomena Mónica provides helpful background with some relevance to the traditional families in her detailed, scholarly analysis of capitalists and industrialists in the formative period of 1870–1914. She delves into family prominence, family links, key figures, and their impact on the economy; see her "Capitalistas e industriais (1870–1914)," *Análise Social* 23 (1987): 819–63. She has also published sixteen interviews with prominent capitalists in *Os grandes patrões da indústria portuguesa* (Lisbon, 1990). For detail on the monopolies in the 1968–1973 period, see Américo Ramos dos Santos, "Economia portuguesa: dez anos. Cinco modelos (1969–1978)," *Economia e Socialismo* 25 26 (April–May 1978): 15–65. See also the insightful analysis by Daniel Nataf and Elizabeth Sammis, "Classes, Hegemony, and Portuguese Democratization," in Ronald H. Chilcote et al., *Transitions from Dictatorship to Democracy: Comparative Studies of Spain, Portugal, and Greece* (New York, 1990), pp. 73–130.

13. See Maria Teresa Patricio, "Industrialization and Communism: The Portuguese Communist Party Confronts the Sines Growth Pole," *Journal of Communist Studies* 6 (September 1990): 44–63, for a study of the industrial petrochemical complex at Sines, on the Atlantic coast south of Lisbon. She reveals the conflict between state-sponsored industrialization and disruptions of socioeconomic life at the local level. The consequences included the expropriation of both small and large parcels of land and the uprooting of families subsisting on the land; a negative impact on the environment which interfered with local fishing industry since marine life was threatened by oil spills; and waste outflows. Since the dominant political force in the area was the local PCP, it adopted positions in both policy and practice that contrasted with the national party, which officially favored the industrial project and opposed labor-intensive small and medium industry and the defense of traditional agricultural and fishing activities. In contrast, the local PCP became not only responsible and efficient, but open to dealing with people's needs and effective in leading or joining with resistance activities to protest the negative consequences of industrialization in the area. See also "Os 'dossiers' secretos de Sines," *O Jornal* 699 (1988). Of the two state petrochemical plants, one was privatized with Finnish capital assuming control, and in 1990 the government was implementing plans to sell its shares of the other.

However, the events of ll March 1975 served as a catalyst and pretext for nationalization of the interests of the economic groups. Three days later their powerful financial base disappeared with the nationalization of the banks and, on the ensuing day, with the takeover of thirty-two insurance firms. During April 1975 the power and oil interests, the steel monopoly, and rail, sea, and air transportation services fell under the control of the state, followed by cellulose and tobacco in May, urban transportation in June and July, mining and chemicals in August, CUF in September, holding companies in October, radio and television in December, and several newspapers in early 1976. The nationalizations continued until 29 July 1976, the process having taken sixteen months to bring 244 firms under state control.[14]

The state moved quickly to reorganize its assets. The Banco de Portugal exercised nearly absolute control (98 percent) over commercial banking in the country (sixteen banks and two banking houses), and it integrated these entities into ten state banks. The state also reorganized its insurance firms, with control over three-fourths of all insurance premiums, into six groups. The state consolidated electric energy under a public entity, Electricidade de Portugal EP, and the four nationalized oil firms, including two refineries, were brought together into Petróleos de Portugal EP. The state organized the paper industry into the Empresa de Celuose e Papel de Portugal (PORTUCEL), and controlled the largest iron and steel enterprise, Siderurgia Nacional EP. By the end of the seventies there were fifty-six "public enterprises" under state administration.

The state sector was economically powerful, although disordered and disarticulated within and affected by a lack of direction and of a rational government policy that would give it dynamism and facilitate the reconstruction of the national economy. One commentator suggested that some industries in the state sector were monopolistic without benefiting from their advantage of being monopolies.[15]

This situation may have changed with the return to power of a technocratically oriented government under Anibal Cavaco Silva and its determination either to liquidate inefficient and unnecessary state enterprises or return them to private ownership. By 1989 real growth was up 5.4 percent, investment increased by 7.5 percent, and unemployment

---

14. The work on the public sector by Maria Belmira Martins and José Chaves Rosa, *O grupo Estado: análise e listagem completa das sociedades do sector público empresarial* (Lisbon, 1979), is detailed and reveals the web of relationships among private and public firms; it focuses on public enterprise in each major sector of the economy. Their information is particularly useful in understanding the strength of the monopoly groups prior to nationalization, the links among them, and how the state reorganized them after the takeovers.

15. Celso Ferreira, "Aspectos económicos do sector público empresarial," *Economia e Socialismo* 40 (July 1979): 23.

had been reduced to nearly 5 percent, the lowest in the EC. Together with increases in personal income and domestic consumption, these advances were reflected in an optimism over the economy, particularly among domestic and foreign investors in the private sector, but there also was a marked growth in sales among public enterprises, in some cases over 50 percent, along with sharp increases in productivity. Roughly a third of the top fifty enterprises in Portugal were public, and many of them had experienced rough times because of poor investment and low productivity, in part attributable to decisions under private management prior to nationalization, but later also to stagnancy under the state. The EDP, for example, suffered from both excessive debt and personnel; QUIMIGAL had invested in oil exploration that had not yielded new resources; the CP needed to renovate its antiquated rolling stock; and Siderurgia Nacional was modernizing its facilities.

By 1990 the Portuguese banking system comprised nine public banks, four private commercial banks, and eleven foreign banks along with three public and two private credit institutions. A year earlier, the BTA had become the first of the state banks to be denationalized, and soon thereafter two of the large public insurance companies, Aliança Seguradora and Companhia de Seguros Tranquilidade, had been privatized.[16]

In 1976 the state created the IPE as a public holding company designed to integrate assets dispersed among some 1,300 firms not directly subsumed to state enterprises. In 1982 the state designated the IPE an autonomous rather than state enterprise, a mere formality because the state maintained complete control; however, this legal change permitted more flexibility in IPE operations, including new investment with political implications.[17]

As the largest group in the Portuguese economy, with participation in one hundred firms, IPE accounted for 6 percent of Portuguese exports. Its activities included agricultural industry, fishing, lumber, paper, cork, mining, textiles, glass, ceramic, cement, chemicals, pharmaceuticals, automobiles, shipping, electronics, telecommunications, maritime transport, construction, insurance, and finance. António Sousa Gomes and a

16. On banking in the early 1980s, see "A banca em Portugal," *Expresso Suplemento* 457 (1 August 1981): 1-S-20-S. The nationalized banks continued under state control throughout the decade, as the Cavaco Silva government strategy was to permit the formation of new private banks. The first of this "new generation" of private banks was the Banco Comercial Português (BCP); see *Sabado*, 5 August 1989, pp. 132–33. In late 1990 the old Mello group, under José Manuel de Mello, revealed its strategy of expanding into "corporate finance" by purchasing a majority share of the Sociedade Financeira Portuguesa, once the government opened its shares for privatization. *Expresso*, 3 November 1990.
17. See analysis by Maria Manuel Stocker in *Público*, 15 November 1990, regarding questionable transactions between IPE and Sociedade de Construções Severo de Carvalho.

team of young entrepreneurs presided over its operations. Gomes envis-aged the IPE as "a state instrument of political economy in the promo-tion of productive investment and the modernization of the Portuguese economy in cooperation with private enterprise."[18]

However, its future was in doubt with a government decision during November 1990 to allow the participation of private capital in units under the control of IPE.[19] Additionally, the Cavaco Silva government attempted to refine and reorganize state involvement in the economy through two new financial groups organized through state entities, the Caixa Geral de Depósitos and the Banco de Fomento Nacional.[20]

The preponderance of the state in the economy was not a deterrent to a rebirth of private economic groups. Among the seven big groups whose holdings had been dismantled by the state nationalizations fifteen years earlier, only the Grupo Espírito Santo under the leadership of Ricardo Espírito Santo had been able to sustain itself and conspicuously reemerge in the new configuration of economic groups that exercised substantial influence on the Portuguese economy by 1990. It had con-centrated its reorganization abroad through two holding companies, one in Luxembourg and the other in the Bahamas. Through joint capital ventures in France, Italy, Spain, and elsewhere, its strategy was to pro-mote a web of international activities while penetrating the Portuguese economy. Its assets in Portugal included financial institutions and insur-ance enterprises, including the Companhia de Seguros Tranquilidade, reacquired in October 1990 through the reprivatization process initiated by the Cavaco Silva government, and it was active in agro-industry, manufacturing, tourism, real estate, food services, and other service areas.

18. Virgílio Azevedo et al., "O renascimento dos grupos económicos," *Revista Expresso*, 8 July 1989.

19. On the new economic groups, see ibid. for important discussion and information. The privatization process was slowed by judicial proceedings and discrepancies between government and arbitration commission values in determining indemnization for the firms nationalized fifteen years previously; for details, see the data in *O Independente*, 4 October 1990. Miguel Quina discussed the nationalization of his property and showed me docu-ments on the 1988 settlement of his claim in the form of bonds that would mature in twen-ty-eight years and leave him little, once inflation was taken into account; he planned to appeal this judgment to the supreme court by seeking remuneration in the form of shares in the old companies as they were privatized. Interview, Miguel Gentil Quina, Lisbon, 2 November 1990. For an analysis by his son, including attention to the nationalizations of 1975, the process of privatization, and the influx of foreign capital in Portugal, see António Calheiros Quina, *Portugal 1990. Conjuncture économique et opportunités d'investissement: con-struction, immobilier, privatisations* Paris, 1990). As an example of this process, in late 1990 the government announced its intention to privatize 60 to 70 percent of the capital of the Siderurgia Nacional without limiting foreign participation and without recognizing any rights of the former owner, António Chamalimaud (*Expresso*, 3 November and 13 October 1990; and *Diário de Notícias*, 13 November 1990.

20. Azevedo et al., "o renascimento."

It also anticipated reacquiring its former bank once the state opened it up to reprivatization.

Even more significant are the many new private economic groups. These include eight major groups, each of them a conglomerate of a dozen or more firms. Together, they are engaged in about every economic activity within Portugal.[21]

Portuguese enterprise has frequently combined with foreign capital. By the end of 1973 some 270 firms were controlled by or integrated with multinational capital.[22] In 1990 multinational capital was conspicuously present among the top corporations, Renault ranking third, Shell seventh, and Mobil ninth, following by Dow, Citroen, Ford, General Motors, Fiat, Philips, Nestle, and Siemens among the top one hundred firms.[23]

The growth and influence of the multinationals in the Portuguese economy was due, initially, to policies under the Caetano regime that aimed to attract foreign capital: minimum fiscal and customs controls, incentives, credit, expatriation of capital, along with the low cost of labor. These firms can be divided into four groups. In the first, are some 150 firms, two-thirds being branches of large foreign enterprises and the other third being integrated with national capital through internal banking credits; they were primarily involved in the exploitation of mineral resources or important substitution activities in, for example, Beralt Tin (wolfram), Standard Eléctrica e Plessey Automática (electrical materials and telecommunications), Lever (detergents), Nestle (food products), Ford, General Motors, Fiat, Renault (automobile assembly), and Secil (cement).

A second group of some ninety-five firms, including Timex, Grundig

21. These eight major groups were: (1) the Grupo Sonae, headed by Belmiro de Azevedo, a conglomerate of sixty firms, including the remnants of the old Grupo Pinto Magalhães, with interests including lumber and wood products, agroindustry, biotechnology, distribution, fast-food, communication services, and tourism; (2) the Grupo Jerónimo Martins, presided over by Alexandre Soares dos Santos, with control over the the supermarket chains of thirty-one Pingo Doce and fifteen Pão de Açúcar stores; (3) the Grupo Amorim, led by Américo Amorim, with sixteen firms and control over more than half the world's cork supply, an enterprise based on a tradition established by his grandfather but now diversified into other lines within and outside Portugal; (4) the Grupo Vicaima, led by Alvaro da Costa Leite, with twenty-five firms in lumber and wood products and construction, and a portfolio that includes financial participation in nine private national banks and a presence in foreign markets; (5) the Grupo Entreposto and its leader, António Dias da Cunha, maintaining interests in commerce, industry, and services in Portugal, Mozambique, Spain, and Brazil; (6) the Grupo RAR, named after its first venture Refinarias de Açúcar, founded in 1942, and headed by Macedo Silva, with majority interest in fourteen firms concentrating on foodstuffs (sugar, chocolate, wines), distribution, finance, and services; (7) the Grupo Interfina, a young group fostered by Jorge Ferro Ribeiro with interests in finance, textiles, insurance, tourism, and construction; and (8) the Grupo Colep and its leader, Illídio Pinho, with a primary interest in packaging foodstuffs. See Ibid for further details.

22. Maria Belmire Martins, *As multinacionais em Portugal* (Lisbon, 1976).

23. See *Expresso*, 27 October 1990, supplement.

Electrónica, Central Data, Philips, General Instruments, and Siemens, aimed at manufacturing for markets abroad and depended on cheap Portuguese labor. A third group of fourteen multinationals imported their products for distribution within Portugal, including pharmaceutical and chemical firms such as Shell, Bayer, and Merck. A fourth group of some twenty firms, including Leon Levy and Costain, was involved in real estate and tourism. These groups exercised substantial control over some economic activities within Portugal.

The Caetano regime had hoped that the opening to foreign investment would be accompanied by technology, capital, and modernization of the Portuguese economy. The multinationals were also encouraged to invest in, exploit the natural resources of, and "colonize" major economic sectors in the African territories. The dominant economic groups within Portugal also envisaged integration of their capital with major foreign corporations as a means of moving toward economic integration with Europe. In her assessment of the multinationals, however, Maria Belmire Martins demonstrated that the presence of the multinationals was not accompanied by any substantial investment of capital nor significant transfer of technology. Furthermore, their penetration and activities in the Portuguese economy were not incorporated into development plans. Indeed decisions were based on multinational interests, impeding any balanced development of the national economy: "The multinationals did not contribute to a real development of our country but led us toward dependency and further separated Portugal from the rest of Europe."[24]

The coup of 1974 and the ensuing revolutionary period and reform legislation were not aimed against foreign capital, and consequently Portuguese dependency on outside capital remained intact. Indeed, more than a decade later the reprivatization schemes of the Cavaco Silva government left the impression that the earlier nationalizations could lead to foreign penetration and control of the Portuguese economy.[25]

Once in power, the Cavaco Silva government promised a rapid divestment of nationalized firms, but in fact it was cautious from 1987 to 1989. New legislation in 1990, however, allowed for the sale of all shares

24. Martins, *As multinacionais*, 62.
25. After the 1974 coup, José Manuel Rolo, in "Transferências de tecnologia e dependência estrutural portuguesa: resultados de um inquérito," *Análise Social* ll (1976): 7–40, emphasized the mechanism of dependency through multinational corporate activity in general, with attention to Portugal and its legislation on foreign-capital investment, which he dissects in detail. A leader of one of the old groups commented that the 1975 nationalizations were aimed at socializing the private means of production without touching foreign capital and that reprivatization under the Cavaco Silva government was leading to foreign control of the domestic economy. Interview with Miguel Gentil Quina, Lisbon, 2 November 1990.

of publicly owned enterprises (previously only 49 percent had been marketable), and this led to the sale of shipping and cement firms, two breweries, and two insurance companies. The caution of the government in moving ahead in other sectors (banking, transportation, steel, communications, chemicals, and paper are principal targets) was due in part to strong foreign demand and the fear that the position of the domestic bourgeoisie is too weak for it to participate in reprivatization.

There were other problems, however. The economy remained relatively flat despite modest economic growth and the neoliberal reform administered by the stable center-right government that consolidated its political hegemony in the mid-1980s. Inflation (13.1 percent) was nearly double that of other EC nations, which discouraged the government from pursuing admission to the European Monetary Union. The rise in domestic prices also affected the trade imbalance, resulting in a gap of $6.5 billion of imported goods over exports in 1989. In its appeal to international capital the government provided cash grants, tax exemptions, and other incentives to lure investors into Portugal as a base for exports to the EC. Foreign investment increased from $156 million in 1986 to $1.3 billion in 1989. With a majority government in power, there is the appearance of political stability, while social pacts with labor ensure a minimum of strike activity and economic disruption.[26]

THE NEW CLASS FORCES

Our second proposition suggests that the dominant classes were weakened by radical reforms, especially the nationalization of private banks during March 1975. Given political space and the possibility for organization and mobilization, the popular classes were strengthened during the 1974–75 period, but after the countercoup of November 1975, they declined in importance. Organized labor in urban centers, for example, succumbed to the pressures and influences of the major political parties, and rural workers suffered from the rollback of the agrarian reform and government inattention to the countryside. This configuration of class forces and their integration in politics shape the ensuing analysis.

The Dominant Classes

What happened to the dominant classes in the period after 1975 and how were they able to reassert their influence in the economy and polity? First, it is important to understand that the countercoup did not signify the immediate dominance of domestic capital, but it allowed the

26. George W. Grayson, "A Revitalized Portugal," *Current History* 68 (November 1990): 373–ff.

state to consolidate its hold: "It represented a step, a pause, an attempt by the state to catch up with itself, to draw its breath, and to generate policies from above to put its house in order."[27]

A glimpse into the few useful studies of the dominant classes suggests some hints as to how the dominant classes used this breathing space. Industrialists under the dictatorship tended to be drawn from the bourgeoisie, some as children of businessmen and landowners who had inherited their enterprise from their fathers, while those who held public office were more likely to be older, middle class in origin, and children of white-collar and professional workers. The main participants in government were technocrats, middle bourgeoisie in origin, many of them academics co-opted into civil service and then into executive positions in the state. Some of them were drawn from the larger, modern corporations in Lisbon, but they tended not to include the wealthier founders, heirs, and owners of traditional industry in the north. Harry Makler believes it would have been difficult for an efficient corporative system to really represent the expanding industrial sector. The state failed to assimilate all the diverse interests because institutional channels of interest articulation were lacking, and special interests tended to align with cliques and become involved in intragovernmental struggles. Many persons in prominent positions in the Salazar and Caetano regimes, however, often became executives in large corporations.[28]

Another observer identified two fractions among Portuguese businessmen: representatives of the large consortia and an ideological bloc of "medievalists" whose survival depended on protectionism under the Salazar regime. This last comprised the large latifundistas in the Alentejo who benefited from subsidies and price controls; small and medium industrialists who imported raw materials from the colonies at prices considerably lower than the world market; investors in the colonies who profited from contractual labor and low wages among African workers; and state bureaucrats.[29]

Capitalism advanced in the late 1950s and in the 1960s because of the need to maintain the colonies. Foreign and domestic capital, mobilized through state initiative and incentives, moved rapidly toward the colonies to exploit natural resources and to offset the threat of the African liberation movements.

27. Phil Mailer, *Portugal: The Impossible Revolution!* (New York, 1977): 344.

28. Harry M. Makler, "The Portuguese Industrial Elite and Its Corporative Relations: A Study of Compartmentalization in an Authoritarian Regime," in *Contemporary Portugal*, ed. Laurence S. Graham and Harry M. Makler (Austin, Tex., 1979), pp. 152–60.

29. Antonio Rangel Bandeira, "The Porguguese Armed Forces Movement: Historical Antecedents, Professional Demands, and Class Conflict," *Politics and Society* 6, no. 1, (1976): 47–48

The initiative of Soares and the Socialist Party (PS) to integrate with the EC would have accelerated foreign investment. It was opposed both by nationalists on the right and Communists on the left in the expectation that industrialists would align with foreign capital in the exploitation of cheap labor and small landowners would disappear as agriculture reorganized.[30]

Under the Caetano period some of the old monopolies entered into joint enterprises with foreign corporations and shifted or complemented their colonial and domestic ventures with more profitable investment in Brazil, Europe, and the United States. The internationalization of the conglomerates represented an undermining of the old alliance between landowners and financial and industrial interests in Portugal as the latter initiated a process of updating and modernizing their activities and the former continued to maintain their traditional properties using old techniques.[31]

Prestigious personalities in the traditional economic groups included Cupertino de Miranda of the BPA, Jorge and José Manuel de Mello of the CUF, António Champalimaud, Ricardo Espírito Santo, and Miguel Quina. Some of these entrepreneurs remained active outside Portugal after their principal holdings had been nationalized in 1975, for example, Champalimaud in Brazil; Quina in France, and Espírito Santo in Brazil, England, Luxembourg, and the United States. Manuel Boullosa built up banking interests in Brazil, while Jorge de Melo moved into vegetable oils and maintained some manufacturing interests in Porto and José Manuel de Mello collaborated with international banking interests and tended his own shipping interests.

Among prominent businessmen of the older generation, Jorge de Brito negotiated state compensation for some of his interests and owned

30. Interview, Rodrigues.
31. Kenneth Maxwell, "Portugal: A Neat Revolution," *New York Review of Books* 21 (13 June 1974): 19. In his *The Crisis of the Dictatorships: Portugal, Greece, Spain* (London, 1976), Nicos Poulantzas sets forth an explicit framework for the analysis of these classes. He sees the dictatorship favoring the comprador bourgeoisie, acting as a conduit for foreign capital, in line with the large landowners in the south of the country. These elements effectively controlled the economy to the disadvantage of the domestic bourgeoisie, which also had benefited from foreign investment and the export market in Europe. Consequently this domestic bourgeoisie sought economic liberalization and elicited support from the popular classes for its program of implementing a competitive political-party system, civil liberties, and a settlement to the colonial wars. Poulantzas believed that after the 1974 coup, the domestic bourgeoisie would not lose control over the democratization process. Its hegemony would remain intact, making impossible a socialist transition. Nataf and Sammis, in "Classes, Hegemony, and Portuguese Democratization," 74–76, dispute his characterization of the domestic bourgeoisie and suggest that some monopoly groups were associated with the comprador bourgeoisie and others with a monopoly domestic bourgeoisie which was not inclined to join with the popular classes.

significant properties in Portugal, while João Mendes de Almeida passed his interests on to his son in Portugal. Still active among big industrialists in the north were Pereira Coutinho, Cupertino de Miranda, Agostinho da Silva, and Teodoro dos Santos.

It was clear, however, that while the nationalizations had eliminated the old monopolies within Portugal, those entrepreneurs who had international interests or who engaged in international commerce and finance had recovered their positions as capitalists. However, those who remained within Portugal attempted to maintain the traditional remnants of their economic groups; for example, textiles tended to become dependent on state banks and consequently to fail.[32]

The new entrepreneurial class included at an upper level Belmiro de Azevedo of the Grupo Sonae, Alexandre Soares dos Santos of the Grupo Jerónimo Martins, Américo Amorim of the Grupo Amorim, Alvaro da Costa Leite of the Grupo Vicaima, António Dias da Cunha of the Grupo Entreposto, Macedo Silva of the Grupo RAR, Ferro Ribeiro of the Grupo Interfina, and Illídio Pinho of the Grupo Colep. A secondary level included important family groups led by Salvador Caetano of the Grupo Caetano, Fernando Guedes of Sogrape, Manuel Violas of the Grupo Violas, Nélson Quintas and six brothers of the Grupo Quintas, and João Mendes Godinho of the Grupo Mendes Godinho.

José Rolo argues that these groups differ from those in the past that were shielded by the state: "Today each group has become a representation of foreign capital . . . simply an expression of foreign interests."[33] António Cardoso confirms this tendency: "The new economic groups are tied to foreign capital and are large potential forces that will impact Portugal. They are not patriotic in their interests, are motivated by profit, and are quite willing to tie into foreign capital. Foreign capital dominates these groups. In real estate foreign capital is substantial, especially Spanish, German, and Scandinavian capital."[34]

One important segment of the domestic bourgeoisie, the textile owners, illustrates the difficulty of capitalists carrying on without outside cap-

32. See Rui Teixeira Santos, "Onde estão e que faxem os empresários do período de Lisboa (1950–1973)," *Semanário*, 1 May 1986, p. 17. Personal perspectives and details of their activities are in interviews with Champalimaud and Quina (see "Entrevista com António Champaimaud," *Seminário*, 8 July 1989, and "Miguel Quina: o triunfo de um banqueiro em França," *Olá Semanário*, 8 July 1989. Entrepreneurial attitudes toward Portuguese politics are evident in the public statements and publications of the Confederação da Indústria Portuguesa (CIP), Associação Industrial Portuguesa (AIP), and the Confederação do Comércio Português (CCP). An example was their disappointment over the election of Socialist Mário Soares as president in 1986; see *Semanário*, 1 March 1986.

33. Interview, José Manuel Rolo, Lisbon, 15 November 1990. For details on entrepreneurs, see Azevedo et al., "o renascimento."

34. Interview, António Lopes Cardoso, Lisbon, 14 November 1990.

ital and technology. Their problems reflect more generally the weakness of the industrial bourgeoisie: "The textile industrialists are simple people, provincial, discreet. They are in trouble. Only Grupo Gonçalves does well because it has adapted to new technology. These are self-made and paternalistic men."[35]

Traditionally Portuguese entrepreneurs were able to flourish through their ties with the state despite limited markets that they controlled in a sort of internal monopoly.[36] Today the economic groups continue to depend on state support (EC funds disbursed by the state ensure this to some extent). One reason for this is the role of the executive and its concessions to the private sector, past and present. Rolo has referred to a series of fiscal pardons, contraband, and other irregularities. He argues that there is an accumulation of foreign reserves so as to offset internal debt and achieve a kind of balance along the lines Salazar always desired. He believes that privatization is also intended to resolve this problem: "Nothing changed in finances. Cavaco is a specialist in finance. He is the Salazar of our times. . . . The quality of finances and the state is completely *salazarista*." Whereas in 1975 the state absorbed national capital as a means of achieving public control over the private means of production, reprivatization under Cavaco Silva was leading to control by foreign capital, a reflection of the inability of the domestic bourgeoisie to absorb the capital gradually being released by the government. Whereas in the past the economic groups were shielded by the Salazar regime, today they represent foreign capital as "simply an expression of foreign interests. Everything is being exchanged with the foreigner at cheap prices. Cavaco knows finances but nothing of business. He believes in the strong role of the state, and Portugal will become another point of contact for foreign investment."[37]

The Popular Classes

After the coup of 25 April 1974, Portugal was embroiled in the mobilization of people in factories, farms, military barracks, and urban neigh-

35. Interview, Maria Filomena Mónica, Lisbon, 14 November 1990.

36. Mónica, *Os grandes patrões* , 21, insists that Portuguese industrialization historically depended on the state, even in periods of strong liberal rule and rhetoric. The state counted on the support of the entrepreneurs (whose capital tended to concentrate in families), and the entrepreneurs needed the state for their business.

37. Interview, Rolo. Thus capital in Portugal was becoming internationalized through foreign investment, especially by the multinationals. International finance and debt problems were affecting capital flows. Foreign investment during the 1980s came from the United Kingdom (23.1 percent); United States (12.6); France (11.4), Spain (10.0); Switzerland (6.1), Brazil (4.5), and Japan (1.0). Nearly half of this foreign investment went into services, especially tourism and real estate, and nearly 30 percent into manufacturing. Complicating these advances is a price inflation of 13.1 percent in 1990 and a budget deficit at 7 percent of gross domestic product. See Grayson, "A Revitalized Economy," 373–74.

borhoods. The urban popular movement included workers' unions and commissions, neighborhood committees, and organizations of soldiers and students. In the countryside farmworkers and landless laborers were mobilized through cooperatives based on land expropriation or the occupation of estates. These popular movements offered the possibility of direct democracy en route to a transition to socialism. The revolutionary left, splintered into a maze of small organizations, favored a strategy of armed struggle or a situation of dual power modeled after Lenin's conception of smashing the state and its powerful apparatuses. Such a confrontation with capitalism probably would have led to civil war, pitting not only the bourgeoisie against most of the urban and rural workers, but also provoking the conservative peasant farmers of the north to resist radical change.

Another strategy was to take over state power through the infiltration of bureaucratic positions, and indeed the MFA and its allies, especially the Communists, resorted to this approach not only to gain power over the entrenched political system but as a means of constraining the radical pressures of the far left.

A further strategy, ultimately adopted and shaped to the political process, was the reformist path through social democracy. This strategy would forestall any intervention by foreign governments and pressures from domestic and international capital, and it offered the possibility of a popular alliance of diverse elements. It also guaranteed a brake on the revolutionary process and deterred the far left and the popular classes from realizing their vision of control through direct democracy. Organized labor in the urban centers eventually succumbed to the pressures and influences of the major political parties, and rural workers suffered from the rollback of the agrarian reform and government inattention to the countryside. This analysis now turns briefly to an examination of these popular classes.

The Portuguese labor movement was formed in the period between 1860 and 1910 when a working class emerged, along with a strengthened industrial bourgeoisie, in the textiles, canning, glass, tobacco, and transport industries. The great mass of this class worked in the countryside, and both urban and rural strikes occurred during this and ensuing historical periods. Anarchism was influential during the First Republic (1910-26), a period characterized as a second stage of the bourgeois revolution in Portugal, when the new commercial, industrial, and colonial middle classes began to enter into conflict with the comprador bourgeoisie tied to the import–export trade and British capital, and with that part of the latifundista nobility that had become capitalist.

This was also the period of the founding of the first labor central in

1913 and the General Confederation of Labor (*Confederação Geral do Tra-balho* or CGT) in 1917. The PCP, founded in 1921, had become influential within the labor movement by 1930, the year of a landmark strike by maritime and glass workers in Marinha Grande. The PCP was active in the labor movement and backed strike activity throughout the Salazar dictatorship.[38]

The tenuous liberalization of the Caetano government gave the PCP the possibility of enhancing its organizational base and by 25 April 1974, its control over labor appeared assured, but the abrupt change in regime and the limits on the state's repressive capacity also led to the unleashing of a wave of spontaneous strikes, factory occupations, and ad hoc workers' commissions and assemblies. The new government, usually supported by the PCP, increasingly mediated and imposed settlements. As a major employer, especially after the nationalizations of March 1975, the government was able to limit wage demands and constrain strike activity. Eventually worker mobilization became subordinated to party politics.[39]

During 1974 and 1975 the PCP controlled most registered unions through the Confederação Geral dos Trabalhadores Portugueses (CGTP-IN), but as its influence in the provisional governments waned and especially after the November 1975 countercoup, other political parties began to compete for union support. By 1984 60 percent, or 208 unions, were affiliated with the CGTP-IN, while 14 percent (48 unions) were under the Socialist-influenced General Union of Workers (*União Geral dos Trabalhadores* or UGT), and 26 percent (90 unions) were independent. Under the Social Democrat government of Cavaco Silva, a third labor central, the Social Democrat Workers (*Trabalhadores Sociais-Democratas* or TSD) was founded.[40] Alan Stoleroff has shown that the relationship of trade unions to enterprises in Portugal can only be mediated through the political arena. He does not see in Portugal, unlike most of Europe, the routinization of labor relations, due in part to an ongoing economic crisis and mutually antagonistic ideologies.[41]

---

38. For a brief but critical history of labor and its ties to the PCP, see Francisco Martins Rodrigues, *Elementos para a história do Movimento Operário e do Partido Comunista em Portugal* (Lisbon, 1975).

39. This thesis of labor subordination to party politics is suggested by John R. Logan, "Worker Mobilization and Party Politics: Revolutionary Portugal in Perspective," *In Search of Modern Portugal*, eds. Lawrence S. Graham and Douglas L. Wheeler (Madison, Wis., 1983), pp. 135–48.

40. See Nuno Pacheco, "Terceira central: os socialistas em xeque," *Revista Expresso*, 8 March 1986.

41. See Alan Stoleroff, *Political Trade Unionism and Industrial Relations Research in Contemporary Portugal* (Lisbon, 1987); idem, "Labor and Democratization in Portugal: Problems of the Union-Party Relationship" (Paper for the Conference on Labor Movements and the Transition to Democracy, South Bend, Ind., 1988).

Moderated by the political parties and potentially a destabilizing force, labor has lost some ground since 1975. John Hammond argues that the destruction of the old oligarchy and their latifundios, the nationalization of the monopoly groups, and the liberation of the colonies had been undertaken in the interest of the working class: "Despite a dramatic leap in political consciousness and organization, the working class did not consolidate power in revolutionary Portugal. It did not create a socialist society or even maintain all the gains which it had made in 1974 and 1975. It was not sufficiently organized or united to transform its society."[42]

Another problem was a reorganization of the work force in some sectors of the economy. The crisis in textiles had affected by 1990 a substantial portion of the Portuguese industrial work force and some twenty thousand families who worked in the mills and who were gradually being laid off in the Vale de Ave. Of twenty-eight firms in the region, two had closed, leaving their 1,450 workers unemployed, three with a total of nine hundred workers were about to declare bankruptcy, and most of the others were behind in salary payments.[43]

A massive influx of capital from abroad also has led to negotiations in search of an accord between business and labor in order to restrain wages and prices. Labor has seen its share of gross domestic product decline, while a drop in state spending has affected workers in public enterprises. The CGTP-IN and UGT managed in 1990 to jointly condemn "the antisocial policies" of the government, and they explored together how to pursue a strategy of improving wages, benefits, and job security for the 2.4 million organized workers.

Finally, the informal economy was having an impact on the work force. In one of the few available analyses of this economy, Manuel Cabral has concluded that family income is larger than represented in official data because of the informal economy. He delves into the delayed and disarticulated character of the Portuguese economy, which is evidenced by an ongoing process of decentralization involving illegal work.[44]

Peasant and farming patterns throughout Portugal, of course, are complex. Cabral has emphasized land tenure and class formation in an

42. Hammond, *Building Popular Power*, 253. In an interview, Francisco Martins Rodrigues (see n. 4 above) argued that the workers' lack of consciousness was due to the legacy of the PCP ("The PCP expressed the incapacity of struggle") and its illusion of establishing an advanced democracy, which "led to the failure of the left in Portugal." During the revolution, he believed, "many workers' commissions were not revolutionary, but were organized to ensure continued employment in their factories, which were abandoned by their owners."

43. See the analysis by Jorge Peixote, "Os cenários e a crise," *Sábado*, 16 November 1990, pp. 38–47.

44. Manuel Villaverde Cabral, "A economia suberranea vem ao de cima: estratégias da população rural perante a industrialização e a urbanização," *Análise Social* 19 (1983): 230–33.

emerging rural capitalist rural economy. Together with Eduardo de Freitas and João Almeida, he identifies a typology of classes in the countryside: big absentee landowners, capitalist entrepreneurs, the peasantry, the semiproletariat, and the rural proletariat.[45]

Fernando Medeiros stresses the dual-society aspect of Portuguese geography, with the Tagus River demarcating the large agricultural properties to the south and the small holdings to the north. In the north and center of the country capitalism decisively established itself in the hands of powerful capitalist interests during the late nineteenth century with the expansion of the vineyards. Family farming, based on renters who give a portion of their production to landowners, was common practice in both the north (where they were known as *pequenos parceiros* or *pequenos renterios*) and the south (*seareiros*). Rural wage earners worked the large farms in the Alentejo. Emigration served as a moderating force in the growth of the capitalist mode of production in agriculture, mitigating the proletarianization of the countryside.[46]

During 1974 and 1975 some changes took place in the agricultural work force. Nancy Bermeo studied farm workers in the south, their challenge to property relations, and their efforts to establish worker control through cooperative units on farms: "These cultivators rebelled with a high degree of autonomy, and their rebellion led, not to trade-unionist demands, but to extensive land seizures and to the emergence of the largest network of worker-run farms in Western Europe."[47] She found that worker-controlled farms were more productive than the units they replaced and that worker-managers were radicalized by workers' control. Cooperative members were also much more likely than nonmembers to participate in elections, parties, campaigns, and demonstrations, but their principal activity concentrated on the defense of their farms: "In Portugal, the success of the rural revolt depended not just on organization and force of numbers but on the force of resistance from the state. The men and women of the Alentejo seized land because they saw that their subsistence was threatened, but they also acted because they recognized that a state weakened by crisis might not move against them." She went on to dispute the prediction by many observers that the era of peasant revolts may be drawing to a close: "The struggle for workers' control in Portugal suggests that this may not be so. The actions of the landless

---

45. Manuel Villaverde Cabral, "Agrarian Structures and Recent Rural Movements in Portugal," *Journal of Peasant Studies* 5 (July 1987): 411–45. Also see Eduardo de Freitas, João Ferreira Almeida, and Manuel Vilaverde Cabral, "Capitalismo e classes sociais nos campos em Portugal," *Análise Social* 12 (1976): 41–63.

46. Medeiros, *A sociedade e economia*, 61.

47. Bermeo, *The Revolution within the Revolution*, 8.

laborers of the Alentejo and the maturation of rural proletariats elsewhere suggest not the decline of rural revolt but rather the potential for more rural proletarian struggle."[48]

The struggle for land in the south led to agrarian reform during 1974 and 1975. Afonso de Barros has assessed the reform and its problems, attributing the persistent agrarian crisis to lack of productive growth, the need to import agricultural products to satisfy internal consumption, and a system of land tenure that blocked development. Agrarian reform was implemented in the Alentejo and Ribatejo, zones with a low population density and a predominance of agricultural production served by salaried rural laborers, who constituted four fifths of the active population. Despite having cut off an important fraction, agrarian capitalism remained strong and in conflict with the reform.[49] Socialist governments reacted by diluting agrarian legislation of its revolutionary potential and permitting former owners to repossess their land. Their motivation was also political, designed to undermine Communist influence in the Alentejo. Gradually the number of cooperatives began to decline, with unemployment on the rise together with the breakup of the cooperative system. By late 1989 Barros had concluded that the agrarian reform project had failed.[50]

State employees constituted another popular sector. Characterized as a "new middle class" or a "new petty bourgeoisie," state employees during 1974 and 1975 were expected to abandon the patronage politics of the authoritarian period while supporting a revolutionary course. In fact, they evolved in a technocratic direction in support of neoliberal policies. One observer attributes this position to the fact that most state employees retained their positions: "The state structures were essentially untouched although democratic processes were implemented. The apparatuses of administration and police for the most part remained in place."[51] Socialist deputy Raul Rego agreed: "All those appointed to administrative posts generally are technocrats – a generation without political formation."[52] Respected leftist intellectual Francisco Louçã noted two successive generations of technocrats: "The principal leaders of the technocratic generation that evolved with Caetano do not now have an important role. They differ from the present generation. Today's

48. Ibid., pp. 219, 222.
49. Afonso de Barros," A reforma agrária em Portugal e o desenvolvimento económico e social," *Revista Crítica de Ciências Sociais* 3 (December 1979): 53–74.
50. Interview, Afonso de Barros, Lisbon, 1 August 1989. A similar view was expressed by the former government minister in charge of the agrarian reform, António Lopes Cardoso (see n. 34).
51. Interview, Rodrigues.
52. Interview, Raul Rego, Lisbon, 19 November 1990.

group is more or less a second line. Cavaco and his associates emerged in the postcoup period."[53]

THE NEW POLITICS

Our third proposition suggests that bourgeois rule has persisted, despite the active participation of other social classes, as a neoliberal and social democratic pact permeated the electoral regime, eventually enabling center-right governments to come to power and marginalize extreme right and left forces, including the Communists. This proposition is examined in the context of electoral regimes and state structures, the continuing importance of executive politics despite efforts to provide the parliament with a major political role, the shift of Socialists from welfare reformers to neoliberal modernizers, and factionalism within the historically important PCP.

Electoral Regimes and the State

Earlier it was asserted that a legitimacy crisis was overcome with the countercoup of November 1975 but that a hegemony crisis persisted well into the 1980s. The Italian Marxist Antonio Gramsci envisaged the state as an arena for ideological and political conflict through which the dominant class seeks popular consensus. He referred to hegemony as a way of explaining the forms of bourgeois ideological and cultural domination. Hegemony implied ideological manipulation and consensus that transcends the state and civil society, and Gramsci employed hegemony to suggest that sustaining of a social order over the long run depended not only on the organization of state power, repression, and violence but also on ideological consensus and popular support. In order to achieve hegemony the interests of the dominant class must become deeply imbedded in the social relations and national traditions.[54]

In the Portuguese case intellectual and cultural life had been limited to a small stratum of the population and in large measure manipulated by the fascist corporate state over nearly a half century. These intellectuals and politicians became intensely involved in the revolutionary interlude after 25 April but their hegemonic role was limited by the legacy of tradition and the mystique perpetrated by the old regime, as well as by a diversity of perspectives on the future of society, to such an extent that their ability to shape popular consciousness also was severely limited.

53. Interview, Francisco Louçã, Lisbon, 19 November 1990.
54. This theoretical discussion of hegemony in the thought of Gramsci draws heavily from the work by Carl Boggs, *The Two Revolutions: Antonio Gramsci and the Dilemmas of Western Marxism* (Boston, 1984), especially pp. 153–98.

The struggle for hegemony was at the center of the MFA, which was permeated with internal conflicts throughout the "hot summer" of July and August 1975. Its hegemony was also undermined by pressures from the political parties, the actions of the PCP, and the demonstrations of the popular left. Dante Pasquino believes this provided an opening to the right.[55] For a brief period the MFA appeared hegemonic, and it not only elicited support for its program from its PCP ally but also was able to obtain a relatively broad consensus among other political groupings. Once it had resolved the question of independence for the colonies and relinquished its authority and power in favor of a parliamentary system, its own ranks divided over how to move toward the socialist transition. In this sense Communist leader, Alvaro Cunhal, correctly surmised that "there was no leading political force, with hegemony over the process. There was no centralized revolutionary power. . . . The MFA and government were unable to define a line for the advance of the revolution."[56]

The countercoup of 25 November served to ensure the unity of the military as an institution. It also assured a dominant role for the moderate politicians favoring social democracy, formal government, and compromises with capital. The revolution rested on a base of agricultural workers in the Alentejo and Ribatejo, where agrarian reform was effective; the industrial workers of the industrial belts around Lisbon, Setúbal, and to some extent Porto; and radicalized soldiers, sailors, and officers. Missing from this alliance were large sectors of the urban petty bourgeoisie and small and middle farmers of the north and center of the country. Paul Fauvet suggests that the PCP strategy precluded any middle road between advancing toward socialism or reverting to an authoritarian state, nor could there be stable bourgeois democracy. Thus, Poulantzas was correct in arguing that what was lost on 25 November was the hegemony of the popular masses over the process of democratization. Divisions in the forces of the left had undermined the popular struggle and "contributed to a stabilization of bourgeois hegemony over the democratization process."[57]

Vitor Ferreira suggested that in the period after 1975 there was a dissociation between civil society and the political class in power. It was impossible for the dominant classes to organize and identify themselves with a coherent political project and exercise any "natural" political hegemony. Under Salazar this hegemonic role was almost always exer-

55. Dante Pasquino, "Le Portugal: de la dictature corporatiste á la démocratie socialiste," Il Politico 42, no. 4 (1977): 703–4.

56. Alvaro Cunhal, A revolução portuguesa: O passado e o futuro (Lisbon, 1976), p. 125.

57. See Paul Fauvet, "Four Years On: The Portuguese Revolution," Marxism Today 20 (April 1978): ll0; Poulantzas, Crisis, 162.

cised in an authoritarian and repressive form on behalf of the commercial and financial bourgeoisie and the latifundistas, through police and military power that would permit a relatively slow but adequate capitalist accumulation.[58]

Parliamentary instability characterized successive governments during the decade after 1976. The breach between the PCP and the PS undermined political alliances on the left, and the minority governments controlled by the Socialists were usually in coalition, in one instance with the right-wing Party of the Social Democratic Center (*Partido do Centro Democrático Social* or CDS). The Social Democrats (*Partido Social Democrata* or PSD) also came to control many electoral regimes, whether in coalition with the PS or the CDS.

Boaventura de Sousa Santos has suggested that "the prolonged nonresolution of the crisis of hegemony could eventually evolve into a crisis of legitimation of the democratic regime." He argued that the crisis could only be averted if a new hegemonic bloc were to emerge to implement a new model of development and provide stability to the political system. There could be no return to the power bloc of monopolistic groups that dominated in the 1960s, but the new bloc would organize around an alliance of "modern sectors of the national bourgeoisie" and "a strong and dynamic economic state sector." Nationalism would serve to mobilize the urban petty bourgeoisie, the working class, and the peasantry in support of negotiations with international capital. These classes would have to be organized into a social pact and provided material concessions and incentives. Without a rapid consolidation of the new hegemonic bloc, the state would disintegrate, the parliamentary system would become more unstable, and repression of the popular classes would be used to check their resistance such that the "boundaries of democratic process will have been bypassed."[59]

This perspective must be examined in light of experience of Cavaco Silva and his PSD government, in office since it won a parliamentary majority in 1987. President Mário Soares, a Socialist elected in 1986 through a rare combination of PS and PCP votes, represented a counterbalance to the PSD majority, but he also served as a consensual and moderate figure, a figurehead limited in his powers of intervention, who stood for reelection in 1990 and was supported by both the PS and PSD. This apparent paradox of politics produced an overwhelming victory and

58. Vítor Matias Ferreira, "A sociedade portuguesa entre a 'anarquia social' e a institucionalização do 'político," *Jornadas de Estudo sobre Portugal Democrático* (Porto), 27–29 April 1980, p. 1.

59. See Boaventura de Sousa Santos, "Social Crisis and the State," in *Portugal in the 1980s: Dilemmas of Democratic Consolidation*, ed. Kenneth Maxwell (New York, 1984), pp. 167–85.

a second five-year presidential term for Soares. Elections on 6 October 1991 also gave Cavaco and the PSD more than half the votes and an absolute majority of seats in the parliament, while the Socialists gained nearly 30 percent and the Communists 9 percent of the vote.

The Cavaco government was successful in implementing constitutional changes that would reduce the size of the state through a process of returning state enterprise to private ownership. Further, it deliberately worked toward policies of economic stability and steady growth and a decline in inflation. As Portugal prepared to fully integrate with the EC, the country continued to face structural problems, including an inflation rate twice that of the rest of Europe and a substantial foreign and public debt. Further, the political majority of the PSD did not constitute an ideological hegemony (in the Gramscian sense and the context outlined by Santos), and the PS was expected to rise to power during the 1990s.

What was significant, however, was the tacit political bloc of forces around the PS and PSD, given their consensus over the decline in state power, deregulation, and incentives for capital investment, and the internationalization of the economy. Additionally, there was the evolution of Portugal as a peripheral part of the European balance of power, leading some analysts to the startling observation: "Financial, economic, and political integration, however, is transferring out of Portugal much of the real decision-making power over Portuguese society."[60] Indeed capitalism, not socialism, was on the political and economic agenda.

Socialists and Communists in the Push for Neoliberalism

The failure of the PS and PCP to coalesce can be largely attributable to two leading personalities. Mário Soares once affirmed: "I am a Marxist, not a dogmatic one, but still a Marxist. As such I have always believed men were instruments or interpreters of history."[61] Alvaro Cunhal was a Marxist and Stalinist whose discipline and orthodoxy had brought success to the PCP, yet had alienated some party militants and intellectuals over the generation or more that he was party leader. Both men were astutely political, maneuvering in the interest of their parties. Soares not only had aligned the PS with the PSD and CDS but supported revision of the agrarian reform and a series of laws that rolled back the advances the working classes had made after 25 April 1974. Soares consistently drew a line between his position of pursuing a democratic and pluralist road and the Leninist position of a single party, united front, or revolu-

---

60. See António Pinto Barbosa, Luís Campos e Cunha, and José Miguel Júdice, "Political Developments, Economic Developments," *Portugal Outlook* 1 (1990): 5.
61. Oriana Fallaci, "Disintegrating Portugal: An Interview with Mário Soares," *New York Review of Books*, 22 (13 November 1975), pp. 24–30.

tionary vanguard advocated by the PCP. He viewed the countercoup of 25 November 1975 as necessary to prevent a Communist military dictatorship. Cunhal, having aligned his party with the MFA and participating in the six provisional governments of 1974 and 1975, nevertheless was suspicious of the far left which he characterized as "an expression of petty bourgeois radicalism, having represented a very negative role in the revolutionary process."[62]

Advocating a national and democratic rather than socialist revolution, the PCP continued to be represented in parliament and in many municipal councils, but in the decade after 1976 its share of the vote was not substantial (less than 20 percent). Its defensive posture concentrated on strengthening internal party organization, keeping a tight rein on the unions under its control, and supporting revolutionary gains in the face of "capitalist recuperation." With the changes in Eastern Europe and the Soviet Union after 1989, the PCP experienced internal dissidence, defections, and expulsions, yet it continued to hold its own in the 1991 parliamentary elections.

The electoral victories of the PSD in 1987 and 1991 left the PCP and PS in the parliamentary opposition. The far left was marginalized, but some of its leadership had shifted to the right, aligning with Mário Soares or with Cavaco Silva. Former Marxist-Leninists such as João Carlos Espada joined Soares as political advisers, while João Freire Antunes became an adviser to Cavaco Silva. José Pacheco Pereira served as a deputy with the PSD, and, together with Espada and others led some important intellectuals in a movement they called the Liberal Left (*Esquerda Liberal*). They had evolved politically within Maoist groups and turned to the right because of their opposition to the PCP and the Soviet Union, which led them to join the PS or the PSD. They were ambitious, aggressive, and disciplined.[63]

Durability of the Existing Political Order?

The discussion thus far has taken a number of directions and suggests a tenuous course for the evolving neoliberal order in contemporary Portugal. Bourgeois democracy has been largely based on a legacy of the past. Eduardo de Souza Ferreira has complained that Portuguese politicians do not understand democracy: "They have the attitudes of Salazar. Those

62. Cunhal, *A revolução portuguesa*, 170.

63. In an interview, Durão Barroso (see n.3), related his personal experience in the revolutionary left, which he joined after April 25 due to his opposition to the PCP. He and others were able to adapt to the PSD because of their desire to remain politically active. Their commitment, political experience, anticommunism, and class origins ("many were of the upper class") provided for an opportunistic shift to the right.

who wish to exercise power in Portugal are not prepared to do so." There is no political tradition, only a small group that has always governed. Cavaco Silva is typical of this tradition: "He does not lead. He does not know how to."[64] Additionally, the parliamentary system did not serve as a means for substantial change. The electoral masses preferred the order of the past, as suggested by Rodrigues: "It was a surprise for the left to discover that the elector supported the right. The mass of the population desired stability and was not prepared for a leftward push. The movement was not led in such a way that it could come to power. There was no unity. The conservative spirit of the great mass of the population wanted a different system, one of order."[65]

The PS inclination to support the neoliberal order can be attributable to its origins in 1973 when it was organized by some 150 intellectuals, mostly lawyers, and middle-class antifascists of liberal and republican bent. Its organization has always been weak, especially in the labor movement. Its early program was progressive and envisaged a society without classes, yet was orientated to political and bourgeois parliamentary democracy. Even during the first four provisional governments the PS never took a firm stand on the process of breaking with capitalism, and the party tended to reinforce Portuguese dependency on Western Europe. The party leadership was largely of bourgeois origin, never took a class position in contending with the dictatorship, and never envisaged a conception of the state as an instrument of class domination. The state was seen instead as an institution above class.

The moderate inclinations of the Socialists were apparent in their social-democratic character and their rightist leadership. They advocated democratization under the leadership of the domestic bourgeoisie. Rather than ally with the PCP or other left parties, the PS leaned toward the PSD and the right. Its anticommunism served to coalesce centrist forces under a facade of democratization. While it showed itself representative of the interests of the domestic bourgeoisie, it did not attempt, however, to represent the comprador or international bourgeoisie or the large landowners. Louçã has affirmed: "A socialist alternative is not possible through the PS within the existing capitalist system. Its socialist project is only to moderate reform in the capitalist system."[66]

Although it has been perceived by the PS and the right as intransigent and revolutionary, the PCP in practice has advocated a path of peaceful democratic socialist change through electoral means and penetrating the state apparatuses. Party strategy has fluctuated between a revolutionary

64. Interview with Eduardo de Souza Ferreira, Lisbon, 15 November 1990.
65. Interview, Rodrigues.
66. Interview, Louçã.

course during the period of dictatorship to democratic parliamentarianism after the coup, a perspective not dissimilar from that of the Socialists. This convergence of views suggests the possibility of various forms of politics under democracy and socialism. At issue is pluralist analysis which assumes that a polity is democratic if it is responsive at least to those who participate in political affairs, whereas Marxist analysis recognizes that all individuals in a society are affected by and therefore must participate in political decisions in order for a polity to be democratic. Antonio Gramsci offered understanding into these differing perspectives in his analysis of democracy and socialism in complex industrial societies.

In the period after 25 April the state has remained dominant. In capitalist and industrial societies there may be an effort to organize social classes collectively through the state so that individual class interests are undermined while the bourgeoisie and its allies are mobilized around national interests. Similarly, the state and its leaders may encourage the disunity of dominant classes so that individual capitalists or capitalist interests do not prevail. Coherent state policy may be possible where the needs, interests, and conflicts of fractions of the dominant class are mitigated.

It is certainly not clear that this process is occurring today in Portugal. Under the dictatorship and the aegis of the corporate state, the bourgeoisie and all its fractions remained relatively cohesive and hegemonic over the economy. Measures of liberalization during the Caetano period did not alter the state structures but resulted in dissension within the bourgeoisie. A change in regime occurred with the 25 April coup, which led to a struggle for control of the state apparatuses, for shaping the political form within which formal and informal democracy could function, and for restructuring the productive system. The appropriation by the state of a good share of national productive enterprise signified its expansion and a greater role for the increasingly influential technobureaucracy. It also represented the decline of the large landowners and the comprador bourgeoisie of urban financial interests, and it signified the decline of the industrial bourgeoisie and the traditional family and economic blocs that had benefited from their sheltered ties beneath the protective wings of the fascist capitalist state.

The period since 1975 has witnessed the elaboration of a hegemonic scenario in which formal competition is seen as enhancing the possibility of state autonomy, in which political relations can develop independently of economic relations, in which the state implements policy formulated within a set of recognized rules, procedures, and institutional bargaining, and in which the outcome in any particular situation may not be predetermined. Outside the state and within civil society, parliamentary and party politics may serve to extend hegemonic rule over the inherently hostile working class, although in times of crisis a social pact between these apparent adversaries may be reached to ensure stability and enhance mutual interests. There may also be the possibility of meaningful informal and direct participation by groups and individuals who influence power and shape policy outside the parliamentary system.

In reality a different arrangement has evolved in which the state continues to dominate together with the emerging capitalist bourgeoisie and the uncertain role of foreign capital. Hammond has deftly characterized this state and bourgeoisie:

> The economic policies adopted in 1976 and after served the interests of the modernizing monopoly bourgeoisie, both its technocratic and its small or medium-sized capitalist segments. This is the civilian class with which the moderate officers who took control after November 25 were by origin and current position most closely identified. The destruction of the power of the old oligarchy through the attack on the latifundios, the nationalization of the monopoly groups, and the liberation of the colonies had been undertaken in the interest of the working class. But in practice all these changes increased state control of the economy. The segment of the bourgeoisie which took power in 1976 could use the centralized economic control to its own advantage.[67]

In the course of the twentieth century, Portugal has seen a succession of six regimes – monarchical, republican, fascist corporate, reformist corporate, democratic socialist, and bourgeois democratic. Through it all, the political structures of a dominant state and the economic structures of a developing capitalism have remained constant. For a brief moment in 1974–75, one regime, that of democratic socialism or popular power, seemed to pose a fundamental threat to these structures. But it did so by increasing the power of the state, only to have, during the succeeding regime of bourgeois democracy, the state then increase the power of the most modern capitalists. The popular part of popular power gave to the democratic part of bourgeois democracy its legitimacy. The power part of popular power gave to the bourgeois part of bourgeois democracy its hegemony. The end result has been to increase both the power of the state and the power of capitalism within Portugal even more than before.

67. Hammond, *Building Popular Power*, 251.

6 GREEK SOCIALISM: THE PATRIMONIAL STATE REVISITED

James Petras, Evangelos Raptis, and Sergio Sarafopoulos

INTRODUCTION

The election victory of the Panhellenic Socialist party (PASOK) in 1981 set the stage for a historical confrontation between traditional social classes and practices entrenched in the Greek patrimonial state, and the modernizing socialist project embodied in the program of *allaghi* (change). Since the end of the civil war in 1949, Greek socioeconomic development had been based upon the mentalities and institutional practices of an ever-growing patrimonial state. By the 1980s, Greek patrimonialism was unable to sustain increased consumption and expanded reproduction of capital in an increasingly integrated and competitive European framework. The patrimonial state was incapable of maintaining its bloated and inefficient structures in a period of socioeconomic crisis. The pressures to transform the structures of the patrimonial state coincided with unique opportunities for challenging its institutional authority. PASOK was capable of drawing on its absolute majority in Congress, its mobilized electoral base, and its large educated cadre of supporters. These potential resources and opportunities had to confront a deeply entrenched patrimonialism that not only permeated state and civil society but was also incorporated in the everyday existence and consciousness of its supporters as well as adversaries.

The resolution of the conflict between the patrimonial state, deeply rooted in the institutional practices of patronage and centralization, and the socialist project, built around the strengthening and growth of the autonomous power of a civil society freed from the fetters of the state, would determine the success or failure of Greek socialism as an innovating project in the 1980s. The outcome depended upon PASOK's willingness to break with the existing state and on elaborate programs aimed at promoting new models of economic development and a new civic consciousness that would respect the distinctness and autonomy of social organizations in civil society.

The elimination of the patrimonial state was the one absolute necessity for a successful implementation of PASOK's socioeconomic modernization project. Within this context, PASOK passed through two distinct phases of "innovation," which coincided with its two consecutive terms in power: a "socialist phase" between 1981 and 1984 and a "liberal phase" in 1985–89. During the first term, PASOK proceeded with a radical plan for social equality and economic development. During the second term, and in the face of a deep economic crisis, PASOK altered its orientation and proceeded with a "stabilization for development" plan along liberal lines.

This essay argues that in both instances PASOK's trajectory followed a course adapting to existing patrimonial practices despite its socialist and modernist ideology; it became the regime that deepened and extended the patrimonial state. PASOK reproduced the traditional practices of the party state in realizing its immediate goals and ended up undercutting the long-term prospects of replacing the patrimonial state. In its first term PASOK propped up the obsolete economic structures of patrimonial capitalism, while it failed to free civil society – and particularly the social movements – from the controls of the patrimonial state. In its second term, PASOK undermined its liberal orientation through its stop-and-go measures freeing the market forces from the constraints of the patrimonial state. In the end, PASOK strengthened the traditional party-state structures and the clientelistic practices associated with it.

PASOK sacrificed its historical role as an innovating force in order to consolidate a powerful electoral constituency. The extension of the patrimonial state was the main factor leading to Greece's descent to the bottom rung in the European economic hierarchy.

POSTWAR GREECE AND PASOK'S RISE TO POWER

The victory of PASOK in the Greek elections of 1981, a mere seven years after the party's foundation, was perhaps the most dramatic breakthrough in the political recomposition of Southern Europe in the late 1970s and early 1980s. Its 48 percent share of the vote and 57 percent of the seats in parliament, almost precisely matching the results the Spanish Socialist party would achieve in 1982, appeared to confirm PASOK's claim to have rallied behind it a new bloc of social forces committed to the modernization of the Greek economy and society.

The rise of PASOK is all the more striking if we bear in mind the onslaught of capitalist-monarchist reaction against the left in the years of repression and civil war that followed the disembarkation of British troops in Athens in the winter of 1944. Under the German occupation the communist-led EAM/ELAS resistance movement had rivaled the strength and penetration even of the Yugoslav partisans, covering the country with a dense network of military and civil counterinstitutions that organized some two and a half million men, women and children.

The subsequent demise of the resistance – first through a fatal pact with George Papandreou's shadowy Center, then through military defeat at the hands of a reorganized right enjoying full British and U.S. support – is too well known to need retelling here. Suffice it to say that by 1949, when the communist guerrillas finally called off the uneven armed struggle, one of the longest and post powerful experiences of popular mobilization in European history had been torn up by the roots, ironically mirroring in the aftermath of world war the destruction of the Spanish revolution that had served as its prelude at the other end of the Mediterranean.

A Franco-style dictatorship was hardly an available option in those immediate postwar years, but as the Cold War descended over the continent, the traditional Greek bloc of army, throne, and capital reasserted its authority over town and country behind a parliamentary facade that excluded the socialist left through an all-pervasive police state and that constantly reproduced a culture of personal patronage even within the bourgeois-liberal opposition parties.

For the early part of the 1950s the principal effort of postwar "reconstruction" was literally designed to put back together the building blocks of the peculiar social and economic structure that had taken shape over the previous century. Greece's age-old specialization within the international economy had gradually given rise to a spectacular concentration of capital among a handful of shipping magnates. Sailing freely in the elite institutions of the West, these families formed a kind of maritime aristocracy whose eccentric pattern of accumulation raised them above the constraints of the nation-state; indeed, the national colors themselves became ultimately little more than a flag of convenience, readily exchangeable for those of Liberia or Panama if covetous land sharks threatened to set up fiscal or other snares. However, it was not as if this fabulous wealth had sprung forth fully grown from the oceans. A sizable part of the workforce that elsewhere in Europe was swept by the Industrial Revolution into factories, mines, or railways came to constitute a highly skilled mariner proletariat, attached in a thousand ways to the country of its own production.

Interlocking on mainland Greece with the empire of shipping capital, two giant corporations, the state-directed National Bank of Greece and the privately owned Commercial Bank of Greece, not only swallowed up virtually the entire shoal of small to medium banking enterprises but

GREEK SOCIALISM: THE PATRIMONIAL STATE REVISITED

established an effective hold over the rest of the economy. Credit policy, potentially a mighty weapon of centralized industrialization, functioned instead to starve manufacturing of the means of modernization, as a plethora of tiny, inefficient firms continued their prewar concentration on low-grade consumer goods. In the countryside, where the interwar period had produced a parcelized agriculture then typical of the Balkans, the peasantry remained trapped in a cost/price scissors for which the banks offered no hope of relief. The swollen apparatus of the state, though heavier and more pervasive than anywhere else in capitalist Europe, had renounced any structural intervention in the productive economy and restricted itself to intermediation within well-worn circuits.

If the shape of the Greek economy and society nevertheless began to change in the late 1950s and 1960s, the impetus overwhelmingly originated in the industrial heartlands of Western Europe. On the one hand, villages and towns delivered up their jobless and underemployed as nearly a tenth of the populace – and considerably more of the working-age population – joined Turks and Yugoslavs on the migration expresses to Munich and beyond, their remittances home helping to create effective demand in Greece itself for the export products of their labor on the assembly lines of the north.

On the other hand, within Greece foreign capital led a significant shift away from investment in traditional industries towards the capital-intensive chemical and metallurgical sectors. By the mid-1960s a third of new investment was in intermediate and certain capital-goods groups. But unlike in other parts of Southern Europe, most notably Spain, no machine-based metalworking industry developed to fuel all-around industrialization, and the new sectors had all the appearance of what Nicos Mouzelis called at the time "capital-intensive enclaves" in a classical land of underdevelopment.[1]

In retrospect those heady years of the 1960s, which, in different ways, placed industrial takeoff on the agenda throughout the Balkans, can be seen as a false dawn. Even in Romania and Yugoslavia, the trend of the world economy in the 1970s and 1980s largely frustrated ambitious industrialization programs. In Greece, where no coherent plan was ever formulated, the early 1970s had already witnessed a rise in the specific weight of the food, clothing, and construction industries, and in the latter half of the decade manufacturing as a whole was contributing less than 15 percent of the annual increase in Gross Domestic Product (GDP), while fully three-quarters of growth in Gross National Product (GNP) came from the inflated services sector. Manufacturing exports,

1. Nicos Mouzelis, "Capitalism and Dictatorship in Post-war Greece," *New Left Review* 96 (March–April 1976), p. 16.

JAMES PETRAS, EVANGELOS RAPTIS, AND SERGIO SARAFOPOULOS

given the small size of the internal market, had originally been conceived as one of the principal keys to success, and at first a number of important openings were found in this area. However, the recessionary tides of the seventies, together with the intense competition of low-wage economies precisely in textiles and other such goods, led to a loss of Greece's market share everywhere except in the Middle East. By 1979, when PASOK was preparing to take over the reins of government, it was possible to talk of an actual tendency of deindustrialization, as the import-to-export ratio of manufacturing goods had risen to 3.2:1 from 2.5:1 in 1974.[2]

It might seem paradoxical that the economic expansion of the 1960s, instead of breaking down the repressive controls inherited from the civil war, led to the creation in 1967 of Europe's first new military dictatorship since the end of the Second World War. Certainly it would be idle to imagine that the colonels' coup somehow corresponded to an inner logic of capital or initiated a Chilean-style economic restructuring; all the evidence shows that, on the contrary, the junta had little or no ambition to alter the previous course of the economy. It "merely" wished to prevent the modern layers of Greek society – including the most dynamic rural strata – from coalescing into a political bloc that would challenge the military-monarchist tutelage of the state. Three years of Center Union government between 1964 and 1967 had given good reason to believe that its return in forthcoming elections would sharpen, if not resolve, the constitutional crisis. But the option of dictatorship proved in the European climate of the 1960s to be one of those traps that history sets for the deluded, whereby they bring about precisely the outcome that their actions are designed to avert. Lacking any popular base to match their totalitarian pretensions, recklessly discarding the second pillar of reaction, the monarchy, the colonels stumbled from repression to *abertura* to still more bloody repression, until their insane plot to force union with Cyprus brought disaster to the island and threw the junta itself into terminal disarray.

When Konstantinos Karamanlis, the grand old man of the Greek right, stepped into the breach and formed the first postjunta government in 1974, it was immediately apparent that there could be no simple reversion to the old model of repressive parliamentarism. It is true that his freshly formed New Democracy party retained and expanded the electoral support that had previously gone to the parties of the right. However, the political discrediting of both the army and the throne, which had in any case regarded with suspicion Karamanlis's 1960s project of modernizing the monarchy, left him with little choice but to seek

2. Constantine Viatos, "Problems and Policies of Industrialization," in *Socialism in Greece,* ed. Z. Tzannatos (Aldershot, U. K., 1986).

164

the consolidation of right-wing hegemony through a populist inflection of internal and external policy.

There are evident similarities here with Adolfo Suarez Gonzalez's mode of operation in the troubled period following the death of Franco, and although Karamanlis had not been implicated in the preceding dictatorship the turnaround was in many ways equally dramatic. Within months of coming to power, the national unity government headed by Karamanlis had withdrawn from NATO's military command structures, legalized the Communist party for the first time since the civil war, organized relatively free general elections, and called a referendum that produced a 69-percent majority in favour of the republic. Subsequent trials of junta leaders – in some cases leading to sentences of life imprisonment – underlined the subordination of the officer caste to normal political activity, while one wing of New Democracy encouraged the secular tendencies that were emerging with the same force as in the rest of the Mediterranean.

Nevertheless, New Democracy was quite unable to satisfy the diffuse aspirations for change that radicalized broad sections of the Greek population in the 1970s. Its nationalist gestures in foreign policy, never carried to the point of open conflict with Washington, sat uneasily with its outspoken commitment to the West and involved it in competition with left-wing opponents on a terrain where it was bound to lose. Internally, its tight grip over the countryside loosened with every year that passed. The peasantry, once awakened by EAM/ELAS and exposed since through migration to numerous outside influences, began to turn to more reliable agencies of economic assistance than the local barons of a party in which a new, organizational structure was rising slowly and inarticulately alongside the cracking edifice of clientelism. In the towns, raging inflation eroded the wages of industrial proletarians and white-collar workers alike, while a new generation of university graduates, often educated abroad in 1968 and after, brought a varied combination of strivings for upward mobility and antiauthoritarian rejection of the status quo.

Before the colonels' coup, the old forces of the Center Union could have expected to sublimate these energies in the higher struggle for parliamentary sovereignty against military and royal encroachment. However, the fall of the junta and the abolition of the monarchy has suddenly rendered obsolete this classic bourgeois-liberal agenda of the 1930s. Blinking itself awake in the postjunta republic, the Center Union managed to win 20 percent of the vote in the first elections, collaborated with Karamanlis in government and then, after a brief reentry as the Democratic Center Union, bowed out forever as an independent entity.

At the left end of the spectrum, the Communist Party of Greece

165

(KKE) rapidly consolidated a strong position in industry and a 10-percent bloc of the electorate, any further progress being blocked more by post-war traumas than by the kind of historic disorientation that shipwrecked their French and Spanish counterparts. In clear distinction from the Center Union and KKE's declines stands the force that has, in several giant steps, come to dominate Greek politics over the past thirteen years.

In both its origins and its formation, PASOK differs markedly from its sister parties in Southern Europe, which can all trace their history, how-ever broken, back to the heyday of the Second International.[3] In Greece, bourgeois liberalism and communism filled for decades the space for opposition to the authoritarian right, and when the hour of Mediter-ranean socialism dawned in the 1970s it here took the form of a disinte-gration of the liberal chrysalis. In fact this coincided with, or found per-sonalized expression in, the generational renewal of the Papandreous: father George aged and declined with the Center Union and left behind no obvious successor upon his death in 1968; son Andreas took over the mantle of charisma and adapted it to the changed conditions of the 1970s.

Trained in the United States as an economist, Andreas Papandreou returned to Greece in 1959 and two years later was offered the director-ship of the Center for Economic Research by Karamanlis. Under the 1964–67 Center Union government, however, he associated himself with the policies of the left and, after the defection of its leader Elias Tsi-rimokos, became its most widely known representative. The colonels' coup then drove him into exile, where he organized a Panhellenic Lib-eration Movement (PAK) whose actions against the dictatorship made it the most widely known, though not the most deeply rooted, of the resis-tance groups.

It was no doubt expected that Papandreou would subsequently rejoin the mainstream of the Center Union, whether as its more or less consen-sual leader or as spokesman of an organic left wing, but once the junta had fallen, Papandreou barely hesitated before rallying militants from PAK and a number of smaller groups and launching the explicitly social-ist PASOK. Breaking with the traditional networks of Greek liberalism, the new party was conceived as a highly centralized instrument speaking with a single voice and under a single command, whose link to the mass-es would rely not only upon semiautonomous local clienteles but also upon the directed activity of the party within Greek society.

In a way, Papandreou's concentration of supreme powers also repro-

3. The Workers' Socialist Party was founded in 1919, with a membership of around a thousand, and reached a peak of 6 percent of the vote as late as the elections of 1936. How-ever, its organization and national presence were effectively destroyed during the following years of dictatorship and war.

duced at the center the type of relationship of personal dependence that had formerly prevailed in systems of local clientelism. For the first ten years of its existence, the PASOK central committee invoked no legitimacy other than its own decisions, nor did it call any congress to exercise even nominal control over its operations. More than any other Socialist leader in Europe at that time, Papandreou kept party appointments under tight personal control and defined the narrow boundaries of legitimate dissent within its leadership and rank-and-file structures.

In the years of New Democracy rule (1974–81) the PASOK central committee fashioned a program that appealed to a broad array of social classes. On one hand, it took up positions considerably more radical than the contemporary mainstream of European social democracy, refusing to integrate itself into the Socialist International (which it held to be too compromised by its fraternization with capitalism) and offering the prospect of full-scale nationalization and "an end to the exploitation of man by man."

On the other hand, particularly as the 1981 watershed approached, its principal emphasis fell first on partial, though still substantial, transformations in the structure of wealth, power, and property, and secondly on an all-around modernization of Greece's productive system that would bring to the fore high-tech industries employing local and expatriate skilled labor and producing for both internal consumption and export. In foreign policy, Papandreou retained his reputation as an intransigent opponent of NATO and of any Greek involvement in the EC, although readers of the international press became aware of an early blurring of this stand, too, in the course of the 1970s. All these themes came together in skillful and insistent propaganda centered on the need for comprehensive change or *allaghi,* the Greek counterpart to the Spanish Socialists' *cambio* or the French Socialists' *changer la vie.* However, important sectors of the electorate continued to believe strongly that a far-reaching socialist transformation would be forthcoming.

The populist-socialist program and organizational dynamism of the new party had already allowed it to win 14 percent of the vote in the elections of autumn 1974, just two months after its foundation. Keeping a severely critical distance from the Karamanlis coalition, it had nearly doubled this to 25 percent by 1977 and, by virtue of Greece's heavily weighted system of proportional representation, raised its share of parliamentary seats from 4 percent to 31 percent. Four years later, with the liberal Center now defunct and New Democracy's share of the vote cut from 54 percent to 36 percent, PASOK swept into power at the end of a masterful campaign that increased its support more or less uniformly in all regions of Greece. Indeed, by the time of the 1985 elections the

Greek countryside, for so long the bastion of the right, was showing a slightly higher allegiance to PASOK than the rest of the country: an average of 47 percent of the vote, against 45 percent in urban and suburban constituencies.

CAPITALIST CRISIS AND BINDING CHOICES: PASOK'S HUNDRED-DAYS PROGRAM

The Panhellenic Socialist Movement promised in its 1981 electoral campaign that if elected it would deal with the nation's two most pressing problems: economic underdevelopment and social justice. Its ideological approach toward socialism rejected both welfare capitalism (leading to shallow income redistribution) as well as socioeconomic statification (leading to short-lived economic modernization). PASOK's socialism was to base its joint developmental and redistributive plan on the principles of socialization, decentralization, and self-management. When PASOK came to power in October 1981 its leadership was expected to implement this preelectoral ideological policy of *allaghi* on the Greek socioeconomic structures. However, it soon became apparent that the socialist government had inherited a deep socioeconomic crisis. After a forty-year period of right-wing leadership characterized by corruption, mismanagement, nepotism, and favoritism towards the capital, and given a global oil crisis with recessionary repercussions unseen since the 1930s, PASOK had to make some hard choices.

The magnitude and immediacy of the economic crisis implied that PASOK's initial policy choices would, to a large extent, be binding for the future. Given the socioeconomic realities of Greece in 1981, PASOK had two options. The first was to see the crisis as an opportunity and seize it in order to pursue a radical restructuring of the economy with a view to long-term development and social justice and redistribution. The Greek capitalist class, after the electoral result in 1981, was in a state of confusion, surprise, and heavy indebtedness to state banks, a situation which would have made it very easy for a new political force to intervene and fundamentally reorganize capital-labor relations.

The second option was to see the crisis as a constraint on the immediate realization of its socialist policies, a constraint which had to be dealt with before any fundamental reorganization of the socioeconomic structure could take place.

The political costs entailed by the first option (further alienation of the capitalist class due to its socioeconomic disempowerment, frustration of the working class because of the need to make new sacrifices for the structural adjustment process) and the high degree of uncertainty for the success of such structural change during a period of global crisis, led PASOK to opt for a "stabilization for development" choice. The gradualist spirit of this choice was encapsulated in PASOK's hundred-day program, the emergency policy that the government announced for the first one hundred days of government. This hundred-day program was one of "economic self-restraint and stabilization, accompanied by a development program and a widening of the participatory processes."[4]

This policy of stabilization with structural adjustment would thus entail a two-pronged gradualist development plan: there would be an incremental shift of resources from domestic consumption into investment and net exports, accompanied by a net transfer of power from the center to the periphery and to the grass-roots nuclei of trade unions and local government.

The fundamental problem with this choice was that by stabilizing the old structures of capitalism, not only did it implicitly accept their survival and continuation throughout the 1980s, but more importantly the PASOK regime would depend on them as the basis of its developmental plan. The end result was that, immediately after PASOK assumed power, it postponed its socialist vision of *allaghi* and accepted the structures, agencies, and mentalities that it had been condemning in opposition and which over the past decades had proved to be detrimental to the long-term modernization of the country.

THE BURNT-LAND STRUCTURES

The economic structures that Andreas Papandreou decided to prop up and legitimize during the first three months of his term in office were those of a capitalism lacking technological innovators and heavily dependent on state subsidies and overseas capital. However, the peculiarities of Greek capitalist development since the nineteenth century – and especially its excessive reliance on "invisible" foreign sources of exchange beyond the control of the Greek government, such as net inflows from shipping and the emigrant population – had prevented the development of an industrial capitalist economy and had instead led to an intermediate state characterized by a backward and undercommercialized agricultural sector, a dependent commercial and industrial entrepreneurial class, and a sclerotic, patrimonial-state bureaucratic apparatus which only accentuated the country's dependency and underdevelopment. Let us examine each of these components separately, as their persistence in the 1980s proved to be detrimental to PASOK's plans for economic and social modernization and development.

4. Gerasimos Arsenis, *Political Testimony* [in Greek] (Athens, 1987), p. 69.

The state structure that the right-wing governments had established and developed over the years was essentially based on clientelistic and patronage practices. The conservative governments, including the military dictatorship (1967–74), which ruled Greece until 1981 (except for a brief period in 1963–65), followed the prewar policy of massive state intervention in the economy. However, the top-heavy government bureaucracies' intervention lacked any element of *dirigisme* (such as in countries like Korea or Taiwan) that could coordinate and promote socioeconomic agents and forces with a view to modernization and prosperity. Instead the state turned itself into a recruiting officer and a petty regulator at the expense of its real responsibilities of providing social welfare and investing in social overhead. The patrimonial state thus exhausted itself by rewarding political loyalty through lifelong positions in government agencies and by promulgating myriad petty regulations for every branch of the economy. It is perhaps indicative of all this that Greece is the only capitalist economy in Europe in which the vast majority of its youth aims at a nonproductive position in the public sector and in which a special branch of the police devotes most of its energies to controlling the prices of consumer goods in local shops and restaurants.

The emergence and development of such a patrimonial state structure, dissociated from the country's developmental process, accounts for many of the socioeconomic distortions observed in Greece during the postwar period. First, although public-sector investment was squeezed in favor of public consumption and social-transfer payments, other forms of state intervention such as subsidies and transfers kept increasing at rapid rates.[5] In terms of GDP they were among the highest in Europe.

However, the wide range of financial assistance to industry, tourism, and various service-related activities, developed to a large extent in an ad hoc way. In the process of selecting industrial branches and sectors as aid recipients the economic and social rates of return were not sufficiently taken into consideration. Accordingly there was considerable wastage of scarce capital and preservation of production patterns with low productivity levels. Thus the very much celebrated industrialization of Greece proved to be of little substance. Although the GDP composition changed (as manufacturing rapidly displaced agriculture), the contribution to overall growth was much smaller. This trend became more evident in the 1967–74 period as the colonels' policies tipped the balance of the economy towards services related to construction and tourism, thus reinforcing the country's image as "Hotel Greece."[6]

5. OECD, OECD Economic Surveys, *Greece 1989/1990* (1990), p. 50.
6. Millicent Schwenk, "The Economy," in *Greece – A Country Study*, ed. Rinn Shin, 3rd ed. (Washington, 1986), p. 165.

Moreover, even the actual growth in manufacturing appeared to be of dubious quality. It was highly dependent on imports of capital goods and energy from abroad and, furthermore, did little to promote an independent, national industrial base, as it either consisted of assembly plants based on foreign imports or of foreign-owned metallurgical and chemical plants (e.g., Aluminium de Grèce, Exxon refineries).

A second phenomenon linked to the burnt-land state structures was the imperfection of public services and infrastructural development. According to the OECD, deficiencies in the public health and education systems not only showed up in poor services but also entailed costs to society at large. Both systems were inefficient and tended to promote rather than reduce regional and distributional inequities.[7] Neither service ever managed to keep supply in pace with demand, while standards remained generally unsatisfactory. Public hospitals and schools were overcrowded especially in the cities. Patients often resorted to private doctors and hospitals or even to treatment facilities abroad.

In the big urban centers it became customary for graduating high-school students to take private evening courses to supplement the poor public schools' standards. Urban education was further burdened by students from the periphery where secondary and higher-education facilities were often nonexistent. Reflecting the unsatisfactory quantity and quality of higher education, many students went abroad, while at home a growing mismatch between supply and demand for various skills was developing, impeding the modernization of the economy and the society.

In the area of public infrastructure the patrimonial state's policies generated an excessive gap between private wealth and income on the one hand, and collective wealth and the provision of public services on the other. Faster population growth after the mid-1970s and rapid urbanization made the need for infrastructure investment even more pressing, since Greece already lagged considerably behind most European countries, especially in the fields of transportation, communications, and energy, as well as in water and sewage systems. Finally, environmental conditions were deteriorating rapidly as unplanned and unregulated urbanization and industrialization led to dangerous levels of water and air pollution, mainly in Greater Athens and the Salonika area.

The third distortion of the patrimonial state concerned the country's external imbalances. The growing gap between consumption and productive and investment capacities led to increasing current account and trade deficits. In order to cover part of these deficits the state had traditionally depended on "invisible receipts" (see table 2★). Over a period of

7. OECD Economic Surveys, *Greece 1989/1990*, 49.
★Tables appear at the end of this chapter, pp. 216–224.

forty years reparations for reconstruction, foreign aid, emigrants' remittances, shipping revenue, tourism, and capital inflow from Greeks living abroad successively financed Greece's growth, consumption, and investment needs. However, these sources did little to develop the country's productive capacities and were highly contingent upon the international business cycle and the political agendas of foreign centers of power. Lacking a sustained commitment to independent economic growth, Greece remained dependent upon economic conditions and sociopolitical agents beyond its national boundaries. The patrimonial state structures of Greece undermined socioeconomic modernization while increasing dependence on foreign capital.

The role and behavior of indigenous capital was yet another factor undermining Greece's development. The Greek entrepreneurial class thrived on state protectionism and short-term speculation. The majority of Greek industrialists lived off state subsidies and contracts while the practice of calculated risk, productive innovation and self-financing were in scarce supply. The high debt-to-capital ratio and deteriorating productivity and competitiveness of industry were clear indications that the Greek private sector was simply borrowing from state banks without any effort to invest in modernizing and efficient technologies. Indigenous capital favored real estate and financial investment that brought quick returns and high profits. Reluctance to make long-term investment was further reinforced by strong family ties. Family businesses avoided long-term expansion that would dilute family control.

As a result of these factors, Greek industry suffered from stagnation in investment (which was often covered by concessions to foreign capital), underexploitation of economies of scale in production and distribution and with speculation. Although the structure of industrial output was altered (see table 4) in some sectors (chemical industries), the basic capital goods industries changed only marginally. Capital formation based on imports was indicative of the lack of depth in the Greek modernization model. Finally, one can observe that despite the shift in industrial production, Greek exports remained undiversified: textiles, for example, represented the same percentage of industrial exports in the 1980s as in the 1960s (see table 5).

A final example of the burnt-land structures inherited by PASOK is agriculture. The agricultural sector absorbed a disproportionate amount of resources and manpower without increasing the export capacities of the country or even achieving self-sufficiency. Although agriculture's share of GDP fell to 14 percent in 1980 (see table 1) it still employed over one million people, 28.8 percent of the active population.[8]

8. Schwenk, "The Economy," 191.

Greek agriculture lacked a technological and institutional infrastructure to increase production and productivity. The holdings were small and fragmented, insufficiently irrigated and grossly underutilized, especially in the mountainous or semimountainous areas where almost half of the farms are located. The processing, packaging, and distribution infrastructure of agricultural crops and livestock was inadequate, if it existed at all. Finally, the cooperative movement was practically nonexistent, or only paper organizations controlled by the government, while relations between the state, the banks, and the individual producers were ones of clientelistic dependency, rather than of cooperative developmentalism.

As a result of these economic structures, throughout the 1960–80 period the rate of Gross Domestic Product growth kept falling despite the fact that investment remained at consistently high levels. Thus despite maintaining an average rate of growth superior to all EC countries (6 percent over the period), by 1980 (when it joined the community) Greece's per-capita Gross National Product (U.S. $3,500) was half the EC average while its socioeconomic indicators were only comparable to those of the Mezzogiorno and the most undeveloped parts of France and Ireland.[9]

Besides these economic impediments, Greece in the early 1980s was experiencing further structural peculiarities, this time in the social realm. Greece's first mass socialist movement has owed much of its vitality to its assumption of the remaining agenda of bourgeois liberalism, an agenda which helped it win the support of decisive sections of the urban "new middle classes." This rising social stratum, whose contradictory class position poses problems for any socialist strategy, included such groups as lawyers, doctors, and other professionals; merchants in the new areas of transport, electronics and so on; public officials in the larger economic enterprises, consultants, educational entrepreneurs, and those in other categories that address the needs of this new class, as well as of other classes who aspire to their position or seek to imitate their life-style.

One striking aspect of the new middle class is the multiple economic and political roles that it combines – specialization in one type of economic activity usually serves as the basis for a kind of initial accumulation, which then leads to a proliferation of activities cutting across the boundaries between public and private, commercial and rentier, urban and rural. This multilateral drive for economic affluence and social status breeds the peculiar Greek phenomenon of the polymorphous operator, familiar with everything, an expert in nothing. More seriously, it produces a chronic inability to fulfill commitments within the original schedule. Tremendous energy, ambition, higher education, and other

9. Ibid., 159.

background attributes go hand in hand with rather unsatisfactory performance of public duties and responsibilities, except insofar as these directly coincide with private interests. The resulting syndrome constituted another major obstacle to economic modernization in contemporary Greece.

Starting life from a position of impoverished subordination in the 1950s, the new middle strata grew rapidly in size and self-assertiveness during the boom years of the 1960s. Their assimilation to the consumerism, social habits and economic behavior of the older oligarchic classes then began to express itself in numerous ways, as summer homes, new automobiles, overseas education, and holidays matched their investments in real estate and employment in nonproductive commerce, the liberal professions and the state bureaucracy. In the absence of commensurate social recognition or political representation, their mimicking of the old dominant classes temporarily made them more radical in their political rhetoric and their advocacy of social programs, but they would soon become as conformist as their life-styles. The new middle classes pride themselves above all on their "modernity' – their valuing of individual fulfillment, their secular, democratic views, their concern with upward social mobility, and their attachment to urban, cosmopolitan society – and the pursuit of the accoutrements of "individual modernization" in Greece has taken place precisely at the expense of the resources required to modernize the productive, educational, and administrative systems.

The rising middle stratum appropriated wealth in large part through windfall gains in real estate, tourism, and related nonproductive services, was able to obtain easy loans from a pliant state, invested in commerce and property, and evaded taxes on a grand scale. Cars multiplied on narrow streets, and evening tutorial colleges often raked in their fees within sight of fast-deteriorating public schools. While massive concrete slabs of apartment blocs scarred the Attic peninsula, Greece was exporting oranges to West Germany and importing orange juice and other products to slake the thirst of "modern" consumption.

It was not that the new middle classes questioned the need for public controls and expenditures: indeed, the polluted air, unpaved suburban sidewalks and chaotic education structures helped to inspire in them a vague demand for change, so long as they did not have to foot the bill for the necessary modernization. The shirking of responsibility was manifest in a sort of pseudoradicalism much purveyed by PASOK in the 1970s which pointed to the upper classes without recognizing that even the confiscation of all their wealth would not begin to make a dent on the investment needs of the public sector.

In reality, the lack of modernization reflected both the misallocation of state loans by the upper class and the fiscal evasion and speculative activity of the *nouveaux riches*, but the new middle class was psychologically unprepared for any sacrifices. Nourished on the myth of being an outsider, it failed to see that it had consumed beyond the productive capacities of the society. Believing that its private gains were simultaneously social gains for everyone, it perceived and aggressively presented any serious revenue-raising by the state as an attack on "the people." This blindness on the part of the new middle class virtually precluded that the bourgeois republic would be able to ground itself on the same social content as the postwar regimes of Northern Europe.

These were the socioeconomic realities that PASOK was called on to face in 1981 with the hope that it would be able to break the vicious circle of burnt-land underdevelopment and social injustice that had characterized Greece in the post-civil war period.

THE 1981–1983 PERIOD

The first two years of PASOK's government showed very little progress in terms of the economic development and social modernization aims of the hundred-day program. Even the stabilization policies failed to restructure the burnt-land structures that PASOK had inherited and had decided to work through. Immediately following the hundred-day program (November 1981–November 1983) the regime indefinitely postponed both stabilization and structural adjustment policies. Political factors account for this inconsistency between the government's discourse and actual policies: PASOK's preelection promises and need to consolidate its political power in the country constrained efforts to back measures promoting capitalist interests at wage-earner expense.

PASOK had committed itself during its election campaign to improve the living standards of the population (through increased income equity, higher social provisions, and expansion of the social security net). Given this constraint, PASOK could not maintain an austerity policy comparable to that of other Western European nations during the period of the second oil crisis. On the contrary, it allowed wages and pensions to rise in real terms by more than 10 percent (see table 8) and it also expanded the social security net to categories of people who had been left without any coverage for decades. Moreover, it pursued highly expansionary fiscal policies, especially in the areas of health and education whose increase in budget share was 26 percent and 39 percent, respectively, in just one year (see table 7). Finally, in an effort to alleviate the social costs of galloping unemployment it increased the level of hiring by the central government by creating thousands of new positions (see table 9).

The other constraint on government policy was Papandreou's desire

175

to consolidate power. Never since the civil war had the traditional elites felt so threatened and disempowered by the political superstructure as in 1981. This rendered them potentially very dangerous, especially since the democratic institutions of Greece were still very fresh and fragile. PASOK had a parliamentary majority but the government moderated its policies regarding the fundamental labor-capital relations in order to neutralize the opposition of the old elites, who still controlled the state apparatus. In order to consolidate state power the government sought to capture the "commanding heights," placing people in high positions who would assure the transfer of political power to the legitimate winner in the electoral process. This necessitated changes in the top administrative positions of all government (police, prefectures, ministerial bureaucracies) and public sector (public utilities, television network) agencies and mass recruitment in lower levels of the state so that party loyalists would eventually be in a position of control. This strategy, however, not only put further burden on the government budget, but it also led to administrative conflicts and an inability to transmit effectively the policies decided at the center.

By the end of 1983, having satisfied some of its populist election promises and consolidated its power, the deteriorating economic situation forced the regime to reconsider the austerity and adjustment policies it had set aside following is ascent to power. By 1983, inflation reached 20 percent, productivity was declining, GDP growth was close to zero, while unemployment was more than three times higher than in the 1970s (see table 6).

Even more worrying though was the fiscal overexpansionism in a period of global recession that had increased the government's debt to unprecedented levels, doubling it in a single decade. It became obvious that change was really needed in the country's productive capacities, the deficiencies of which were increasingly being subsidized by unrestrained domestic and foreign borrowing. After a fundamental cabinet reshuffling, Gerasimos Arsenis emerged as the tsar of the government's economic policy. As Minister of Finance he supervised the ministries of the National Economy, Industry, and Trade. The enactment of the first comprehensive plan for the economic and social development of the country was under way.

THE FIVE–YEAR PLAN FOR ECONOMIC AND SOCIAL DEVELOPMENT (1983)

A five-year "Economic and Social Development Plan" for 1983–1987 was approved by Parliament in November 1983, despite opposition from both the left (KKE) and the right (New Democracy). The plan was patterned on the hundred-day program unveiled two years before. Its main objectives were to decrease unemployment and inflation; improve the quality of life and status of the underprivileged through better environmental conditions and social services; mobilize provincial resources for balanced regional development; develop research-and-development facilities and high-technology industries; and increase the participation of individuals in local government, the cooperative movement, unions, and public enterprises.[10]

According to the EC, the public sector would play a major role in the strategy by undertaking the responsibility for high-risk investment that private enterprises were unwilling to assume.[11] The program of public investment was to take place through the decentralized framework of the country's prefectures (*nomarhies*) and public enterprises. Industrial and investment policy has a threefold aim: the stimulation of new, regional, and decentralized private (including foreign) investment through government subsidies and state participation in the share capital as a form of incentive; the improvement of the technology, international competitiveness, structure, and capacity utilization in Greek manufacturing; and the restructuring and rehabilitation of the overindebted "problematic" firms in the traditional industrial sectors (textiles, mining, construction).[12] Special emphasis was also given to energy policy and to the reorientation of tourism and shipping. Agricultural policy aimed at fostering economic and social progress in the rural periphery while increasing self-sufficiency in food production and developing high-value-added food products.

In terms of income policy, the five-year plan had a twofold aim: achieving greater social equality and lowering the rate of inflation. A wage-indexation system which offset in full the inflationary erosion of the purchasing power of the lower income brackets (while only partially compensating higher ones) combined with a deliberate increase in transfer payments for health, social insurance, and education, was perceived as reconciling these two aims.

Public expenditure was reorganized so as to increase the share of capital expenditure relative to that of current expenditure, the emphasis of which shifted towards health, social insurance, education, and quality of life. Expenditure on staffing would be contained while agricultural subsidies would decline. To offset the net increase in expenditure, overall

10. Center of Planning and Economic Research (CPER), *The Five-Year Economic and Social Development Plan 1983–87* (Athens, 1983), pp. 10–11.
11. *European Economy*, no. 19 (December 1990), p. 56.
12. CPER, *Development Plan 1983–87*, 7.

taxation was to rise with the implementation of a uniform Value Added Tax (VAT) while property taxes and penalties for tax evasion would increase. The main source of financing would still be bank credit, but additional sources would be provided by certain forms of regional self-financing and the issuing of special certificates.

THE ACHIEVEMENTS OF THE FIVE–YEAR PLAN

The economic benefits of the five-year plan were substantial but were mainly concentrated in the areas of short-term income redistribution and economic spurts rather than long-term prosperity and sustainable development. The rates of growth were very encouraging by comparison to those of most other European countries, while investment (mainly public) and productivity turned substantially positive. The expansionary fiscal policy had vigorous stimulating effects on general government and private consumption, thus leading to lower levels of unemployment. All that took place, moreover, with only minor increases in the inflation rate (see table 6).

In addition, the five-year plan maintained the trend of increased standards of living that was established in the 1981–83 period, thus compensating to a large extent for the loss of income due to the two oil crises and the contradictory and inegalitarian policies of the right in the 1970s. As tables 7 and 8 show, real wages increased through indexation while the increased amount of transfer payments (old-age and agricultural pensions, social security, health, and education) further improved the lot of those in lower income brackets.

Although the economic and redistributional successes of the five-year plan were not firmly anchored and easily reversed, the social achievements of PASOK, both within and outside the framework of the five-year plan, were of some substance. Institutional reforms in many areas of social life led to much needed modernization of the country's civil society. Laws were passed instituting civil marriage, decriminalizing adultery, and liberalizing divorce; extensive efforts were made to formulate city plans for all urban areas, to solve Athens' traffic problems and to combat the smog (known as *nefos*) that covered the greater Athens area. Voting rights were granted eighteen-year-olds, and athletic installments and programs, free theater tickets to students, programs to reduce unemployment and for the rehabilitation of drug users contributed to increasing opportunities for young people. The number of people helped through the Labor Housing Organization increased impressively. The welfare benefits of the elderly were expanded, as the pension level was elevated and the KAPI (old-age recreational centers) were instituted. Finally, some halting steps were taken by PASOK toward gender equality and the enhancement of the social activity, recognition, and integration of women, including changes in the family code.

PASOK's social modernization program focused on promoting decentralization of administrative functions away from central authorities to municipalities and communities, especially in regard to planning, as well as the socialization of the key sectors of the Greek economy. Decentralization implied the empowerment of citizens at the local level vis-à-vis the central government. Towards the realization of that aim PASOK set up councils, composed of representatives from municipal councils, farmers, workers and employers, to advise the governors, and reduced the governors' control over local councils. PASOK increased almost threefold central government funding to these councils, giving them financial independence (see table 10). New institutions for decentralization and popular participation in the decision-making process were created and began to operate, initially with the project of implementing popular meetings, developmental associations, program contracts, municipal radio, and development conferences.

Socialization was the functional equivalent of decentralization in the economic realm. In public sector enterprises, this took the form of advisory committees composed of workers representatives, local or central authorities, members of public interest groups, and shareholders. The aim was to replace the bureaucratic management systems that were dependent on the ministries of Athens with a democratic form of social control. In the private sector, socialization initially covered the "problematic" enterprises, as well as some key sectors such as the banking, insurance, mining, shipbuilding, steel, cement, fertilizer, pharmaceutical, and defense industries.

The socialization and decentralization program of PASOK had a major impact on the education and health systems. The immediate expansion and improvement of the educational apparatus and the intensification of its social role came through student councils and parent committees which were established in each school. Decentralization was also implemented in the highest level of education with the founding of three new universities in the provinces. By the end of 1983 the legal framework for a national health system (ESY) was already in place and within the next year and a half firm steps were taken toward its realization. Its goals were decentralization, preventive care, an adequate supply of nurses and government physicians, outpatient health centers, and the improvement of hospital technology. Plans for the construction of 185 rural clinics, 25 hospitals, and 18 nursing schools were well under way.[13]

13. Schwenk, "The Economy," 135.

Government allocations for both education and health continued to rise, albeit at a slower pace than in 1981–83, but were still higher than under the preceding right-wing government (see table 7).

THE FAILURE OF THE FIVE–YEAR PLAN: STRUCTURE AND POLICY

In terms of economic development and modernization, according to the EC, the five-year plan treated the alleviation of the country's structural disequilibria as a gradual and secondary process, and not as an urgent requirement.[14]

Three overall problems can be identified with this economic strategy. The first was that the patrimonial state structure that was to conduct the implementation of the five-year plan had in the past repeatedly proved incapable of coordinating the multifaceted aspects of a structural developmental process. The EC subsidies in agriculture (see table 13) were not complemented with the infrastructural measures (irrigation, transportation, distribution, and marketing) required for the productive utilization of these funds, something which led to a substantial wasting of resources.

As a result, by 1985, i.e., two years after the implementation of the five-year plan, there was still no sign of agricultural self-sufficiency or even of an increase in agricultural productivity. If anything, during that two-year period the country's imports in meat and dairy products increased by 11 percent and 9.5 percent, respectively, while its production of such key products as wheat, oranges, and apples fell by 32.5 percent, 6.1 percent, and 24.6 percent, respectively.[15]

Another example of the government's inability to coordinate the developmental process is education. Despite increased spending to improve the quality of education, the Ministry of Education made no effort to coordinate its developmental policies with those of the newly established Ministry of Research and Technology in order to direct the human capital of Greece in directions of greater economic promise. Thus, instead of pursuing careers in information systems, biotechnology, or alternative energy production, university graduates still sought the security of employment in the state bureaucracy.

The second problem concerned private investment and industrial development. In these areas the five-year plan proceeded from the mistaken assumption that there was already a demand for investment in the market and that if the economic incentives were provided, the private

---

14. *European Economy,* no. 23 (March 1985), p. 64.
15. Dimitrios Chalikias, *Bank of Greece-Annual Report of the Governor for the Year 1985* [in Greek] (1986), p. 56.

sector would take advantage and invest productively. What in fact occurred was that Greek entrepreneurs continued to invest in the types of projects which merely replicated the structural deficiencies of the burnt-land manufacturing sector without exhibiting any spirit of innovation. Thus by 1985, according to data gathered by the Bank of Greece, the bulk of productive investment was still directed towards the food and beverage and electrical appliances industries; the first was linked to the country's traditional low-value-added agricultural production and the latter consisted primarily of assembly lines which imported both the equipment required for the assembly process as well as the parts to be assembled. The fact that in 1985 capital goods production fell by 3.9 percent is also very indicative of the propensity to imitate old structures and to limit any prospects for the development of an independent and competitive manufacturing base (see also table 12).[16]

The third problem is directly related to PASOK's policies of fiscal overexpansion during the 1981–83 period that, by the time the five-year plan was implemented had generated growing public-sector financial imbalances and a chronic, self-generating public debt (see table 6). The adverse implications of this for the five-year plan were numerous. First of all, since the financial imbalances of the government were largely financed by the savings of the private sector, this squeezed the credit available to small-scale entrepreneurs. In other words, the fiscal appetite of the public sector deprived investors who had little or no access to government loans from benefiting from the provisions of the five-year plan. Secondly, the policies of scaled wage indexation (which were not accompanied by plans for increased production or productivity for the aggregate economy) resulted in unacceptably high costs of production and therefore in decreased competitiveness for Greek products as a whole. Thus imported goods started squeezing out domestically produced ones since their quality was superior and the increase in disposable income made them easily affordable (the deterioration of the trade balance is illustrated in table 6). Consequently, not only was there no shift of resources towards export industries as the five-year plan had intended but even domestic producers found themselves in a very disadvantaged position.

In other words, soon after the implementation of the five-year plan, the PASOK government had to confront not only the deficiencies it had inherited from previous decades, but also a set of rapidly deteriorating macroeconomic and microeconomic conditions resulting from their own previous policies.

The socialization and decentralization processes did indeed produce substantial institutional changes but were unable to modify the arrange-

16. Ibid., 60.

ment of social power in Greece. One reason was that PASOK's social base (small and medium-size entrepreneurs, the working class) still clung to paternalistic mentalities cultivated by centuries of Ottoman rule and patronizing right-wing governments and thus remained suspicious toward PASOK's social experimentation initiatives. As a result, the five-year plan was not seen as an opportunity to increase popular input into the decision-making process or to alleviate regional and class disparities, but rather as an opportunity to benefit personally as much as possible, as fast as possible, and with as little pain and work as the situation would permit. The lack of class consciousness and the pervasiveness of the "cunning fool" attitude of the popular classes, especially those in the party's grassroots – the local communities and the trade unions – proved to be detrimental to the implementation of the socialization and decentralization aspects of the five-year plan.

The decentralization process was seen by local officials in purely parochial terms and was perceived to be an opportunity to gain personal prestige rather than as the delegation of authority to modernize and enrich the locality. Within a matter of months, thousands of local notables became "presidents" or "secretary generals" of local organizations, councils, or committees. This title entailed personal access to public funds and personal favors from the local Socialist party machine (*kladiki*), which still retained control at the local level. The billions of fresh funds from the government and the EC transferred directly to local agricultural cooperatives and municipal and community enterprises were not invested in long-term development (see table 13). Rather, the funds were seen as a temporary blessing to be used for personal benefits and perks such as office restructuring, costly conferences and banquets, trips abroad, extensions in rural property and housing, and the purchase of Jeeps and VCRs for personal consumption.

The socialization process had a very similar fate. The worker advisory committees that PASOK tried to establish in the gigantic public-sector companies, starting with the Public Power Corporation (DEI), the Hellenic Telecommunications Organization (OTE), and the Hellenic Railways (OSE), could not be transplanted to the highly unregulated and fragmented private sector consisting of self-employed professionals, farmers, and manufacturers and comprising more than 50 percent of the labor force. However, even in the areas where there was an effort to implement the principles of socialization (commercial banks, shipyards, defense industry), local union leaders did not use the opportunity to control the means of production and improve (for their own benefit) the productive capacities of their sector, but instead appealed to the party state for short-term benefits and favors that in the long run would prove to be detrimental both for their enterprises as well as for the economy as a whole.

For example, the trade unions in the Hellenic Shipyards, one of Greece's largest employers, made a major effort to have their enterprise considered a "problematic" one, so as to have it transferred from private ownership to public, and thus enjoy the security and laxity of the state bureaucracies.[17] For them socialization was an opportunity to increase the level of state subsidy and protection of their firm by transferring ownership of the means of production to the government instead of trying to acquire control over production for themselves, increasing their productivity and their independence as a social force. Thus, for the trade union movement socialization soon became synonymous to a series of demands on the state for decreases in working hours, laxity in productivity controls, the prolongation of summer vacations and massive hirings of underemployed university graduates in the public sector.

THE FAILURE OF THE FIVE–YEAR PLAN: POLITICAL CHOICES

The structural impediments to the economic development of Greece were compounded by numerous intentionally distortive political choices by the government. To begin with, PASOK did nothing to discourage the statist and protectionist mentalities of the Greek entrepreneurial class, which depended on government subsidized loans and contracts in order to avoid international competition. If anything, PASOK encouraged state dependence in an effort to lure capitalists to the socialist electoral camp and away from their traditional support of the right-wing New Democracy party.

PASOK did little to directly challenge the monopolistic, tax-evading, and overinvoicing practices of the capitalist class in order to correct Greece's deficient capital-labor structures. On the contrary, PASOK bought into the capitalists' threat to disinvest and promised to help them recover from their current crisis with additional government grants, subsidized low-interest (and often at negative rates) loans, and accelerated depreciation allowances (see table 11).

The entrepreneurial class, of course, gladly accepted these windfall benefits but then turned its back on the government's modernization vision. Under the pretext of inconsistent economic policies (which to a large extent were a result of their own unreasonable demands), labor unrest (which was much lower than during the period of right-wing rule), and redistributional promises (for which they did not in any case

---

17. Dimitrios Stergiou, "A Year of One-Sided Austerity, A Blueprint for Irrationality" [in Greek] *Oikonomikos Tahidromos*, 22 October 1986, p. 11.

have to bear an especially large part of the burden) they turned disinvestment into self-fulfilling reality and directed the funds they received into a speculative short-term investment and capital flight (see tables 6 and 11). Thus, the private sector's share in fixed investment fell by almost 1 percent of GDP in just two years (1984 and 1985), while in that same period capital flight reached almost a third of a billion U.S. dollars (see table 14).

The best illustration of the antidevelopmental outlook of Greek business and its cozy relation with the state is PASOK's policy toward the overindebted enterprises of the private sector. The liberal leading policies of the rightist governments of the 1970s to the industrial elites in the more traditional sectors (textiles, metallurgy, construction, beverages), paired with a complete disregard for diversification, efficiency, and increased competitiveness, led to a number of firms becoming insolvent in the economic crisis of the 1980s.

As the owners declared themselves unable to pay their debt to the state banks (mainly to the National Bank of Greece and to a lesser extent to the Commercial Bank, the Agricultural Bank and ETVA) they threatened to close down their plants and fire their employees, approximately forty-thousand workers. The PASOK government decided to step in and assume their debt burden. By the end of PASOK's first term some 39 companies, with some 27,000 employees, and with a total debt of 167 billion drachmas, had been officially recognized as subject to state intervention.[18]

Rescue operations usually involved the conversion of at least 50 percent of the company's outstanding debt into equity shares owned by the government via the state-owned commercial banks that had initially issued the loans. The most notable conversions included the Skalistiri group of companies (which manufactured products for use in the metals and cement industries), Piraiki Patraiki (the largest textile manufacturer in Greece), and Heracles General Cement company (the largest cement company in Europe). These companies on which conversions were imposed constituted the backbone of the traditional burnt-land industrial base.

This conversion and rehabilitation process of problematic companies essentially implied that the former owners avoided paying their debts while financial mismanagement went unpunished, and unprofitable, inefficient firms continued to function in the old way with more state subsidies. In the second year of the five-year plan approximately five hundred firms had investigations pending preliminary to state intervention and restructuring, a clear indication of the failure of private-sector utilization of state loans and a major reason for the plan's blatant inadequacies in the economic sphere.

18. Schwenk, "The Economy," 169–70.

184

Moving beyond the economic failure, PASOK's organizational apparatus distorted and asphyxiated the socialization and decentralization processes. First of all, its leadership interpreted the people's call for redistribution simply as a call for additional material benefits. Thus, without touching the privileges of the economic elites, PASOK offered an increase in goods and services at the expense of the state budget and financed by internal and external borrowing. Pensions were raised and extended to groups which up to that point were left outside the social security net, wages were raised at rates substantially higher than those of inflation, spending on health and education went up in real terms, and hiring in the public sector steadily increased (see table 9).

However, all these measures aiming at decreasing social inequities were taken without concern for how they would be financed. The productivity of both the public and the private sector continued to fall (see table 6), the entrepreneurial class was not forced to share the burden of social equity and modernization, and government revenues were not increased by means of higher property or corporate-profit taxes. If anything, PASOK reduced the industrialists' burden in the government's developmental and redistributional effort: corporate and property taxes constituted 4.5 percent and 9.2 percent, respectively, of total public revenue in 1974–81, declining to 3.2 and 5.9 percent by 1985.

In effect, redistribution under PASOK came to mean the irresponsible use of public finances in order to establish its own electoral, clientelistic relationships with both the upper and the lower classes. By attempting to satisfy all sectors of the Greek society without making anyone accountable for the cost of this fiscal expansion, the regime generated a major fiscal crisis.

PASOK manipulated the socialization process to maintain control over civil society and improve its chances of future electoral successes. Party leadership realized that a real transfer of power through decentralization and socialization would trigger the growth of autonomous social movements. These forces, in turn, would challenge the power that PASOK had consolidated during the 1981–83 period. In order to avoid such a scenario, PASOK progressively established a party-state structure which would penetrate and firmly control Greek civil society. PASOK sacrificed the success of the socialization and decentralization process by retaining central state control and maintaining the existing configuration of socioeconomic power. PASOK exploited the new organizations in order to broaden the paternalistic control of the emerging party-state structure. The first signs of these new tendencies, which were to become pervasive in the second term, slowly appeared in PASOK's policies vis-à-vis the student movement and the labor unions.

185

One of the most important measures within the socialization process was the creation of student councils at the primary and secondary levels. These councils, though, soon degenerated into instruments of the party state. PASOK used student elections in order to flex its political muscle and establish partisan control over the student body through its youth organization. New Democracy and KKE imitated these practices and the whole process became an object of partisan competition. Constructive cooperation towards the improvement of the educational system was replaced by the same state control that had operated in past decades.

Another example of the contradictions between PASOK's public discourse on socialization and its actual paternalistic practices is its policy toward the trade unions. Despite the institutional changes that we have already examined, PASOK was no better than the governments of the right in manipulating the labor movement and trying to install union leaders who would favor its policies. In fact PASOK was in a better position to impose its will than New Democracy because PASOK has come to power as a champion of the working class and not as an enemy. Despite its rhetoric PASOK's labor policies were geared toward reinforcing the state's domination over civil society and reducing the space of autonomous institutions.

By mid-1982, PASOK had intervened for the first time in the labor movement. The right-wing leadership of the National Confederation of Greek Labor (GSEE) was deposed by a dubious court injunction and replaced with an appointed provisional council which had thirty-five PASOK members out of forty-five. PASOK, under pressure from the Federation of Greek Industrialists, the Athens Chamber of Commerce and Industry, and the Confederation of Artisans, later empowered the government to refer strikes to binding arbitration, a measure which clearly limited the independence and effectiveness of the labor movement.

Moreover, under the pretext that public enterprises were becoming "socialized," PASOK continued the practice of tying trade-union finances to the Ministry of Labor and subjecting union election slates to control by the party's inner circle. In the same way, PASOK made it increasingly difficult for public sector employees to go on strike by requiring a majority vote of union members. Finally, strike funds were not established, despite pressure from the rank and file, thus continuing to limit labor unrest to ineffective one-day warning strikes, or one-hour stoppages.

ASSESSING PASOK's FIRST TERM

The five-year plan for social and economic development became in effect PASOK's vision of *allaghi* during its first term in office. It was the most ambitious and comprehensive policy initiative that a Greek government had ever presented in the course of the country's modern history. Its two-pronged developmental strategy (social equity and economic growth) implemented through a framework of decentralized popular participation and socialization provided a reasonable basis for the country's modernization within the European Community.[19] The initial implementation of the program provided encouraging results. The Greek economy seemed to be coming out of is deep crisis, income disparities decreased substantially, and social change was visible in some sectors of society.

However, in the months preceding the 1985 parliamentary elections PASOK decided to abandon the five-year plan and returned to the populist policies of the 1981–83 period. This decision demonstrated the continuing strength of the existing socioeconomic structures in Greece and how little PASOK was committed to eradicating them by means of socialist reconstruction. The rejection of the five-year plan created a socioeconomic and political framework that was detrimental to PASOK's second-term efforts as well. The economic successes were reversed within a matter of months to the point that, even before the 1985 elections, one could discern growing internal and external imbalances. Even the social successes evaporated in the face of the populist-induced economic crisis and the growing power of the party-state machinery. In sum, putting the five-year plan in what Andreas Papandreou often called "the file cabinet of history" proved to be the occasion for undermining most of PASOK's past achievements and most of its future efforts.

The reasons for the plan's rejection were structural as well as political. Structurally, PASOK's socioeconomic vision of development was constrained by the old structures, agencies, and practices of Greek capitalism and the Greek state. The choices that Papandreou had made in the first hundred days of his term had legitimized these constraints and had given them the opportunity to overcome the initial shock of his 1981 electoral victory. Thus, by the end of 1983, when the five-year plan was announced, there were no alternative structures or agencies on which PASOK could have based its development plan. Even worse, clientelistic mentalities, bureaucratic apathy, and entrepreneurial speculation were already in a position to obstruct development and to turn it to their advantage, strengthening their position within the Greek economy and society. Tied to past structures, agencies, and mentalities, PASOK not only was unable to promote the processes of *allaghi* through socialization

---

19. Louka Katseli, *Structural Adjustment of the Greek Economy*, Center for Economic and Policy, research discussion paper no. 374 (Athens, 1990) p. 92.

JAMES PETRAS, EVANGELOS RAPTIS, AND SERGIO SARAFOPOULOS

and decentralization, but it also became an accomplice to the forces undermining and distorting its initial programmatic goals.

Politically the PASOK government was equally at fault in undermining its development program. The gap between its public discourse on socialism, economic development, decentralization, and socialization, and its actual policies of fiscal populism and partisan overcentralization widened over time. Instead of trying to increase national wealth and redistribute it according to the notions of socioeconomic equity and justice, PASOK decided to redistribute in a wasteful and sectarian manner the existing limited wealth and to resort to the cultivation of demagogic rhetoric as an easy way out of the crisis. These tactics reached their climax in the 1985 electoral campaign. PASOK further fueled the public's euphoria and escapist proclivities by promising "even better days" (*akoma kalliteres meres*), meaning greater consumption, an overtly demagogic claim given the magnitude of the public deficits.

Superimposing a welfare state (through increased public allocations and borrowed wealth) on a dependent and underdeveloped economy without fundamentally restructuring its deficit or capital-labor relations implied that when the populist economic crisis arrived, the government would then take back what it had delivered. PASOK would soon have to ask for even greater sacrifices from those who had earlier been the beneficiaries of its populist consumer allocations and who had assumed that they were permanent gains.

PASOK's intentional distortion of the aims and means of the five-year plan for short-term electoral gain did not limit itself to the economic aspects of their policies. As Greek citizens in a matter of a few years became highly dependent on state transfers based on a shaky budget rather than through the expansion of productive capacities, they ended up victims and clients of the emerging party state. Short-term consumption became the easy substitute for a real social transformation. Instead of giving people real control over the means of production, PASOK merely increased social transfers without providing the independence and sovereignty that was necessary for long-term development and prosperity to sustain the social gains. Thus, when state allocations and provisions reached their limit, those who had accepted their clientelistic position for immediate gratification found themselves even more dependent on the state and worse off vis-à-vis the upper class.

By the end of PASOK's first term in office, the government of Andreas Papandreou was burdened with a set of structural weaknesses that followed it throughout the course of its second term in office. The basic structural weaknesses were located in the economy. As Table 6 shows, the cost of the economic revitalization of the five year plan in

188

terms of public finances was immense. Within just four years, the gross government debt more than doubled while most of the macroeconomic indicators did not give much reason for optimism. During PASOK's first term the economy grew at a rate half of that of the 1974–81 period, with higher inflation, lower productivity, and an unemployment rate almost four times higher than during the New Democracy period. Furthermore, despite the government's incentives and the accelerated rates of public investment, gross fixed capital formation remained negative while private disinvestment became endemic. In addition, the country's dependency on overseas markets increased both in terms of imports of consumer and capital goods (see the trade balance deterioration) as well as in terms of foreign lending and EC transfers. Finally, as table 12 shows, during PASOK's first term, there was little industrial diversification while even the limited preexisting heavy industrial base, started to shrink.

The contradictions between a socialist developmental discourse and a populist practice sanctioning the structures of capitalism had led to a disastrous and explosive economic situation by 1985. In addition to the parasitical capitalism of the previous decades absorbing state resources, there was now the imposition of a populist state apparatus which distributed money in all directions, without any specific plan, and with the sole purpose of creating a mirage of modernization and social equity for narrow and immediate electoral ends.

The second problem facing PASOK after 1985 was social. The country experienced substantial institutional change in the social realm, but this change remained solely at the institutional level. The contradiction between the socialist discourse of socialization and decentralization and the clientelistic centralization practices of an emerging party state prevented the real empowerment of the masses. Changing values and ideas constitute the only viable course toward an irreversible and irrevocable modernization of Greek society, but these did not change. The institutional changes were very shallow and fragile, specially as they were imposed from above by party-state bureaucracies rather than organically developed from below by the independent will and participation of the people.

PASOK's third problem was electoral. In the elections of June 1985, PASOK won a landslide victory and argued that it had been successful in consolidating and maintaining a firm electoral base. Yet Papandreou's antiright rhetoric and policy of populist allocations, which neutralized the KKE, could not be sustained in the post-1985 period. PASOK's acceptance of the constraints posed by the traditional structures and agencies allowed it to immobilize the right, yet hindered its efforts at developing any innovative and progressive alternatives to IMF-style solutions to the impending economic crisis.

PASOK had won another term in office and secured a mass base to proceed with the consolidation of its state-party apparatus, yet by June 1985 it had come full circle. Not only had PASOK been unable and unwilling to implement its socialist policies of socioeconomic modernization and development, it had laid the foundations for the emergence of what it had so openly condemned while in opposition: a new version of clientelistic dependent capitalism based on a centralized state.

THE POPULIST CRISIS OF 1985 AND THE STABILIZATION PLAN OF OCTOBER 1985

The populist fiscal overexpansion that characterized PASOK's first term, which had culminated with the "better days" election campaign, had led by the end of 1985 to a full-blown economic crisis. The success in building and consolidating a party-state machinery during the 1981–85 period was clearly the result of populist spending. PASOK seemed to be aiming at the maintenance of a state which was dissociated from the country's economic development process. A second characteristic of the emerging party-state structure was a growing tendency towards an "inverse determinism," that is, a total subordination of the economic structure to the political (and especially partisan) superstructure for reasons of power consolidation and electoral success. These two characteristics resulted in 1985 in a populist economic crisis that combined serious internal and external economic imbalances.

The most pressing domestic problem was the mounting public-sector deficit, a direct consequence of PASOK's populist fiscal overexpansion and of its effort to establish its party-state apparatus. As table 16 shows, in 1985 the gross government debt grew exponentially and, as a result, so did the government's net borrowing requirements, especially in the sectors of social security, public utilities, and transportation.[20] The repercussions of this public overindebtedness were already being felt by August 1985 throughout the economy.

First of all, the government's effort to finance its deficit through printing money resulted in a debt-growth–money-growth spiral. The increasing growth rate in money supply for reasons of debt financing produced widespread inflationary pressures. The government tried to deal with these pressures by keeping the prices of utilities and other public services at artificially low levels, that is by running additional public deficits. This in turn created increased money-supply needs, increased inflationary pressures, higher deficits, and so on.

20. Pavlos Klavidanos, "The Failure (?) of the Stabilization Program Is an Omen for a Prolonged Period of Tight Policies" [in Greek] *Oikonomikos Tahidromos*, 3 July 1986, p. 33.

The second repercussion of the government's overindebtness was in private investment. As the growing deficits were consistently being covered by domestic commercial bank credit, by 1985 an extensive credit crunch for private entrepreneurs had been created. Thus the falling investment rates observed in 1985 were not to be attributed simply to the disinvestment tendencies of Greek industrialists but also to the lack of credit availability for many parts of the private sector.

The above internal disequilibria were complemented by even more threatening external ones. To begin with, the capital-account deficit increased by almost 40 percent in a matter of a few months due to a combination of lower capital inflows and higher capital outflows. However, the most telling indicator of the country's economic crisis was the doubling of its current-account deficit in the course of 1985. By December 1985, the deficit amounted to $3.3 billion, or almost 10 percent of the country's GDP.

Two factors account for this rapid deterioration. The first is once more related to the public (and to a lesser extent to the private) deficit. Domestic savings were inadequate to sustain the growth of these deficits because of the negative real interest rates that the banks offered to depositors (see table 15) which led to dissaving among the population. The PASOK regime increasingly turned abroad to satisfy its borrowing appetite. As a result, in 1985 the external deficit jumped by 45.3 percent vis-à-vis its 1982–84 levels. This meant higher net factor payments abroad (24 percent of the country's total services and goods exports) and widening current-account imbalances.

The second factor responsible for the current-account deficit was that of the deteriorating trade balance. As table 16 shows, Greece's trade balance was improving at an average annual rate of 7 percent in the 1982–84 period. Then, in 1985, the deficit skyrocketed a spectacular 17.1 percent.

The reasons for this deterioration are to be found on both the imports and exports sides. In terms of exports, Greek products were considered uncompetitive abroad because of the high real labor costs at home and because of the overvaluation of the drachma in the course of 1985. On the imports side, there was a rapid increase in the volume of imports of both capital and consumer goods, as well as of oil. The fiscal expansionism of PASOK and the increases in the level of disposable income among population created demand in both the public and private sectors. However, as domestic supply proved to be highly inelastic in regard to this growing demand (in fact, as already noted, the rate of private investment fell), the country turned abroad.

The import penetration tendencies of the economy took explosive

191

dimensions by the end of the summer of 1985, with massive speculation on a postelectoral devaluation, which caused many people to try to make "last fling" purchases of imported goods. It is estimated that, as a result of this "import mania," by the last quarter of 1985 the country's foreign-currency reserves were as low as $868 million, the equivalent of thirty days' worth of imports.[21]

The rapid increase of both internal imbalances and external disequilibria (a current-account deficit fueled by growing debt-servicing requirements and trade deficits) necessitated immediate action and a radical policy reorientation. The party-state structure had to at least temporarily shelve its populist policies and return to conservative orthodox austerity policies. PASOK faced two options in proceeding with the economic restructuring. The first was an economic restructuring along socialist lines, the second an economic restructuring along neoclassical lines.

The first option was already out of the question for two reasons. First, the five-year plan, which had been intended to be one of socialist restructuring, had never really got off the ground, while the deficit economic structures of burnt-land capitalism had remained intact, if not strengthened. The second reason was that, at the social level, the socialist transformation had no real basis of support, since changes were limited to the institutional level and were imposed from above. Therefore it could not provide political support for the burden of an economic restructuring.

Since PASOK did not want to pay the political cost of a socialist restructuring, it chose the second option, that is, an IMF–style stabilization-liberalization package. This package, besides dealing with the current-account deficit, served another purpose as well: it satisfied the policy prescriptions of the EC, OECD, and other foreign creditors and thus assured new lending to the PASOK government. This realignment of Greece with the Western financial powers was seen by Papandreou as a necessity because it would assure PASOK a substantial part of the funds it needed for the rest of its second term in office.

The major targets of this stabilization policy, which Papandreou implemented voluntarily without the mediation of the IMF, included a decrease in the net public-sector borrowing requirements; a decrease in the current-account deficit in order to alleviate the burden of debt service payments; containing of inflation to reestablish normal investment and savings behavior; limits on domestic credit expansion; and a reduction in unemployment with the aim of reaching full employment and thus maximum efficiency in resource allocation.[22]

21. Bank of Greece, *Monthly Statistical Bulletin* (March 1990), pp. 52–53.
22. Yannis Spraos, "Means and Aims of Macroeconomic Policy," in *The Policy of Economic Stabilzation* [in Greek], ed. Costas Simitis (Athens, 1989), pp. 63–65.

Income, trade, fiscal, monetary, and exchange policies were all supposed to be utilized during the stabilization program. The wage-indexation system (ATA) was modified to exclude import prices, and wages were adjusted on the basis of projected inflation instead of past price rises. Thus in January and May 1986, the maximum indexation was 4.5 percent and 1.2 percent respectively, rather than 14.8 percent and 6.4 percent as the previous ATA calculation scheme would have called for; this resulted in a substantial loss in buying power for wage earners.[23] This ceiling on the nominal rate of wage increase was to be implemented across the board in both the public and private sectors and was aimed at bringing inflation down from 25 percent at the end of 1985 to 19 percent by the end of 1986.

In terms of trade policies, the stabilization program promulgated obligatory six-month non-interest-bearing deposits on certain imported goods as a means of imposing an additional tax on luxury items and consumer durables of foreign origin. This measure was complemented by a 15 percent devaluation of the drachma. The combination of the two was aimed at reducing import penetration and improving competitiveness of Greek exports and, in general, the overall balance of trade.

In terms of fiscal policy, the stabilization plan curtailed public expenditures, increased prices on public goods (e.g., a 50 percent increase in urban transportation fares) and utilities. In addition it increased tax revenues through higher rates, the abolition of exemptions, and greater efforts at curbing tax evasion. This tight fiscal policy aimed at halting the growth of government deficits and decreasing the PSBR approximately 8 percentage points (from 18 percent of GDP to 10 percent) in the course of two years.

Finally, monetary and credit policies were to be tightened as well by limiting Central Bank–lending to public creditors for debt financing, by increasing interest rates on consumer loans, and by limiting the growth of the money supply (from 24.4 percent to 11 percent). Moreover, real long-term interest rates were to be brought up to a positive level (see table 15).

The stabilization plan was to last for two years (1986–87) and it immediately obtained the full support of the EC Commission, which granted a 1.75 billion-ECU (European Currency Unit) loan to finance its implementation. Politically, in pursuing this orthodox program the PASOK regime was clearly taking a further step away from its original socialist commitments and orienting itself toward a rapprochement with overseas and local investors and bankers; the populist interlude was in retrospect a stopover on the road to political and economic conformity.

---

23. Yiannis Marinos, "The IMF Is Cautious for the Results of the Measures of October's austerity" [in Greek] *Oikonomikos Tahidromos*, 11 September 1986, p. 55.

THE SUCCESSES AND FAILURES OF THE STABILIZATION PROGRAM

By the end of 1987, the official benchmark for measuring the performance of the orthodox stabilization program, some of its aims had been realized to a certain extent, and this was recognized and applauded by most international creditors and financial organizations such as the EC, the IMF, and the OECD. Thus, as table 15 shows, the current account deficit decreased almost fourfold, the growth of the trade deficit was largely constrained (at least in 1986), while the capital account improved just as sharply as it had deteriorated previously. Moreover, the cooling down of the economy had lowered the inflation rate to the 15-percent target. Economic constraints did not affect the country's employment level; on the contrary, unemployment during the stabilization process fell by approximately 1 percent.

The Greek government and its international creditors failed to see (or refused to admit) that behind these apparent successes, the structural inadequacies and disequilibria that had caused the populist-induced economic crisis of 1985 still remained unchallenged. During the two-year period of austerity and "structural adjustment," PASOK temporarily adjusted its external disequilibria in order to pacify its international creditors, while it let the economy drift into a recession. By 1987 both economic growth and productivity had turned negative, against the general economic trends of most Western European nations during that period. Moreover, fixed investment showed a spectacular decline throughout the 1986–87 period, thus incapacitating Greece's potential for future growth and economic recovery. As table 17 shows, industrial production in key sectors such as capital goods and food and beverage manufacturing kept declining at even higher rates in the years of the stabilization program.

Last, but not least, the public sector, the major cause of internal disequilibrium, had failed to limit its fiscal appetite or its propensity toward waste. By 1987, not only was the PSBR as high as 13.5 percent of GDP (as opposed to the 10 percent intended in the stabilization program), but it was estimated that even this modest decrease was mostly due to the fall in international oil prices rather than to fiscal restraint.[24] As table 15 shows, government debt kept growing, and by 1987 it had surpassed 60 percent of GDP. In sum, the stabilization program sacrificed domestic growth and economic stability for the sake of short-term improvements in the country's external accounts.

24. *European Economy*, no. 30 (November 1986), p. 81.

STRUCTURAL AND POLICY REASONS FOR THE FAILURE OF THE STABILIZATION PROGRAM

The IMF–style orthodox stabilization package that the PASOK government adopted in October 1985 was incompatible with the socioeconomic realities of Greece and thus led to the usual contradictions and inefficiencies that such packages have demonstrated throughout the 1980s in many countries, especially in Latin America. The so-called "structural adjustment" policies brought about economic stagnation since any additional income and output was diverted towards the repayment of stabilization loans. This pushed the country into a debt trap that only weakened its economic structures and worsened prospects for growth.

The orthodox stabilization recipe (tight monetary policies to reduce internal imbalances; export-oriented growth to reduce external imbalances) soon proved to be ineffective. The size of the public debt (over 50 percent of GDP) simply did not permit the kind of fiscal and monetary tightness required for its reduction. As the central government's debt service requirement jumped from 280 billion drachmas (15.8 percent of total budget expenditure) in 1985 to 650 billion drachmas (24.3 percent) in 1987, it became absurd to talk about fiscal restraint.[25] If the government had to pay a fixed 25 percent of its budget toward servicing its debt, there was not much left to cut.

The monetary policy aspect of stabilization stumbled on the same obstacles and contradictions. The government had had to increase commercial bank interest rates in order to attract savings to finance its deficits; this boomeranged because the government itself then had to pay higher interest on its debt-service requirement to the commercial banks. To avoid this the government increased the level of money growth in 1987 (see table 15), thus falling into a vicious circle of higher debt requirements and looser monetary policies.

The above ineffectiveness of the fiscal and monetary aspects of the IMF recipe forced PASOK to rely almost exclusively on an unorthodox wage freeze based on a social pact with the trade unions. This excessive reliance on income policy for the achievement of structural adjustment ended up serving the interests of the capitalist elites at the expense of the working class, which had to carry a disproportionate share of the austerity burden. Average earnings from wages and salaries in 1986 and 1987 fell in real terms by 10 percent and 4.7 percent respectively, while during the same period, the net rate of return on capital was between 4 and 6 percent.[26]

25. Bank of Greece, *Statistical Bulletin* (1990), pp. 53–54.
26. OECD Economic Surveys, *Greece 1989/1990*, 27, 80.

What made this injustice even more pronounced was that the burden of the income policy was borne principally by the working class and especially the salaried employees of the public and, to a lesser extent, private sector, which constitute less than half of the country's productive force. The remainder, self-employed professionals and farmers, operated outside the framework of the wage freeze and thus had the luxury to continue transferring the effects of inflation directly onto the rest of the nation's citizens. Thus wage and salaried workers were exposed to lower earnings and higher prices under the PASOK stabilization plan.

Besides failing to deal with the public debt while widening socioeconomic inequalities, the stabilization program also distorted investment behavior. As we have already noted, during 1986–87 fixed investment declined by 14 percent. Two factors can account for this phenomenon. The first is the 50 percent fall in public investment. The government tried to curtail its fiscal overexpansion and deal with its growing debt-service requirements in a way that would minimize its short-term political and electoral costs rather than cut down on its administrative spending and waste. It did so by decreasing the public sector's share of gross fixed capital formation and thus sacrificed the future productive capacities of the country for the sake of presenting to foreign creditors some semblance of fiscal restraint.

The stabilization program's impact on private sector investment was also negative. As table 15 shows, the compression of working class wages and the continued oversubsidization practices of the five-year plan failed to translate increased capital profitability into an equivalent increase in private investment. Two reasons account for this. First, the rise in interest rates led to an increase in the debt-servicing requirements of the private sector (since it relied heavily, like the public sector, on borrowed funds from commercial banks), as well as to a lower rate of return in its investment projects. Furthermore, since the rate of return on government bonds issued for the financing of the public debt was much higher than the rate of return on industrial investment (bonds offered a tax-free 21 percent per annum rate of return), foreign as well as domestic investors preferred not to take any risks but rather place their money with the government. Because of the huge public deficits we observed throughout the duration of the stabilization program there was a net transfer of resources from the private to the public sector, which contradicted the rationale behind the implementation of austerity measures and which exacerbated the declining rates of productive investment.

The poor investment performance of the private sector cannot be explained simply by high interest rates and high yields on government bonds. Greek businessmen still considered PASOK's Greece an unsafe place for investment. The wave of antiausterity strikes in 1986 and especially in 1987, together with the nationalization of the oil facilities in Prinos despite successive government declarations to the contrary created the foundation of the disinvestment trend. The revelation of the first financial scandals involving prominent government officials further discouraged new investments. The most important scandal included PROMET (a public company involved in extensive public procurement scandals) and the Stamatelatos affair, in which a bank official embezzled public funds to finance his favorite soccer team.

In the final analysis even the improvements of the external imbalances were largely illusory. The improvement of the current account balance, both in 1986 and 1987, had nothing to do with an improved export capacity on the part of the Greek economy, which would have indicated an increase in international competitiveness. Rather, it was the result of a mass increase in invisible receipts (30.8 percent in 1986 and 44.3 percent in 1987)[27] concentrated in tourism, worker remittances, and EC transfers that were highly contingent upon an international financial environment controlled by foreign capital. Moreover, the spectacular increase in capital inflows (see table 15) was mainly a one-time transfer due to the introduction in Greek financial markets of the concept of "foreign currency accounts." Thus, this money was not new foreign capital seeking investment opportunities but rather the repatriation of speculative local capital. Overall, the net improvement in the country's balance of payments (whether current or capital account) was extremely shallow since it had no prospects of continuation and since it did nothing to promote the productive development of Greece.

POLITICAL CHOICES: THE END OF THE STABILIZATION PROGRAM

PASOK's stabilization program and its implementation (and nonimplementation) was above all a political question, susceptible to manipulation according to the political and electoral contingencies in Greece as well as to the external financial needs of the state. By looking at the stabilization program from this political vantage point one can make sense of the zigzags and apparent inconsistencies in its application and of its eventual abandonment.

Notwithstanding all these structural constraints, mistakes, and contradictions in policy, an IMF–style austerity program could have been implemented and the economy could have been liberalized had the

27. Dimitrios Chalikias, *Bank of Greece-Annual Report of the Governor for the Year 1987* [in Greek] (1988), p. 160.

PASOK government been committed to that aim. If Andreas Papandreou were indeed an IMF capitalist crisis manager, not only could he have pursued more vigorous stabilization policies than the ones he implemented in his 1985 austerity plan, but he could have complemented it with an IMF–style restructuring of the country's economy along liberal lines.

To begin with, he could have increased the role of market mechanisms in determining wage levels by linking wage compensation to labor productivity, and he could have limited state control over the structure of the labor market by abolishing regulation of the number of firings, work schedules, and part-time and seasonal job contracts. He could have liberalized the price system and increased profit margins, especially in the public utilities that constituted approximately 25 percent of Greece's consumer price index. Furthermore, he could have liquidated, restructured or privatized – on a case-by-case basis – the inefficient and ailing firms under public control that promoted market rigidities while overburdening public finances. Finally, he could have decreased government controls over the banking system, especially over interest-rate determination and the rationing of credit.

However, Andreas Papandreou did none of the above. On the contrary, within a year of implementing the stabilization program he initiated a new round of populist expansion. PASOK's defeat in the municipal elections of October 1986 (New Democracy won an absolute majority in the three largest municipalities of Athens, Salonika, and Piraeus) signaled a substantial decline in its support. This decline, if not reversed, would cost PASOK the parliamentary elections of June 1989. As a result most of the austerity provisions were reversed in the fiscal 1987 budget in an effort to recapture part of the lost electoral base discontented with the stabilization program. Widespread price freezes in public services and utilities and tax reductions for targeted segments of the population indicated PASOK's intention to return to 1982–85 patterns of macroeconomic management.

This change in policy illustrates PASOK's tactical use of the stabilization program to pacify growing demands from creditors on one hand and from Greek society on the other, with a view to an electoral victory in 1989. Stabilization was not seen as part of a strategic move for long-term socioeconomic modernization and development. In other words, Andreas Papandreou in his second term maintained his populist discourse, with its antioligarchical, antirightist, anti–West rhetoric, for domestic consumption purposes, but complemented it with a stabilization and liberalization discourse, for external consumption, for European and overseas creditors, allies, and economic partners. Thus, what was bellowed from a balcony in Constitution Square in central Athens as socialist *allaghi* was presented as orthodox stabilization in the conference rooms of Brussels, Paris, and Washington.

However, even this double discourse began to ring hollow as the actual self-contradictory policies of PASOK undermined both. Real decline in the wages of the working class, increased favoritism towards unproductive and tax-evading local capital, and higher dependency on foreign borrowing were not indications of socialist progress. On the other hand the continuation of high-spending practices in a period of deep fiscal crisis and continuous growth in the public sector could not be considered as positive steps toward stabilization and liberalization either. Just as socialism was abused, distorted, and rejected in the course of the first term and especially after the promulgation of the austerity plan in October 1985, so was neoliberalism abused after the electoral failure of October 1986.

The implementation of a stabilization and a liberalization program, apart from being too costly in political terms, would entail the net transfer of power from the bureaucratic apparatus to the market. Papandreou was not willing to give up his capacity to maintain his electoral clientele through public expenditure, nor was he willing to decrease the paternalistic role of the state within civil society and institutions. If anything, he had to expand both the clientelistic capacities and the paternalistic role of the party state, in order to assure another electoral victory in 1989.

In the course of PASOK's second term, and particularly after October 1986, there was a conscious effort on the part of the party leadership to maintain and expand the party-state structure in an attempt to assure a successful transition into a third term. However, it soon became obvious that a gigantic, all-penetrating party-state bureaucratic apparatus would not be sufficient. The state of the Greek economy in the mid–1980s required foreign help which was contingent upon some kind of a stabilization program that would improve the country's external imbalances. Given this constraint , PASOK was not able to meet the demands of its social base. As a result, party-state-structure patronage was complemented by the encouragement of a vast underground economy. This gave the public the impression that stabilization and structural-adjustment sacrifices could easily be bypassed with a pool of "hot money" circulating beyond the reach and understanding of any international creditor.

This combination of a paternalistic party state and an unregulated underground economy was PASOK's answer to the problem of satisfying the "irreconcilable" interests of Greek society and international creditors in order to maintain its electoral base.

JAMES PETRAS, EVANGELOS RAPTIS, AND SERGIO SARAFOPOULOS

PARTY–STATE STRUCTURE AND THE STABILIZATION PLAN

Although the overall size of public-sector expenditures during the stabilization program grew moderately by comparison to PASOK's first term (see table 18), this actually hides the real growth of the party-state structure. If we take into consideration the fall in public-sector investment and a lower government wage bill (the result of real salary compression) (see tables 15 and 19) we realize that even though the public sector did not grow, there was a change in the composition of its expenditures so as to satisfy some critical sectors, that is, critical according to PASOK's paternalistic and electoralist criteria. This change in expenditures can be clearly seen in the areas of government grants to overindebted public utilities and social security funds (an increase of 58.2 percent in 1987 against 11.8 percent in 1986), and in agricultural subsidies (an increase of 15 percent in 1987, up from 1.75 percent in 1986).[28] The electoral failure of 1986 does not seem unrelated to this growth in allocations by the expanding party state.

The agricultural sector is an excellent case study of manipulatory spending aimed not at enhancing the productive capacities of a segment of the economy but at the cultivation of a political clientele which would hopefully translate into votes. Apart from increased government and EC agricultural subsidies (see table 20), Greek farmers were favored in various ways without any control as to the efficient use of the resources acquired.

First of all, they were given access to the EC's newly established Integrated Mediterranean Programs. Moreover, the tax system was modified in such a way so as to favor farmers: in 1987, farmers were relieved of the newly imposed VAT on the sale of agricultural products, while their tax-deductible income was raised from 1.2 million drachmas to 1.6 million. Finally, the debts of the cooperatives were "regulated" (which means that many were written off, at the expense of the state budget and the Agricultural Bank of Greece), while at the same time the retirement age was further reduced to the point that a farmer could start reaping full social security benefits at the "advanced" age of forty-six.[29]

During the stabilization period the government bureaucracy, with all of its satellite enterprises and public-utility companies, not only imitated the clientelistic practices of previous right-wing governments but substantially enhanced them. Thus the consolidation of national allegiance to PASOK came not so much as a result of a general acceptance of its programmatic guidelines and policy successes but through the establish-

28. Ibid., 132.
29. Stergiou, "A Blueprint for Irrationality," 11.

200

ment of an expansive state apparatus where the party and the state would fuse into one entity and become inseparable. Within this context, not only were there no efforts to democratize, decentralize, and modernize the public sector, but rather decision-making became increasingly concentrated in the party-state machinery.

Although the severe oppression that the country had experienced during the post-civil-war period under pro-U.S. rightist regimes decreased, a different, subtle yet pervasive control was introduced: every activity that was even remotely related to the ever-expanding authority of the public sector needed to be examined under the magnifying glass of PASOK's "local commissions." In the state-owned companies a political payoff triangle developed between administrative elites, public procurement suppliers, and party officials. This turned government bureaucracies into agencies of partisan favoritism. Employment in the public sector, free plane tickets during elections, construction licenses, all became privileges which citizens could lay their hands upon and often abuse if they had the right partisan connections.

This state of affairs was exacerbated by the overt interference of the party in the selection process of the top administrators in public enterprises in favor of party officials over labor leaders or technocrats. Party-hired executives rendered the public sector an obedient subject to party dictates and proved to its employees that recognition of their services had nothing to do with their social contribution but was simply a function of their partisan affiliation. Even services that were supposed to be provided equitably to the whole population, such as access to a telephone, became subject to party favoritism, especially since the growing demand for public goods and services was not met by an increase in production. The scarcity of public services allowed corrupt bureaucracies to enforce their own criteria for rationing.

Typical of the use of arbitrary partisan political power were the procurement policies of OTE, the state telecommunications firm, and its notorious director Anastasios Tobras. He and his closest associates were able to appropriate substantial kickbacks from local contractors and foreign multinationals for selling equipment at prices substantially greater than international norms. The government tolerated this behavior because Tobras had established an extensive telephone-tapping network, eavesdropping both on Papandreou's foes and his associates, something invaluable to the leader of PASOK. This mutually beneficial cooperation led to the nomination of Tobras as one of PASOK's candidates in the June 1989 elections.

Within this context of corruption and party favoritism, the Greek businessman knew that it would be more lucrative to spend his mornings waiting outside the office of the minister of trade to secure export subsidies (especially if he had promised a campaign contribution) than if he devoted his time at his "productive unit" trying to find ways to improve its international competitiveness. By 1987, state grants and interest-rate subsidies amounted to about two-thirds the value of the approved investment projects (nearly all projects that were submitted were approved) and represented 3 percent of GDP.[30]

The subsidization of anyone willing to collaborate with the party-state structure led not only to public sector overindebtness and an expansion of the tradition of political cronyism, but it also created a dependency in the population on a state-subsidy mentality to the detriment of independent initiative (at least within the context of legality), productivity, and a sense of social responsibility. Traditional notions of shrewdness and ingenuity were channeled away from the search for productive means of wealth acquisition into the search of sophisticated means for appropriating of public subsidies.

The case of George Koskotas provides the best illustration of how the requirements of party-state control were fused with private corruption and greed at the highest reaches of government and finance. Koskotas was a business man who arrived in Greece in 1979 and in 1984 acquired the Bank of Crete using funds of dubious origin. By the end of 1987 he had expanded his activities to equipment leasing, newspaper publishing, and the control of one of the biggest athletic associations in Greece. This personal empire was achieved through the embezzlement of Bank of Crete funds and through his close ties with the PASOK government. His ability to maintain his illegal activities for so many years was a result not only of his bribing of top government officials, but mainly through his political allegiance to the party of Andreas Papandreou. In exchange for turning a blind eye to his illegal empire-building, Koskotas mobilized his publishing empire to serve PASOK's party-state propaganda and electoral campaigns.

PASOK's handling of problematic companies and pension funds were two areas that undermined the stabilization plan. In its first term PASOK had assumed control of the most inefficient and overindebted problematic companies of the private sector. Problematic firms included those enterprises whose financial obligations to public commercial banks did not permit continued operation under their previous owner. The understanding under which the government undertook this responsibility was that it would liquidate nonviable companies while it would socialize, modernize, and render competitive the remaining ones. During the sta-

30. OECD Economic Surveys, *Greece 1989/1990*, 67.

bilization period, none of that happened. The government systematically exploited the socialization process in order to put these companies under the command of party members whose main concern was not the improvement of productivity but the establishment of firm partisan control over the employees.

As a result, these companies stagnated and, if anything, their competitiveness and financial solvency deteriorated. In fact, the Organization of Business Reconstruction (OAE), the bureaucratic framework created in 1983 to oversee their modernization and privatization, ended up overseeing only the perpetuation of a policy of inaction toward resolving their problems.

The government spent about 1 percent of the country's GDP, about 50 percent of total government grants and subsidies and 20 percent of total bank credit, in order to finance the exponential growth of the problematical firms' losses during 1985–87.[31] The principal reason was not just to prevent further unemployment, which would discredit PASOK domestically. Rather, the party state desired to establish political influence over thousands of families whose income depended on the employment of one of their members in those firms, thus maintaining economic (and thus political) control over key electoral constituencies (northern Greece, Greater Athens) and some strategic productive sectors (shipyards, construction material, mining).

In its effort to incorporate an ever-growing portion of the population under the partisan state, PASOK used (or rather abused) the social security system, to the point that some of the biggest funds, such as OGA (farmers), NAT (the maritime industry) or IKA (general), which had been breaking even or showing profits in 1980, had a deficit by 1987 of approximately 5 percent of GDP, more than half of which was financed through government grants.[32] In a matter of years PASOK had transformed a system of social security into one of social welfare without developing its financing capacities through the greater participation of the entrepreneurial class. Thus, in eight years (1980–88) the number of people employed per pensioner fell from 2.8 to 2, while the pension fund's deficit was increasing annually at the expense of the state budget at a rate of 0.4 percent of GDP.[33]

Large segments of the population (peasants, refugees from Turkey, Egypt, and Eastern Europe, left-wing participants in the anti–German resistance) received pensions without having made prior contributions and without any specific government plan to secure the financial solven-

31. Ibid., 61.
32. Bank of Greece, *Statistical Bulletin* (1990), 59.
33. OECD Economic Surveys, *Greece 1989/1990*, 47–48.

cy of the pension funds which were allocating these additional benefits. Moreover, selective electoral groups saw their level increase substantially. As a result, not only did the ratio of contributors to pensioners fall radically, but essentially this situation gave incentives to the Greek population to retire as early as possible and enjoy the benefits of this all-encompassing welfare system,. As for PASOK, it established a firm clientele among the immigrants, the aged, and the peasantry, who felt that the most insecure part of their lifetime was at last becoming the state's responsibility.

THE POLITICS OF THE UNDERGROUND ECONOMY

The continued expansion of the party state as a means of ensuring electoral dominance faced a severe challenge because it developed during a period of deep crisis and substantial financial constraints. The party-state structure was unable to continue providing all the benefits that were required for the maintenance of its electoral clientele. Thus, some kind of a market mechanism had to step in and complement the state's allocation of goods and services. Since a neoliberal economy favoring the elite would alienate most of the state-subsidized capitalist class as well as workers and salaried classes and run counter to the principles and requirements of the party-state model, the PASOK government encouraged the growth of the underground economy, an even more ruthlessly competitive, profit-oriented, and unregulated market structure than even the neoliberal model suggested by the IMF and OECD.

The financial locomotive of the Greek underground economy was mass tax evasion practiced by practically every segment of the population. The leading tax evaders were self-employed professionals such as lawyers and private doctors. Then came retail-trade entrepreneurs who, as has already been noted, managed to bypass the VAT constraint by failing to issue register receipts for the purchases by the public, and therefore hid most of their actual earnings.[34] There was also the whole range of medium-sized handicraft enterprises and retail shops (approximately 430,000 of them) that, according to the rough estimates of the Ministry of the National Economy, ended up declaring only 30 percent of their gross earnings.[35]

It is interesting to note that in 1987 the estimated number of unregistered, and therefore untaxed, handicraft units in the greater Athens area alone amounted to three thousand. The operation and viability of such

34. Yiannis Marinos, "Undermining of the Private Initiative" [in Greek] *Oikonomikos Tahidromos*, 2 July 1987, p. 5.
35. Ibid., 6.

enterprises depended upon this massive tax evasion. Otherwise, given the extremely high real rate of return on government bonds for the financing of the fiscal deficit (approximately 6 percent) Greek entrepreneurs would have totally disinvested from the industrial sector, whose rate of return was often negative. Thus, the private sector's participation in the country's gross capital formation would have ceased, unless the government tolerated tax evasion, indirectly subsidizing private investment. This also explains the boom in the construction, restaurant, and night club industries, all activities which are extremely conducive to tax evasion and related underground activities.

In addition, since the salaried sector of the population, especially employees in the public sector whose income tax was directly deducted by the internal revenue service, had to bear a disproportionately high share of the stabilization sacrifices, it resorted to tax evasion in order to maintain its standard of living and finance its increasing consumer needs, leading to the emergence of an underground labor market (without any tax or social-welfare deductions). Practically all salaried employees had a second or even third source of income, sometimes related, sometimes not, to their "visible" employment. Thus internal revenue service employees worked as financial accountants in the private companies of the tax district they supervised; highly skilled architects in the ministry of public works became invisible partners in major construction firms; public high school teachers offered private lessons to students who wanted to supplement inadequate training acquired in the deteriorating public educational system in order to gain a competitive edge over their fellow students in national examinations; technicians in the Public Power Corporation (DEI) operated neighborhood electrical appliance repair shops; policemen – the only citizens legally allowed to carry guns in Greece – became private bodyguards of rich celebrities. Others were willing to do any work that was at hand: bookstore salesmen become late-night videoclub clerks; hairdressers served as waitresses in jammed summer bars; bus drivers baked hamburgers in small fast-food restaurants.

In short, the expansion of the underground market satisfied all the unfulfilled needs and desires of the national economy while at the same time compensating for the income lost during the stabilization process. Even the state itself engaged in some kind of underground deals (at least in terms of national accounting) with is employees, thus undermining the austerity that it had imposed on them. Instead of giving full indexation to protesting public-sector unions, the government often offered them additional social security concessions (further decreases in the retirement age, subsidized social tourism) as well as public-service benefits (deductions in the electricity bill for the National Electricity Company employees, free passes to public transportation employees and their families.)

Apart from the tax-evasion aspect of the underground economy, the state intervention in the trade and financial mechanisms of the market spread the parallel-market structure to other parts of the economy as well. The unregistered barter of goods and services became endemic as monetary tightness squeezed legal economic activity. An electrical appliances importer and an official of OTE would often exchange a Japanese VCR for a speedy telephone connection (which usually takes five to seven years); a successful plumbing repair would be paid for with a bottle of imported scotch. These all became common practices and necessary means of providing and rationing goods and services that the paternalistic capitalist model was either unable to provide or incapable of allocating. The major casualty in double and triple jobholding was the quality and quantity of work in one's primary job, a point infrequently discussed by the proponents of the informal economy.

Finally, there was a boom in the illegal currency and loan markets, abetted by PASOK policies. Monopolistic centralization in the commercial banking allowed the government to secure cheap credit to finance its debt, constricting the credit market. Even though the investment needs of the private sector were substantially decreased, its financial needs for current transactions and obligations had to be financed. Since public banks were often unable to do this, a parallel financial market developed. The exorbitant interest rates charged by loan sharks, often 20 percent per month, created new financial elites in Athens as well as in the agricultural periphery.

The growth of this parallel financial structure illustrates the liquidity problems of the private sector and the tremendous amounts of hot money floating around the economy as a result of government practices. A similar phenomenon was observed in the foreign-currency markets. A substantial part of the invisible receipts in shipping and to a lesser extent in tourism were absorbed at higher than official exchange rates by a currency black market made possible because the state had overvalued the drachma. Hard currency was then sold at a profit to Greeks heading abroad who wanted to spend more in foreign species than the government would allow them, to importers who had no access to Central Bank reserves, or even to speculators who wanted to establish or increase their Swiss bank accounts.

Thus, while the underground economy served as an escape valve for discontent, it also undermined the operation of the legal economy, and, more importantly, contributed to undermining social services and public infrastructure by evading payments. Again, short-term electoral and political gains were made at the expense of medium and long-term socioeconomic welfare.

EROSION OF SOCIAL ACHIEVEMENTS

The inconsistencies between public discourse and actual practice, the accumulated financial problems of the public sector, and the ossification of malfunctioning administrative structures, were all characteristic of PASOK's second term in office. As a result, not only was the stabilization program undermined, but even much of the progress made in the social realm during the first term was reversed. The growth of the party-state apparatus and the widening of the underground economy dashed hopes for the successful implementation of previously initiated reforms in health, education, and labor relations.

During its first term, PASOK took various steps in restructuring, modernizing, and planning the educational system. However, in the second term education became one of the victims of PASOK's austerity program. As tables 7 and 21 show, the average percentage share of the budget devoted to education was even lower than during the New Democracy regime in 1981. This put an end of PASOK's effort to improve the quantity and quality of education and to reduce the social and regional inequalities of the existing system.

As a response to this neglect of education by the government, professors engaged in a bitter struggle against the austerity program, resulting in a further decline in educational standards, since their prolonged annual strike at the end of every academic year aimed at the undermining of the national university admission examinations. Throughout the academic year, university students engaged in sit-ins at their schools and marches on the ministry of education, resulting in endless days of lost classes and educational decay. As a result of this constant turmoil in higher education, the learning process itself degenerated. Class attendance became optional, interfering with lectures became a regular occurrence, and, in general, university education was reduced to a mere "paper chase." PASOK's budgetary cuts increased tensions and induced administrative chaos. The government, instead of mediating in an impartial manner to reduce sociopolitical tensions, continued to promote its student and faculty followers, turning education into an arena of partisan confrontation.

The most problematic situation that emerged during PASOK's term though, was that of "parallel," or underground, education. Although the number of university students rose from 14,600 in 1981 to 23,000 in 1988,[36] universities were still unable to grant admission to all applicants,

36. PASOK, *Social Contract* [in Greek] [Pre-electoral informative publications of the 1989 campaign], p. 17.

especially given the growing demand for postsecondary education. Those who were unable to secure a place in a university and who did not have enough resources to follow thousands of other Greek students abroad, mostly to Italy, Britain, France, and the United States, enriched the so-called "centers of study." These institutions, with high fees but not necessarily high standards, provided some sort of a professionally oriented training and diploma public sector, though not one officially recognized by the state or public-sector employers.

The bulk of the parallel education market took place at the high-school level. Parents, realizing that the competition for university admission was becoming more and more acute, increasingly paid exorbitant sums to private preparatory schools to compensate for the inadequacies of the public school system. The *frontistiria* – private preparatory night schools aimed at the national admission examinations – which had existed since the 1970s, mushroomed throughout the country in the 1980s. These were complemented by foreign-language institutes preparing students for foreign examinations such as the SAT (for the U.S.) or GCE (for Britain). On top of all this, those who could afford it hired a professor for individual instruction of their children at home. It would not be an exaggeration to say that families with children between the ages of fifteen and nineteen spent a substantial fraction of their monthly budget to this thriving underground economy, which undermined PASOK's effort towards the establishment of an egalitarian and high-quality public education system.

In the area of health (tables 7 and 21), PASOK maintained its budgetary commitment to improving the country's public health system. The National Health System (ESY) was implemented during the second term, and through it the government funneled substantial funds to improve both material infrastructure and human resources, especially in the provinces. PASOK's accomplishments in the health field were sustained and expanded through the evolution and expansion of a public health network.

However, the evils of statification and the underground economy eroded many of the positive results accompanying the transformation of the health system. The relatively low wage level (imposed by the state) for doctors in public hospitals resulted in the flight of most prominent doctors to the private sector. Since doctors were not permitted to perform in both public and private hospitals, the private hospitals, offering higher wage rates, attracted the most skilled, experienced and well-educated surgeons. This reality significantly weakened people's confidence in the public health system and those who could afford it turned to foreign countries or private hospitals for critical and urgent operations or treatment. Moreover, despite the decentralization of health, patients rushed to the metropolitan centers for medical coverage as the regional hospitals were not yet fully operating or presented severe organizational inadequacies.

The accumulation of patients in the cities, along with the lack of doctors and staff, led to extreme congestion in public hospitals. As a result, patients would receive cursory attention or wait months for surgery. A widespread underground economy for health services emerged. The profiteering mentality of doctors and people's willingness to accept their exploitation enhanced the commercialization of health, already practiced during the preceding rightest government. The doctors in the National Health System, apart from accepting bribes (*fakelaki*) for preferential treatment in public hospitals, also maintained clandestine private offices where they provided treatment to those who were able to pay more than their social security contribution. The end result of this situation was that despite PASOK's positive efforts they were still unable to cure many of the evils of the health system and did not eliminate its social inequalities.

With regard to the rights of the labor movement, PASOK took greater legal measures than any other postwar Greek government to promote an effective union movement. The centerpiece of its labor policy was the union law of 1982. It granted protection from layoffs to union officials and required employers to furnish facilities for union meetings at work sites having over one hundred union members. It also prohibited lockouts, legalized sympathy strikes, and strengthened the right to strike by reducing required notice to one day and eliminating the necessity for formal negotiations with employers. Finally, labor centers and federations affiliated with GSEE were obliged to inscribe more than a hundred unions, largely communist, that had been excluded under previous governments.

Despite these legal successes, the trade-union movement was constantly undermined in practice. We noted earlier how manipulative PASOK proved to be vis-à-vis the unions during its first term. The situation deteriorated during the second term. As a result, by 1987, the working class of Greece was unable to effectively resist the stabilization program from which it had experienced only one-sided sacrifices and economic recession. When some labor unions decided to stage a series of strikes protesting against the National Collective Labor Contract of 1987 (thus breaking the social pact signed with PASOK) their actions were undermined by the PASOK union bureaucracy, which was following the directives of the party state.

PASOK's policies were partially successful in eroding labor's capacity to mobilize. The expansion of the underground economy prevented a fall in the living standards of some workers and also weakened working-class unity by encouraging individualistic tendencies that blocked effective social action. Many trade-union leaders were under the control of PASOK and obstructed any mobilization against government policies.

Party-state control over the labor movement soon brought about its fragmentation along the lines of party allegiance. While left-wing sectors engaged in a direct confrontation against PASOK in an effort to maintain the worker's standard of living and social role, the rest of the unionists either sided with New Democracy and pursued obstructive policies or attached themselves to PASOK's party state in an effort to artificially sustain their authority over the workers movement.

The net result was that by the end of PASOK's second term, the trade-union movement was very far from performing its role representing the working classes as defenders of their socioeconomic interests. Divided with one sector subordinate to the party state and its austerity policies, the union movement was unable to put forward any coherent and substantial alternative to those of PASOK or New Democracy. Effectively, PASOK had come full circle: from being proponents of an independent and class-conscious working class struggling against the patrimonial state it became a party obsessed with controlling and subordinating the trade unions to the shifting policies of the party state.

POST-STABILIZATION CRISES AND THE EXIT OF PASOK

At the beginning of 1988 the stabilization program officially reached its end and it was at that point that its inherent contradictions intensified and its superficial successes were reversed. Domestically, although the country experienced an upturn in economic growth and a revitalization in both public and private investment (see Table 15) this only took place at the price of growing fiscal imbalances. Gross government debt increased by 24 percent in just two years and it became evident that this deficit was on an unsustainable trajectory that elevated it from the status of a serious macroeconomic problem to that of a major structural constraint.

The repercussions were soon felt. Debt-financing needs compelled the government to increase real interest rates by more than 100 percent in 1988–89. This increase in the cost of borrowing, paired with a lack of confidence in the government's ability or willingness to restrain its fiscal appetite, severely affected the quality of private investment and patterns of private consumption. Thus, real-estate speculation skyrocketed (the growth of construction's share in gross capital formation rose from 4.9 percent in 1987 to 7.5 percent in 1989) while consumerism became very widespread (gross-private-consumption growth was 4.1 percent in 1989 as opposed to 0.7 percent in 1987). In completing the vicious circle of internal imbalances, these speculatory and consumerist tendencies over-heated the economy to the point that strong inflationary pressures (like those of 1985) started appearing once more by early 1989.

These internal imbalances were of such a magnitude that they ended up reversing the stabilization program's external achievements as well. Growing import penetration and debt-servicing requirements more than doubled the current-account deficit, while fading confidence in the drachma and government economic policy as a whole led to a rapid fall in capital inflows and invisible receipts. Despite all the sacrifices of the austerity period, the macroeconomic successes achieved by 1987 proved to be short-lived. Public deficits and the country's dependence on for-eign and highly volatile sources of inflows meant that when the govern-ment decided to aim for economic expansion in 1988–89, the economy was unable to achieve it without further economic imbalances.

By mid-1989, the end of PASOK's term in office, the economic situ-ation was deteriorating. Nothing reflects better PASOK's contradictory, zigzag policies than the macroeconomic indicators given in table 15. In the course of just four years, the country experienced annual rates of growth which were anywhere between 4 and −0.5 percent. At the same time, investment varied from −8 to 9 percent of GDP, while inflation fluctuated between 14 and 22 percent. The constantly changing cycles of economic recovery and recession, apart from handicapping any prospect of economic stability, demonstrate that PASOK's two consecutive terms in office did little to confront the deficient economic structures that it had inherited in 1981. Greek economic performance remained equally if not more dependent upon external contingencies and centers of power and upon local political and entrepreneurial monopolies than under New Democracy. The only consistent macroeconomic indicator was that of the mounting government debt, a testimony to PASOK's biggest economic "achievement": the creation of a gigantic party-state apparatus which thrived upon the burnt-land structures of the paternalistic state capitalism that the governments of the right had created and developed since the postwar period.

During Papandreou's second term in office, in the aftermath of the failed five-year plan and stabilization program, a growing number of vot-ers came to realize that PASOK was incapable of resolving the basic socioeconomic problem facing the country and was ineffective in dis-mantling the prevailing structural impediments to the country's growth and prosperity. Even loyal supporters of PASOK felt that the party lacked a coherent developmental vision and a clearly articulated, feasible strategy for tackling the country's major problems. Papandreou's govern-ment never had the political will to overtly confront the burnt-land structures and consistently prosecute a radical plan for the ultimate restructuring and modernization of the Greek economic system and society. PASOK adapted to the traditional patronage and paternalistic tactics of Greek political and economic life that its right-wing predecessors had developed. More importantly, it perpetuated and even enhanced these tendencies, thus undermining some of the earlier promising social and economic initiatives.

During 1988–89 a process of rapid electoral decline for PASOK was irreversibly set into motion. Earlier the PASOK regime had substituted welfare reforms for basic shifts in social power and economic transformation and had successfully retained and even expanded its electoral base. During its second term it increased its patronage activity and state transfers in the course of losing its capacity to sustain its welfare program, holding on to a substantial sector of its electoral clientele. In the end, however, its questionable manipulation of public-enterprise funding and blurring of public and private use of state resources had led to pervasive and highly visible corruption practices, and charges along these lines unhinged enough voters to provide the opposition with a slim plurality.

Despite deep disillusionment among its electoral followers it took a series of sensational scandals to finally erode PASOK's hold on the voters. In large part PASOK's continued high vote (40 percent and over) reflected the voters' perception of the unattractiveness of the opposition, as well as PASOK's rhetorical threats about the return of the right.

A series of events during the last year in power marked the tortuous course of PASOK's decline. Andreas Papandreou's sickness and three-month hospitalization created a state of confusion and a power vacuum in PASOK's highly personal and centralized government, which was now characterized by irresolution and ineffectiveness, unable to tackle even the most immediate problems. Papandreou's illness in a period of economic stagnation shortly after the failure of the austerity program eroded public confidence in PASOK's leadership. The unfavorable political climate was exacerbated by the simultaneous explosion of a momentous bank scandal involving PASOK–linked businessman Koskotas, the owner of the Bank of Crete, who was accused of embezzling some $210 million. The investigation revealed a chronic and chaotic state of corruption in the political arena, encompassing ministers and government officials. The opposition and the press, both domestic and foreign, engaged in an aggressive campaign against the PASOK government in a coordinated attempt to discredit its political authority. Amid charges of political corruption and disillusionment with the state of affairs in the social sphere, parliamentary elections took place in June 1989.

In this unfavorable context PASOK, after an eight-year term of government, lost power in the June elections. What was a surprise was its still impressive 39.2 percent of the vote (New Democracy received 44.2 percent, and the Communists 13.2 percent), one of the largest for a socialist party in Europe. PASOK demonstrated that it had established an enduring political clientele.

As soon as the results of the elections were made known, PASOK proposed a long-term coalition government of the left with the Communists and others, which had the requisite parliamentary majority, totaling over 52 percent of the vote. However, the Communist party, with 28 M.P.'s at its disposal, in one of its most bizarre tactical moves, formed a government with its archenemies on the right, New Democracy. "The two-party government, due to the fact that it lacked a common platform, declared itself to be a government of short duration (three months) and limited objectives."[37]

With all domestic and foreign-policy issues frozen, the coalition proclaimed a salvage operation, freeing the political world from all contaminating scandals. The alliance proceeded to launch a legal campaign against PASOK leaders. Andreas Papandreou and a number of former cabinet members were to stand trail before a special tribunal. The allegations were that in 1988 Papandreou received more than six million dollars in stolen Bank of Crete funds, that he abused his public office by forcing public agencies to deposit more than $3.3 million in the Bank of Crete, and that he tapped the telephones of opposition leaders and his own cabinet.

However, at the grass-roots level the prosecution provoked reactions contrary to those expected by the new government. The trend was to rally around PASOK and come to its rescue. A parallel political association of liberal and left personalities (prominent elements of the independent left, politicians from the center-right, and ex-PASOK supporters) appeared in opposition to what was perceived as a political persecution of PASOK.

The results of the second election on 5 November 1989, in which New Democracy received 46.2 percent, PASOK 41 percent, and the Coalition of the Left 11 percent, failed to create a viable parliamentary majority for any party. The results were a victory of sorts for PASOK, which managed to regain approximately two percentage points. Through this election result PASOK realized all its goals: (1) preventing New Democracy from achieving an absolute majority in parliament; (2) expressing voters' disapproval of the Communists' experiment with a right-wing alliance in order to minimize a repeat; and (3) restoring self-confidence among party loyalists.[38]

37. Alexandros Papanastasiou, *Demos: The PASOK Review*, no. 1 (April 1990), p. 15.
38. Ibid., 23.

In the political deliberations following the November 1989 elections, the Coalition of the Left again steadfastly refused to form a coalition with PASOK. Upon the insistence of the Communists that the right also participate in any formula to form a government, PASOK proposed a compromise plan whereby all three parties agreed to an ecumenical government with a mutually acceptable nonparty personality as prime minister. This government was a compromise dictated by national necessity, made feasible by the existing balance of political forces and by the serious and complex issues Greek society was facing. Dr. Xenophon Zolotas, a member of the Greek Academy of Letters and a conservative economist, headed the government which lasted until April 1990, when the withdrawal of the New Democracy ministers led to new elections.

In the elections of April 1990, New Democracy at long last succeeded in winning 150 seats in Parliament (of a total of 300), and secured one more vote from the small center-right DIANA (Democratic Renewal) party. The electoral system which allowed Theodoros Katsikis, who merely won 388 votes, to become DIANA's pivot M.P., established the margin for a New Democracy majority.

In conclusion, one could assert that by the end of 1988 a critical situation of political corruption, economic stagnation and public disillusionment with the lack of social vision was widely experienced within Greek society and precipitated PASOK's fall. PASOK retained, however, a substantial sector of its electoral base in part because the opposition was perceived to be even worse in terms of democratic freedoms, social welfare, and economics. PASOK also retained widespread support in part due to early reforms and, more importantly, from extensive populist payoffs, which had created a vast net of electoral supporters. Macroeconomic failures were compensated by micropolitical favors. The November 1989 election results established PASOK as a permanent, stable political force still capable of capitalizing on popular antirightist sentiment. Nonetheless, by April 1990, a plurality of citizens were sufficiently troubled by the political and economic impasse to vote for New Democracy, as the right managed at least temporarily to convince a plurality of the public that it could provide viable and effective government.

CONCLUSION

The course of PASOK's development in Greece differed substantially from that of its Mediterranean counterparts and of its initial ideological identity. It did not pursue the vigorous neoliberal policies of Spain's González nor did it move to realize any deep structural changes envisioned in its original program. Instead, PASOK essentially pursued a welfare-patronage approach largely geared toward building and consolidating an enduring party state on the basis of existing configurations of power. Hence, Greece experienced neither the neoliberal restructuring of Spain nor the enduring welfare reforms of Northern European social democratic governments. In essence, Papandreou pursued what can be described as "heterodox orthodoxy" – the pursuit of political power on the basis of a mixture of traditional clientele-patronage organization and radical populist-nationalist rhetoric. PASOK 's orthodoxy becomes evident the further one moves along its political trajectory: beginning with a radical socialist program, it quickly adopted a series of populist-welfare reforms, followed by an inconclusive stabilization program (and reversal of earlier reforms) and ended with a shifting set of liberalizing reforms for private capital accompanied by spurts of state spending.

The incapacity of PASOK to transcend the historical constraints of traditional patronage politics and transform and modernize the state was not predetermined. As has been shown, opportunities abounded for consequential changes; political mandates and economic crises were not effectively exploited. The failures of PASOK were as much the result of political choices as they were structurally conditioned. At each political conjuncture (the hundred-day program, the five-year plan, stabilization crises), the PASOK leadership squandered historical moments to implement measures that could have modernized the Greek economy and society.

Nonetheless, despite its failures, PASOK's capacity to retain the electoral support of four out of ten voters is testimony to its organizational ability to manipulate outside resources and popular symbols and dispense state patronage.[39] Neither the left nor the right was able to provide a powerful countermessage or convincing ideological appeal to undermine PASOK's electoral machinery in the countryside or even in the urban centers. The many who were nourished by the party state had either lost their ideological idealism or had found in PASOK an adequate instrument for satisfying their particularistic needs. Papandreou's capacity to transform PASOK from an innovative political movement into a centralized party patronage machine while retaining the core of his electoral support testifies to his political cleverness, a quality, however, that aided little in preventing Greece from tumbling into last place among Western European countries and into the hands of the traditional right.

---

39. As this book goes to press, Papandreou holds an almost insurmountable lead in the polls over Greece's right-wing prime minister Constantine Mitsotakis.

Table 1: Burnt-Land Structures: General Economic Indicators (1960–80)

	1961–65	1966–70	1971–75	1976–80
GDP Growth	7.68	6.62	5.72	4.18
Fixed Capital Investment (FCI)	24.00	27.00	27.00	23.00
Agriculture	24.00	19.60	19.70	14.00
Industry	14.40	17.00	20.30	21.40
Services	49.80	50.60	50.50	52.50

As percentage of GDP.

SOURCE: Andrew Freris, *The Greek Economy in the Twentieth Century* (New York, 1986), p.156.

Definition of burnt-land structures: in the development literature, a term referring to an economy characterized by a backward and undercommercialized agriculture, a dependent commercial and industrial entrepreneurial class, and a patrimonial state that tends to accentuate underdevelopment.

Table 2: Trade Deficits and "Invisible Receipts" (1960–80)

	1961–65	1966–70	1971–75	1976–80
Trade Deficit	481	836	2319	4908
Invisible Receipts	330	679	1488	3426

In millions of U.S. dollars; current prices.

SOURCE: Freris, *The Greek Economy*, 188.

Table 3: Sectorial Growth (1960–79)

(1) Average annual percentage change in output of industry and services
(1970 prices)

	1960–73	1974–79
Industry	10.8	4.4
Services	7.5	4.8

(2) Contribution of sectors to GDP increase (= 100)

	1960–73	1974–79
Industry	25.8	14.7
Agriculture	10.6	4.7
Services	50.1	77.2
Energy	13.4	3.4

SOURCE: Freris, *The Greek Economy*, 157

Table 4: Structural Changes in the Composition of Industrial Output (1953–79)

	1953	1963	1974	1979
Textiles, clothing, shoes	34.7	26.4	25.5	27.2
Food, beverage, tobacco	26.8	22.3	17.8	18.8
Metallurgical	0.6	1.7	7.0	5.9
Mechanical, engineering	12.3	13.2	13.0	11.1

As percentage of total industrial production.

SOURCE: Freris, *The Greek Economy*, 158.

Table 5: Structure of Exports (1965–80)

	1965	1970	1975	1980
Textiles	21.7	15.3	25.9	34.8
Alumina	13.7	19.3	6.1	6.1

As percentage of total exports.

SOURCE: Freris, *The Greek Economy*, 190.

Table 6: Main Economic Indicators of the First Term

	1974–81	1982	1983	1984	1985	1982–85
GDP growth	3.1	0.4	0.39	2.7	3.1	1.6
GDP per capital growth	1.9	-0.15	2.5	1.6	2.8	1.7
Gross capital formation[1]	-1.9	-1.9	-1.3	-5.7	5.2	-0.9
Fixed investment total[1,2]	15.2	14.5	14.8	14.8	14.7	14.7
– Private sector	10.0	8.8	8.0	7.4	7.2	7.8
– Public sector	5.2	5.7	6.8	7.4	7.6	6.9
Inflation	16.8	20.7	18.1	17.9	18.3	18.7
Productivity	1.7	1.2	-0.6	2.4	2.1	1.3
Unemployment	2.3	5.8	9.0	9.3	8.7	8.2
Gross government debt[1]	26.3	36.1	41.2	49.5	57.9	46.2
Trade deficit growth		-11.5	-9.1	-0.6	17.1	

[1] As percentage of GDP.
[2] Housing excluded.

SOURCES: OECD Economic Surveys, *Greece 1984/1985* (1985), p. 36; International Monetary Fund, *International Financial Statistics: Yearbook 1990* (1991), pp. 378–81; European Commission, *European Economy: Annual Economic Report 1990–91* (November 1990), p. 281.

Table 7: Education and Health during the First Term

	1981	1982	1983	1984	1985	1982–85
Education	7.9	10.0	9.1	8.3	9.7	9.3
Health and Social Security	8.9	12.4	11.9	8.9	9.2	10.6

As percentage of total budget expenditures.

SOURCE: National Accounts of the Greek Government (Years 1981, 1982, 1983, 1984, 1985).

Table 8: Wages and Pensions during the First Term

	1981	1982	1983	1984	1985
Wage	27.0	33.5	19.0	26.0	20.0
Minimum Wage	23.0	48.0	15.5	26.0	18.0
Government Pensions	23.0	35.0	19.0	29.0	24.0

Gross percent change from previous year.

SOURCE: OECD Economic Surveys, *Greece 1984/1985*, 13, 27.

Table 9: Employment by the Central Government

1981	1982	1983	1984	1985
0.4	3.95	4.35	6.0	11.2

Percentage growth of ordinary budget expenditures by the central government devoted to wages of its employees.

SOURCES: Bank of Greece, *Monthly Statistical Bulletin* (November 1985), pp. 54–55; Demetrios Chalikias, *Annual Report of the Governor for the Year 1985,* p. 122.

Table 10: Local Government Transfers from the Central Government

1981	1982	1983	1984	1985
2.79	4.0	4.13	6.4	6.7

As percentage of total budget expenditures.

SOURCE: National Accounts of the Greek Government (Years: 1981, 1982, 1983, 1984, 1985).

Table 11: Borrowing and Investment of Greek Industrialists by the State

	1981	1982	1983	1984
Investment*	108	101	111	28
Credit*	540	664	765	18
Real interest rate**		–9.7	–7.1	–5.4

*In nominal billions of U.S. dollars
**Nominal interest inflation.
SOURCES: OECD Economic Surveys, *GREECE 1984/1985*, 59; Bank of Greece, *Statistical Bulletin* (1985), p. 42.

Table 12: Industrial Output: Burnt-Land Era vs. PASOK Era

	1974	1985
Textiles, clothing, shoes	25.4	18.3
Food, beverage, tobacco	17.8	15.4
Metallurgical	7.0	0.1
Mechanical, engineering	13.0	8.4

As percentage of total industrial output.

SOURCES: Katseli, *Structural Adjustment*, 96; Freris, *The Greek Economy*, 158.

Table 13: EC Transfers during the Five–Year Plan

	Growth (% Change)		
	1982/83	1983/84	1984/85
Regional Fund	28.1	4.9	97.2
Agricultural subsidies	54.3	18.8	26.4
Transfers to public corporations	113.5	17.4	6.5

SOURCES: Dimitrios Chalikias, *Annual Report of the Governor for the Year 1983 (1984)*, p. 98; idem, *Annual Report*, 131.

Table 14: Capital Flight Approximation

1981	1982	1983	1984	1985
–364.5	70.6	357.2	312.3	–22.4

In millions of U.S. dollars.

SOURCES: Chalikias, *Annual Report of the Governor for the Year 1983*, 102; idem, *Annual Report of the Governor for the Year 1985*, 136.

Table 15: Major Economic Indicators during the Second Term

	1985	1986	1987	1988	1989	1985–89*
GDP growth	3.1	1.2	-0.4	4.0	2.5	2.08
Gross fixed capital formation**	5.2	-5.7	-3.2	9.0	6.6	2.38
Inflation	18.3	2.2	15.7	13.9	14.3	16.8
Fixed-investment growth	5.2	-6.2	-7.8	2.0	–	–
– Public	10.0	-18.3	-29.2	3.0	–	–
– Private	2.3	1.7	3.5	11.2	–	–
5. Productivity	2.1	0.9	-0.3	2.8	1.8	1.46
6. Unemployment	8.7	8.2	8.0	8.5	8.5	8.4
7. Current-account deficit**	8.2	5.2	2.5	1.5	3.4	4.16
8. Capital-account deficit growth	39.1	-35.0	0.01	3.8	5.9	2.76
9. Trade–deficit growth	17.1	-9.3	22.0	10.0	12.7	10.5
10. Gross government debt**	57.9	58.3	63.3	70.3	78.1	65.6
11. Money growth (M3)	27.3	19.1	24.6	23.0	–	–
12. Long-term real interest rate	-2.5	-6.2	1.7	2.7	3.7	-0.12

*Annual average for the second term.
**As percentage of GDP.

SOURCES: OECD Economic Surveys, *Greece 1989/1990*, 18, 22; IMF, *Yearbook 1990*, 378-81; European Commission, *Annual Economic Report 1990–91*, 281.

Table 16: The Populist Crisis of 1985

	1982–84	1985
Internal imbalances		
Money growth (M1)	19.1	24.4
Growth of real labor costs in production	0.93	2.7
Gross government debt★	42.2	57.9
Fixed investment in private sector★	8.0	7.1
Net general government borrowing	8.6	13.8
External imbalances		
External debt★★	10.8	15.7
Current account★	-4.46	-8.2
Trade deficit growth	-7.0	17.1
Capital account deficit growth	-0.1	39.1

★ As percentage of GDP.
★★ In billions of U.S. dollars.
SOURCES: OECD Economic Surveys, *Greece 1984/1985*, 24, 36, 41–42; idem, *Greece 1989/1990*, 18, 22, 38, 123; European Commission, *Annual Economic Report 1990–91*, 281.

17: Industrial Production and the Stabilization Program

	1985	1987
Nonagroalimentary manufacturing	96.5	96.4
Metal products	89.7	82.0
Capital goods	81.1	75.9

(1980=100)

SOURCE: OECD Economic Surveys, *Greece 1989/1990*, 118.

Table 18: Size of the Public Sector

	1981	1985	1988
General government expenditure	39.7	47.8	49.4
Public enterprises' expenditure	9.9	14.4	13.2
Total public sector	49.6	62.2	62.5

As percentage of GDP.

SOURCE: OECD Economic Surveys, *Greece 1989/1990*, 42.

Table 19: Employment by the Central Government

1986	1987	1988	1989
1.7	2.2	1.25	3.0

Percentage growth of ordinary budget expenditures by the central government devoted to wages of its employees.

SOURCE: Bank of Greece, *Statistical Bulletin* (1990), pp. 54–55.

Table 20: EC Transfers during the Second Term

	1986	1987	1988	1989
Mediterranean Integrated Programs	–	823	52.3	-53.3
Regional Fund	421	-6.7	4.0	72.8
Agricultural Subsidies	79	8.5	6.0	32.1

As percentage change from previous year.

SOURCES: Dimitrios Chalikias, *Annual Report of the Governor for the Year 1987*, 142; idem, *Annual Report of the Governor for the Year 1989* (1990), 141.

Table 21: Education and Health during the Second Term

	1986	1987	1988	1989	1986–89
Education	8.8	7.6	6.6	6.8	7.5
Health and Social Security	9.0	10.5	11.2	11.9	10.7

As percentage of total budget expenditures.

SOURCE: National Accounts of the Greek Government (1986, 1987, 1988, 1989).

7 A TALE OF TWO PERIPHERIES: SOUTHERN EUROPE AND EASTERN EUROPE

James Kurth

EASTERN VARIATIONS ON SOUTHERN THEMES

"Europe stops at the Pyrenees," said Talleyrand, as we noted at the beginning of this volume. At about the same time, Metternich observed that "Europe stops at the Landstrasse," the street leading east from Vienna. As it turns out, the two great peripheral regions of Europe, the southern and the eastern, have had many features in common during the past 175 years. Some of these common features have been apparent during the past tumultuous four years, the period of the great transformation of Eastern Europe from communist regimes to democratic polities.

When they had first established their independent statehood, several countries in Eastern Europe went through phases of development similar to those in Southern Europe. This was first the case with the Balkan countries of Bulgaria, Romania, and Serbia (later the nucleus of Yugoslavia), which achieved statehood during the nineteenth century and therefore had time enough to follow Southern Europe through several phases from the 1850s to the 1930s. This pattern also pertained in the more northern countries of Hungary, Poland, Lithuania, Latvia, and Estonia, which achieved statehood only after the First World War but which also followed Southern Europe during the 1920s and 1930s. Like Southern Europe, Eastern Europe has also been characterized by patrimonial authority and delayed development, features which continue to shape the politics and social structures of these countries in the contemporary, postcommunist era.

The Balkan countries and the Greek model. Greece in particular provided a model for the Balkan countries in the nineteenth century. A small part of Greece achieved independence from Ottoman rule in 1827. This territory became a core state, known as the "old kingdom," which steadily expanded in the course of the nineteenth century up through the 1910s, reclaiming other territories with Greek populations from Ottoman rule and incorporating them into the Greek state.

225

In later decades, this process was repeated among other Balkan peoples who were under Ottoman rule and who were close to Greece geographically, historically, and culturally. A small part of what would become Romania achieved independence in 1858, followed by Serbia in 1867 and Bulgaria in 1878. In each case, a core state or "old kingdom" was created which then expanded through the 1910s, in its own "gathering of the peoples."[1] All three countries thus went through a phase of liberation and unification similar to that of Greece and, to a lesser degree, Italy.

This phase of liberation and unification was in turn followed by a phase of political practices similar to the *trasformismo* and caciquism of Southern Europe. The Balkan countries, however, had experienced rather more repressive rule under the Ottomans than Italy and Spain had experienced under the Habsburgs and the Bourbons (sultanism rather than patrimonialism, in Max Weber's terms), and the Balkan economies were even more delayed in their development – they were, indeed, utterly backward – than those of Italy, Spain, Portugal, or even Greece. This meant that there was a good deal of caciquism and not very much trasformismo in the Balkan countries, compared with Southern Europe.

The northern countries and the Italian model. Before the First World War, Eastern Europe north of the Balkans was divided among three great multinational empires, Austria–Hungary, Russia, and Germany. The collapse of these empires at the end of the war brought into being several new states – Hungary, Czechoslovakia, Poland, and the Baltic states of Lithuania, Latvia, Estonia, and Finland.

What is remarkable about most of these new states is how quickly they conformed to the political patterns then developing in Southern Europe. This was particularly the case in countries with large Catholic populations (Hungary, Poland, and Lithuania). After a brief and chaotic parliamentary period, several Eastern European states established authoritarian regimes and, at least in rhetoric, corporate states. Indeed, Mussolini, who came to power in 1922, was seen as a model in Eastern Europe, as he was in Southern Europe. Authoritarian regimes were established by Józef Piłsudski in Poland (1926) and Antanas Smetona in Lithuania (1926); while they were similar to the Italian example, they were even closer to the pattern established by Primo de Rivera in Spain (1923) and Salazar in Portugal (1926). Hungary had had a more traditional authoritarian regime under Admiral Miklós Horthy since 1919. Overall during the 1920s and 1930s, Poland would remain the Eastern European country most like Southern Europe.[2]

1. Robert Lee Wolff, *The Balkans in Our Time* (New York, 1967).
2. Joseph Rothschild, *East Central Europe between the Two World Wars* (Seattle, 1974).

The Great Depression brought a second wave of authoritarian regimes, similar to those that had been set up in the 1920s. In the Balkan states, the monarchs established royal dictatorships – King Alexander in Yugoslavia (1930), King Carol in Romania (1930), and King Boris in Bulgaria (1934). In the Baltic states, elected presidents also established authoritarian rule – Karlis Ulmanis in Latvia (1934) and Konstantin Päts in Estonia (1934). Only Czechoslovakia and Finland remained democratic systems throughout the interwar period.

As of the 1930s, then, the political development of most of Eastern Europe was very much like that of Southern Europe. Both regions were dominated by authoritarian regimes, which were legitimized by the rhetoric of corporate states and which carried out policies of landlord protection and labor repression. Under the impact of the Great Depression, the two regions also became similar in their economic development. In both regions, the state assumed a large role in supporting industrialization. Since much of Eastern Europe was even more backward than Southern Europe, the role of the state (as one would expect from Alexander Gerschenkron's thesis) was even more pronounced. By the end of the 1930s, most Eastern European countries had entered into the initial stage of industrialization, that of the production of consumer non-durables.[3]

The great catastrophes and the great divide. It was in the 1930s, however, that a fundamental difference in the situations of the two peripheries reappeared. Since 1815 (and even before), Southern Europe had been on the periphery of the great powers of the day. Eastern Europe, however, had been between, indeed in the middle of great powers. With the defeat and collapse of these great powers – Germany, Austria–Hungary, and Russia – as a result of the First World War, Eastern Europe was suddenly given enough breathing space to emerge into independence.

In the 1930s, however, the reappearance of Germany and Russia (now the Soviet Union) as great powers put the countries that lay between them in a terrible dilemma, one which had no obvious solution. At best, they were doomed to be dominated by either one or the other power. As it happened the outcome was even worse; they were dominated first by one and then by the other, with the transition between the two consisting of the greatest war in history being fought

---

3. Hugh Seton-Watson, *Eastern Europe Between the Wars, 1918–1941,* 3rd ed. rev. (New York, 1967). On the successive stages of industrialization, see James Kurth, "The Political Consequences of the Product Cycle: Industrial History and Political Outcomes," *International Organization* 27, no. 1 (1979): 1–34; and idem, "Industrial Change and Political Change: A European Perspective," in *The New Authoritarianism in Latin America,* David Collier, ed. (Princeton, N.J., 1979), pp. 319–362. On Gershenkron, see ch. I of the present volume.

on their territories. Of course, the Second World War in Italy and Greece and the civil wars in Spain and Greece were terrible too. The decisive divergence between Eastern Europe and Southern Europe came in 1944–1945 when the former was conquered by the Red Army and the latter was conquered by the American and British armies (Italy and Greece) or not even invaded at all (Spain and Portugal).

THE COMMUNIST ERA IN EASTERN EUROPE

With the Soviet occupation and the subsequent establishment of communist regimes, Eastern Europe was driven down a radically different path than that of Southern Europe. The Soviet model of politics, the communist party state, was the extreme solution to the problem of political power. Just as sultanism had been different from patrimonialism, so, too, was Stalinism, and in much the same ways. Similarly, the Soviet model of industrialization, state led and forced draft, was the extreme solution to the problem of delayed development. Yet, as the decades wore on, the Soviet model faded, and the Soviet domination diminished. By the early 1970s, three decades into the communist era, versions of the earlier Eastern European approaches to patrimonial authority and delayed development began to reappear. As such, Eastern Europe in some ways began to converge once again with Southern Europe.

Within the long communist era of Eastern Europe's history, we can distinguish several phases of political and industrial development.

From early industrialization to communist party state. The social structures and the national traditions of most Eastern European countries in 1945 made it most unlikely that a government friendly to the Soviet Union would issue from a wholly indigenous or independent political process, be it democratic or authoritarian. As we have noted, most of these countries at that time were still in the initial stage of industrialization, that of the production of consumer nondurables. Their working class was small, their middle class was weak and divided, and their landlord class was powerful, i.e., they looked rather like Spain and Portugal at the time. This was the case in Poland, Hungary, Romania, and Bulgaria.[4] In these countries, it was likely that, in a few years after World War II, the old conservative elites would regain their political power, just as they had after World War I. Being anticommunist by class interest and anti–Russian by national tradition (except in Bulgaria), these elites would then

---

4. Yugoslavia and Albania had social structures similar to these countries, but they were not occupied by the Soviet Union. Rather, communism came to power in these two countries through indigenous guerrilla movements. Conversely, Lithuania, Latvia, and Estonia were not merely occupied but totally annexed by the Soviet Union.

readily ally themselves with the current great power to the west, the United States, and would once again become a threat to the Soviet Union.

This meant that the Soviets had to replace the natural social structure with an artificial one, that the Soviets would have to manufacture their friendly governments by a revolution from above and from without, and they would have to impose communist-party rule and maintain it by authoritarian, even totalitarian means. This was the pattern and the process in Poland, Hungary, Romania, and Bulgaria (and also the Soviet zone of Germany) in the years immediately after the Second World War.[5]

Missing from this list were Czechoslovakia and Finland, the exceptions that prove the rule. For these nations were considerably more industrialized in 1945, had maintained democratic rather than authoritarian systems in the interwar years, and had large mass-based communist parties. These differences in social structure preserved Czechoslovakian democracy from a Soviet-imposed revolution for three years until 1948, when the division of Europe and the polarization of the Cold War caused the Soviets to end this particular state of exception. Similar differences in social structure, however, and a less strategic location, preserved Finnish democracy throughout the long Cold War.

From communist party state to forced-draft industrialization. The political logic in Eastern Europe soon turned into an economic one. The communist parties of the Soviet Union and its new satellites were committed to a particular economic program, that of rapid, forced-draft industrialization, particularly in the production of capital goods (such as the steel, chemical, and electrical industries). This process in turn resulted in rapid urbanization and a rapid growth in the number of industrial workers, bureaucratic employees, and urban professionals. These social changes had something in common with those that occurred in Spain in the 1960s under the Franco regime.

The capital-goods stage of industrialization is a peculiar one. It requires the generation and mobilization of vaster amounts of capital than in the preceding stage of consumer nondurables. The construction of heavy industry is a heavy burden on a society and normally requires a rather heavy-handed politics. A communist party, Marxist in social ideology and Leninist in political organization, is in many respects the most effective agent for driving a society through the capital-goods stage of industrialization. In Spain, however, a similar function was performed by the Franco regime and its state enterprises.

5. Joseph Rothschild, *Return to Diversity: A Political History of East Central Europe since World War II* (New York, 1989); Hugh Seton-Watson, *The East European Revolution,* 3rd ed. (New York, 1964); James R. Kurth, "Economic Change and State Development," in *Dominant Powers and Subordinate States: The United States in Latin America and the Soviet Union in Eastern Europe,* Jan F. Triska, ed. (Durham, N.C., 1988), pp. 85–101.

From forced-draft industrialization to economic obsolescence. The very fact that the Marxist–Leninist party is such a perfect agent for bringing about the capital-goods stage of industrialization means, by a dialectical logic, that it is an imperfect agent in what is normally the next stage of industrialization, the production of consumer durables (such as automobiles, appliances, and consumer electronics). It is no accident that countries ruled by communist parties normally experienced growth rates in capital-goods industries that were greater than those in capitalist countries, and growth rates in consumer-durables industries that were lower than those in capitalist countries. The communist pattern of industrialization is a period of dramatic and dizzying growth, followed by a period of pronounced and prolonged stagnation.

The paradigmatic example of this pattern was of course the Soviet Union itself. The consumer-durables stage or "autoindustrial age" of the Soviet Union stayed fixed on an ever-receding horizon, and the Soviet economy remained what it had been since the first Five–Year Plan in the 1930s, a great monument to the leading industries of Europe between the world wars – steel, chemicals, electricity, and armaments.

The most effective agent for bringing a society through the consumer-durables stage of industrialization is neither a full communist party state, as was the case in Eastern Europe, nor even a full free-enterprise system dominated by foreign multinational corporations, as has been the case in Southern Europe. Rather, it is probably a system of "organized competition," in which the national state and perhaps a hegemonic party define the framework in which a half-dozen or so enterprises operate and compete. This has been the case with a number of successful East Asian countries (Japan, South Korea, Taiwan, and Singapore).

From economic obsolescence to political obsolescence. The economic obsolescence of the communist party state was compounded by its political obsolescence. It was difficult to govern an industrialized and urbanized society, a "civil society," with a small authoritarian party, even a highly organized communist one. The Soviet army and the communist party brought into being in Eastern European countries a new society that then pressed upon the bounds of the party and on occasion broke into open rebellion. Thus, there were rebellions of workers in East Berlin in 1953, of workers and intellectuals in Hungary in 1956, of intellectuals in Czechoslovakia in 1968, of workers and intellectuals in Poland in 1956, 1970, 1976, and 1980–81, and finally of virtually all of civil society in every Eastern European country in 1989.[6]

Most of these earlier rebellions were put down through military inter-

6. Rothschild, *Return to Diversity*; Timothy Garton Ash, *The Uses of Adversity: Essays on the Fate of Central Europe* (New York, 1989).

vention by the Soviet army. But in Poland in 1981, the Soviet-style system was maintained by a new form of military intervention in a communist state, i.e., by the local military itself. With this political innovation, Poland entered into a military-based authoritarian regime, at about the same time that Spain, Portugal, and Greece were leaving theirs. Once again, as in the 1920s and 1930s, Poland was the Eastern European country most like Southern Europe. However, the Polish military regime had a particular quality absent from its Southern European counterparts: it was supported (and surrounded) by two Soviet divisions in Poland, twenty Soviet divisions in East Germany, and ninety Soviet divisions in the European USSR. When that support became doubtful in 1989, the future of the Polish military regime became doubtful as well.

FROM STEEL COMMUNISM TO YUPPIE COMMUNISM: THE GREAT TRAJECTORY OF EASTERN EUROPEAN INDUSTRIALIZATION

The great and sudden change in Soviet policy toward Poland and its other Eastern European allies in 1989 had its origins in the great and long trajectory of Soviet-style industrialization from the 1950s to the 1980s. Undermining the apparent stability of the communist political system was a steady decline in its industrial performance and therefore in its legitimacy. Each successive decade from the 1950s to the 1980s saw a decline in the rates of economic growth of the Soviet Union and of its Eastern European allies.

Steel communism. For the Soviet bloc, the 1950s were a decade that perfectly fit the Stalin formula. Indeed it might be called the decade of steel communism (Stalin had chosen this name as his pseudonym because it meant "man of steel," and for the rest of his life he saw steel as the solution to virtually every military or economic problem). It was the true and pure decade of forced-draft industrialization, of rapid growth in heavy capital-goods industries. It also brought into being a large class of industrial workers, which was supposedly the suitable mass base for communist rule.

During this period, Soviet and Eastern European annual growth rates often exceeded 6 percent and were among the highest in the world at that time. This impressive economic performance gave great legitimacy to the Soviet model. When the Soviet Union exceeded the United States in steel production in 1958, it seemed as if the communist system might indeed overtake and surpass the West. But the great project of capital-goods industrialization, of steel communism, was already reaching its limits.

231

Sputnik communism. The 1960s might be called the decade of Sputnik communism (after the dramatic success of the Sputnik space program in 1957). The emphasis was now on high-technology industrialization. There was also a vast expansion of higher education and the creation of a large class of managers and professionals.

Annual economic growth rates remained high in this period – 4–5 percent – but they were lower than they had been earlier. They were not much above the growth rates in Western Europe, and were now exceeded by those of Japan and the newly-industrializing countries of East Asia. The Soviets had adopted a standard of legitimacy that was closer to the values of the West, and their advantage on this standard was much less pronounced.

Goulash communism. The 1970s might be called the decade of goulash communism (after Nikita Khrushchev's description of János Kádár's Hungary, which he saw as something of a model). Now, for the first time, the emphasis was on consumer-durables industrialization. In order to bring this about, the Soviet bloc opened itself to Western loans, joint ventures, licensing agreements, and even a few multinational corporations, i.e., the first beachheads of the international market. A prime example was the arrangements with the giant Italian enterprise, Fiat, to reorganize and expand Soviet production of automobiles (the Lada model line). But these half measures were insufficient to build a successful consumer-durables economy.

By now, the annual growth rates of the Soviet bloc had fallen to 3–4 percent. The new standard of legitimacy was virtually identical to one of the central values of the West and the international market, consumerism, but on this standard the Soviet bloc was obviously at a marked disadvantage.

Yuppie communism. Finally, the 1980s might be called the decade of yuppie communism. By now, the annual growth rates of the Soviet bloc economies had fallen to 1–2 percent or less. It became clear that the communist regimes were not able to fulfill the promise of mass consumption, and they retreated to a promise of elite consumption, i.e., consumption by the "new class" of bureaucrats, managers, and professionals. Most of these were products of the great expansion of higher education in the 1960s.

The communist parties of the Soviet bloc had always been a grand coalition of the old class, industrial workers, and the new class, organizational bureaucrats. But in the beginning these bureaucrats normally were former workers and were a rather thin stratum on top of a large worker mass.[7]

---

7. Milovan Djilas, *The New Class* (New York, 1957); Max Haller, ed., *Class Structure in Europe: New Findings from East-West Comparisons of Social Structure and Mobility* (Armonk, N.Y., 1990).

By the 1980s, however, the new class had expanded enormously in size, in part because of the vast expansion of higher education. It had grown considerably in scope, by now including professionals and managers as well as bureaucrats, and it had expanded significantly in depth, including young persons whose parents had been members of the new class and who thus were second-generation members.

By the late 1980s, the youngest two-thirds of communist-party members were people who had been born after the Second World War, who had become adolescents after Stalin, who had been university students in the 1960s or later, and who were now in mid-career and middle management positions. They were thoroughly imbued with the aspirations, tastes, and desires of professional people, not industrial workers; they identified specifically and intensely with their counterpart professionals in the West; and they craved the benefits of international trade, especially consumer durables. Formally, they were members of the communist party; in fact, they were members of what might be called the yuppie international. Red on the outside, white on the inside, numbering in the millions, they appeared on the political landscape as a vast field of "radish communists."

Whereas in the 1940s the communist parties had been thin strata of bureaucrats on top of large masses of industrial workers, in the 1980s they had become thin strata of gerontocrats on top of large masses of yuppies. The only growing and dynamic force in these otherwise stagnate societies was this mass, this class, and in the course of the decade, the aging communist leadership began to yield more and more to their demands.[8]

At first, the professionals demanded cultural liberation, and the communist governments of Eastern Europe gave it to them with heavy spending upon the restoration of cultural monuments of the past and the virtual elimination of restrictions on cultural imports from the West. Then, the professionals demanded consumer liberation, and the communist governments gave them a larger and larger share of a smaller and smaller economic pie; they paid off the new class at the expense of the old class of industrial workers. Finally, in the epic and epoch-making year of 1989, the professionals demanded political liberation. The communist governments of Eastern Europe, after years of yielding to professional demands and ignoring worker problems, now found themselves utterly without any loyal support. They gave into this last and ultimate demand with a suddenness and a completeness that astonished the world.

Debt burdens and the dynamics of liberalization. The inability of the communist party states of Eastern Europe to bring about the consumer-

8. Stephen R. Graubard, ed., *Eastern Europe... Central Europe... Europe,* special issue of *Daedalus* 119, no. 1 (1990).

durables stage of industrialization was thus one major factor leading to their collapse in 1989. Yet, it was not the only one. A second major factor was the debt burden that these regimes had assumed in the 1970s.

When in the 1980s the Eastern European countries needed to renegotiate the terms of their debt payments, they faced a grand alliance of financial institutions (international banks, the International Monetary Fund, and the World Bank) with a clear and common program for sweeping changes in their economic and political systems. These changes included such familiar measures as liberalization of financial markets, privatization of state enterprises, elimination of state subsidies, and more. Together, they added up to a full market economy, operating within and legitimated by a formal liberal democracy. The financial institutions of the Western world exerted a relentless pressure first for economic liberalization and then political liberalization.

The Eastern European country with the heaviest per capita debt burden was Hungary, most of which was owed to German banks. Hungary was also the country that moved the furthest toward liberalization during the 1980s. By May 1989, this had reached the point that the Hungarian government, strongly encouraged by the German government, dismantled the "iron curtain" of frontier barriers between Hungary and Austria. This led to first the flood of East German refugees across that frontier in the summer and fall of 1989, then the destabilization of the East German government, and finally the fall of the "wall" around East Germany itself.

Similarly, the Eastern European country with the next-heaviest debt burden was Poland, and it was also the country that moved most rapidly toward liberalization during the first eight months of 1989. By August, this had reached the point that the communist military regime agreed to give up control of most of the government to Solidarity, the anticommunist opposition. This provided an example for other Eastern European countries in the fall of 1989, as their own communist regimes gave up power to opposition movements.

THE EASTERN EUROPEAN TRANSITION IN COMPARATIVE PERSPECTIVE

The few years since the collapse of the communist regimes have been a tumultuous period in Eastern Europe. To many observers, this transition seems to have been utterly unique. Yet there have been similarities to transition periods in other times and in other places. Some comparisons with these other periods may provide some perspective on the future.

The Southern European comparison. The most obvious and immediate comparison is with the Southern European transition of the 1970s, as

Spain, Portugal, and Greece went from authoritarian regimes to democratic systems.

In their final years, the Polish and Hungarian communist regimes themselves considered the Spanish transition in particular to provide something of a model. The Polish communist leader, General Wojciech Jaruzelski, hoped to manage a moderate transition by turning the parliament and much of the government over to Solidarity while retaining the commanding heights of the military and the police under communist control. The Polish presidency, held by Jaruzelski, was to continue to perform a moderating role similar to that of the Spanish monarchy as played by King Juan Carlos. Within a year and a half after the beginning of the transition, however, the communists lost control of the military and police, and the opposition leader, Lech Walesa, assumed the presidency himself, bringing an end to the Spanish-style experiment in Poland.

The Hungarian communist leaders held similar hopes for a Spanish solution, but this, too, was overwhelmed by the flood of events. It is clear that the upheaval in Eastern Europe in 1989–1990 was far greater in depth and scope than the one in Southern Europe in the 1970s. Instead, the rejection in popular elections of the communist presidencies in Poland and Hungary had more in common with the rejection in popular referendums of the conservative monarchies in Italy and Greece after the Second World War, during a more radical period of transition.

The new postcommunist governments of Eastern Europe adopted the same economic liberalization policies that had been adopted by the postauthoritarian governments of Spain, Portugal, and Greece.[9] The earlier Southern European liberalization had still been constrained to a degree by the continuing existence during the 1980s of something of a Marxist alternative. With the collapse of the communist parties and even of the Soviet Union in 1989–1991, however, the power and credibility of a Marxist alternative collapsed also, at least temporarily. Consequently, the Eastern European economic liberalization has been even more rapid and extreme than in Southern Europe. Consequently, too, there has been an even greater destruction of national industries in Eastern Europe than in Southern Europe. These economic upheavals also testify to the more radical nature of what has transpired in the East.

What happened in Southern Europe in the 1970s was a transition; what has happened in Eastern Europe since 1989 is a revolution, and it bears comparison with other revolutions earlier in this century. In lengthening our perspective in time, we must also broaden our perspec-

9. Peter Gowan, "Old Medicine, New Bottles: Western Policy toward East Central Europe," *World Policy Journal* 9, no. 1 (1992): 1–33; Mark Kramer, "Eastern Europe Goes to Market," *Foreign Policy*, no. 86 (1992): 134–157.

tive beyond the peripheral regions of Eastern Europe and Southern Europe, to look at their place in Europe as a whole and even in the global international system.

THE EASTERN EUROPEAN REVOLUTION IN HISTORICAL PERSPECTIVE

The Eastern European revolution of 1989 was the third Eastern European revolution in this century. Like the earlier two revolutions of 1918 and 1945, that of 1989 came at the end of a world war, in this case the Cold War. The settlement after each of these wars and revolutions has brought about great shifts in power, both international and domestic, political and economic. In understanding the consequences of the end of the Cold War and the revolution in Eastern Europe, it will be helpful to place them in the historical perspective of the two earlier postwar and postrevolutionary settlements.[10]

It is useful here to distinguish between the apparent and the real victors of the war. For in each of our three cases, those who appeared to be the victors in the great struggle immediately afterwards were not the same as those who were the real victors from the perspective of later years.

The post–First World War settlement. In 1918–1919, it certainly appeared that the Western allies, particularly France, Britain, and the United States, were the victors over Germany, and this was incorporated into the Versailles Treaty and the system which it established. France and Britain, however, had fought the war so long and so hard that they were exhausted by their victory, and it soon became clear that the real inheritor of the fruits of victory was the United States. The United States first created the League of Nations (which it almost immediately abandoned) and then the Dawes Plan (large-scale bank loans) for reconstructing Central Europe and especially Germany in its own liberal-democratic and liberal-capitalist image. From the perspective of the 1920s, then, the United States was the real victor of the First World War. At the end of the 1920s, however, it turned out that the U.S. victory, too, was only apparent. With the onset of the Great Depression in 1929, the Dawes Plan and the American project for Germany collapsed.[11]

The real and fundamental strategic legacy of 1918 was now revealed. Before 1914, Germany had been haunted by the "nightmare of encirclement," of being trapped between France and Russia. During the First

10. James Kurth, "Things to Come: The Shape of the New World Order," *The National Interest,* no. 24 (1991): 3–12; idem, "The Post–Modern State," *ibid.,* no. 28 (1992): 26–37.
11. Charles P. Kindleberger, *The World in Depression, 1929–1939* (Berkeley, 1973).

World War, however, Germany had defeated Russia, as demonstrated in the "forgotten peace" of Brest-Litovsk in March 1918. For two decades thereafter Russia remained isolated behind the *cordon sanitaire*, composed of the new and weak states of Eastern Europe, and preoccupied with its "socialism in one country." Thus, after 1918, Germany was confronted with only one major continental adversary, France, rather than with two.

The economic legacy of 1918 was much the same. Despite its long succession of economic miseries – defeat, revolution, occupation, inflation, depression – the underlying reality of the German economy was that it remained the largest, the most advanced, the most efficient, and the most competitive industrial complex in Europe, just as it had been before 1914.

When the Weimar Republic was displaced by the Nazi regime in 1933, it was not long before these underlying strategic and economic strengths were recognized and realized. While Adolf Hitler and the Nazi elite were fixated upon the strategic strengths, the economic strengths were well understood by the conservative elites of German industry and finance. These soon composed the Schacht Plan (based upon organized foreign trade and controlled currency exchange) for reconstructing Eastern Europe in their own corporatist-authoritarian and organized-capitalist image. They conceived much of what we have called Eastern Europe to really be Central Europe or *Mitteleuropa*, centered upon that most central of European powers, Germany. This grand project for German hegemony in Mitteleuropa through economic power, which very well might have succeeded, was instead overtaken by Hitler's own ambition for German domination of all of Europe through military conquest.[12]

The post–Second World War settlement. A similar but simpler pattern of apparent and real victors occurred after the Second World War. In 1945, Britain, the United States, and the Soviet Union were the obvious victors over Germany and Japan, and this was demonstrated in the Yalta–Potsdam system. Britain, however, had fought the war longer and harder than any of the other Western allies, so long and hard, in fact, that it was again exhausted by its victory, and the real inheritor of the fruits of victory was again the United States. The United States then composed the Truman Doctrine, the Marshall Plan, and the NATO alliance for reconstructing Western Europe, including Italy and Greece, in its own liberal-democratic and liberal-capitalist image, now modified by the New Deal welfare state. In this grand project, Britain had a special relationship but played only a secondary role.

12. Albert O. Hirschman, *National Power and the Structure of Foreign Trade,* expanded ed. (Berkeley, 1980, originally published in 1945); Antonin Basch, *The Danube Basin and the German Economic Sphere* (New York, 1943).

JAMES KURTH

There was also no doubt that the other real victor was the Soviet Union. As we have seen, it proceeded to carry out the Eastern European revolution of 1945, a revolution from above and from outside. It also imposed forced-draft industrialization and devised a Molotov Plan to reorient the Eastern European economies toward the Soviet one. The Soviet Union thus reconstructed Eastern Europe in its own Stalinist and state-communist image. In doing so, it re-created an Eastern Europe in much of what had previously been seen, especially by the Germans, as Central Europe.

The post–Cold War settlement. In the last few years, political commentators have repeatedly proclaimed that the United States has won the Cold War, but, in a pattern similar to that of Britain earlier, the United States fought the Cold War longer and harder than any of the other Western allies, so long and hard, in fact, that its economic health has been depleted by its military expenditures,[13] and in many ways the real inheritors of the fruits of victory have been Germany and Japan. It is likely that Germany will come to compose a Mitteleuropa project, if not quite a Kohl plan, reconstructing Eastern Europe in its own liberal-democratic and social-market image (and thereby reconverting Eastern Europe back into Central Europe). In this grand project, the United States will have a special relationship but will play only a secondary role.

This Mitteleuropa project could recapitulate the economic goals and methods of German industrial and financial conservatives between the 1880s and 1930s and the political goals and methods of German social democrats of the Weimar and Cold War periods. It would also represent the reversal of the military defeats of the 1940s with the economic achievements of the 1990s. De-Stalinization would reach its logical culmination in the reversal of Stalingrad not long after 1993, the fiftieth anniversary of that great climactic battle.

THE MITTELEUROPA MODEL: A THIRD WAY BETWEEN EAST AND WEST

At the present time, it is conventional wisdom that Eastern Europe aspires to become like Western Europe or even like the United States, i.e., to acquire liberal democracies and capitalist economies. This is the famous "end of history."[14]

Economic deformation and political reaction. The great transformation from Eastern to Western, authoritarian to liberal, communist to capitalist, however, shows more and more signs of being a great deformation

13. Paul Kennedy, *The Rise and Fall of the Great Powers: Economic Change and Military Conflict from 1500 to 2000* (New York, 1988).
14. Francis Fukuyama, "The End of History?" *The National Interest,* no. 16 (1989): 3–18.

238

instead. By now there have developed in several countries two political blocs or tendencies, one that is Western and capitalist and a second that is national and social (not yet socialist, given the continuing bad memories of the old regime). The first tendency predominates in the more developed countries (Hungary, the Czech Republic), the second predominates in the less developed ones (Romania, Bulgaria, and Slovakia), and they seem to balance or even stalemate each other in Poland and the Baltic states. These two tendencies could eventually result in something like the conservative and socialist political parties of Southern Europe or like the Christian Democratic and Social Democratic parties of Germany. In any event, the devastating economic consequences of the free market and liberal capitalism are now producing an organized political reaction. This social tendency in much of Eastern Europe is likely to become a more powerful and credible restraint on liberal capitalism than the socialist parties of Southern Europe.

It is probably only a matter of time before the nations of Eastern Europe reject the extreme of liberal capitalism as decisively as they rejected the extreme of state socialism and seek a third way. An alternative future is that Eastern Europe will become *Mitteleuropa*. This would be the return, rather than the end, of history.

The civil society, cultural standards, and even life-styles of much of *Mitteleuropa* were shaped either by the Catholic church (Poland and Lithuania), by the Habsburg empire (the Czech lands of Bohemia and Moravia), or by both acting together (Hungary, Slovakia, Croatia, and Slovenia). These countries have long found their social and cultural models in Germany (whose southern region is Catholic) and Austria.

This could become true for their economic model as well. This model could become not the free market but the social market, as it has existed in West Germany and Austria since the early 1950s. This includes (1) a substantial part (40–50 percent) of the gross national product passing through the state sector, i.e., through either federal, state, or local governments; (2) "societal corporatism," or close and continuous cooperation between state agencies, business corporations, and labor organizations; and (3) a universal system of social-welfare benefits.[15]

Catholic social teaching. The ideas of the social-market economy are completely in accord with Catholic social teaching, as articulated in a

---

15. On Germany as a model for other European countries, see the excellent and innovative analysis by Andrei S. Markovits and Simon Reich, *The New Face of Germany: Gramsci, Neorealism, and Hegemony*, Harvard University Center for European Studies Working Paper Series, no. 28 (Cambridge, Mass., 1991). A shorter version is idem, "*Modell Deutschland* and the New Europe," *Telos*, no. 89 (1991): 45–63.

century-old tradition of papal encyclicals·[16] The first papal encyclical on social questions, *Rerum novarum* (whose English-language edition is entitled "*On the Condition of the Working Classes*"), was promulgated just over a century ago by Pope Leo XIII. It has been followed since then by a half-dozen comparable encyclicals, each focusing on the social questions of the time. They include *Quadregesimo anno ("Social Reconstruction,"* 1931) by Pius XI, *Mater et magistra ("Christianity and Social Progress,"* 1961) by John XXIII, and *Laborem exercens ("On Human Work,"* 1981) by John Paul II. To commemorate the centennial of *Rerum novarum* and to direct the application of this Catholic social tradition to the new emerging Europe, John Paul II designated 1991 as the "year of Catholic social teaching," in which he promulgated a new encyclical on contemporary social questions, *Centesimus annus,* and convened a synod of bishops that formulated a social project for the new Europe.

The papal encyclicals and the social teaching of the Catholic Church have consistently criticized both state socialism and liberal capitalism as incomplete and flawed ideologies. In their place, the church advocates such conceptions as society's need for both business organizations and labor unions, but also the "principle of the priority of labor over capital;" the need for meaningful work and a "just-wage" for the full development of the human person; and the need to limit state power to its proper role by the "principle of subsidiarity," which devolves power and responsibilities to intermediate institutions between the state and the individual.

The new encyclical of John Paul II continued and expanded this tradition. *Centesimus annus* celebrated the fall of communism in Eastern Europe in 1989, but it also condemned two forms of capitalism, the "national security state" (such as existed in Latin America from the 1960s until the 1980s) and "consumer society" (such as exists in the United States and increasingly in Western Europe). Instead, the pope praised "a democratic society inspired by social justice," such as that pursued in much of Western Europe for most of the period since the Second World War.

The papal encyclicals and the social teaching of the Catholic church could fit the economic realities of the new Mitteleuropa for many years to come. It is possible that they might provide an intellectual order, political legitimation, and policy guidance to governments in Mitteleuropa, after the collapse of state socialism and out of the turmoil of liberal capitalism.[17]

16. Eric O. Hanson, *The Catholic Church in World Politics* (Princeton, N.J., 1987).
17. James Kurth, "*Rome à la reconquête de l'est,*" *Politique Internationale* (Paris), no. 54 (1991–92): 369–377.

THE ITALIAN MODEL: A THIRD WAY BETWEEN EAST AND SOUTH

One model for the Eastern European periphery may be found in the European center, *Mitteleuropa,* itself. It is possible, however, that another model may be found in that other periphery, Southern Europe.

It is commonly assumed that the contemporary Eastern European transition from a state economy to a capitalist one is unlike anything that has occurred before and, accordingly, that there are no lessons to be drawn from past economic transitions. This is a curious presumption, however. In actuality, after the Second World War most of Western Europe underwent a comparable transition from a wartime, state-run economy to a capitalist one. Of course, that capitalist economy was not a pure market one, as is now often envisioned for Eastern Europe. Rather, it was a mixed economy, complete with a "social compact," welfare state, state enterprises, and, for more than a decade after the end of the war, extensive controls on foreign exchange. We have already discussed the most successful of these mixed economies, the social-market economy of West Germany, and have suggested that the German experience provides a better model than the free-market economy for Eastern Europe.

Another relevant model, however, is the Italian experience after the Second World War. In 1945, the Italian economy was as decrepit and backward relative to the rest of Western Europe as the Eastern European economies are today. Furthermore, the major Italian industries were directed by the state. This immense state sector dated from the Great Depression, and it has continued down to the present time. Yet, Italy soon developed an extremely vigorous private sector composed of both a few large corporations and many small flexible enterprises. The very vitality of the private enterprises has rested upon the predictability provided by the public ones. Postwar Italy, then, could have provided an excellent economic model for contemporary Eastern Europe. What explains why this was a "path not taken?"

Italy in the late 1940s was the major case of a Western country containing a strong communist party; indeed, the Italian one was the largest and most powerful communist party in Western Europe. The existence of a credible and powerful Marxist alternative put serious constraints upon capitalist leaders and forced them to compromise with labor unions and other popular organizations. In addition, the Italian capitalist class was then mainly national, rather than international, in its interests, and it sought protectionist economic policies. The result of these pressures was the mixed economy, Italian-style.

The current absence in Eastern Europe of both a credible Marxist alternative and a national capitalist class has thus far prevented that region from taking the Italian path. The excesses of the free-market economy, however, may bring a reconsideration. In particular, Hungary, which was long the leader in Eastern European economic reform during the communist years, has begun to examine and emulate aspects of the Italian experience.

In the early 1990s, Europe no longer stops at the Pyrenees, Italy is no longer only a promontory which links Europe to Africa, and Greece no longer lies beyond the pale of civilization. The four countries of Southern Europe in the past generation have each entered Europe itself. In doing so, however, they have also entered dependent development upon a higher stage.

In the early 1990s, however, Europe still stops at the Landstrasse. The countries of Eastern Europe are even more eager to enter into Europe in the next generation than those of Southern Europe were in the past one. The road they are now on leads toward a free-market economy and liberal capitalism, that is, more toward America than toward Europe itself. At the end of this road, Eastern Europe may as last enter into Europe, but it will do so upon an even more dependent stage than did Southern Europe.

The true road to Europe does not meander through yet another, even if very different, periphery of Europe, the far western one across the Atlantic (or even across the Channel). It is a more direct and more straightforward route. Europe ends at that street leading east from Vienna. The journey to Europe also begins on that street, leading west to Vienna and to the great and ancient capitals of the continent beyond.

BIBLIOGRAPHY

SOUTHERN EUROPE: COMPARATIVE STUDIES

Giovanni Arrighi, editor, *Semiperipheral Development: The Politics of Southern Europe in the Twentieth Century* (Beverly Hills, Calif.: Sage Publications, 1985). Essays interpret Southern Europe from a dependency and "world-system" perspective.

Suzanne Berger, editor, *Organizing Interests in Western Europe: Pluralism, Corporatism, and the Transformation of Politics* (Cambridge and New York: Cambridge University Press, 1981). Contains an excellent essay on Spain by Juan Linz, as well as a comparison of the 1968-1969 crises in France and Italy by Michele Salvati.

Suzanne Berger and Michael J. Piore, *Dualism and Discontinuity in Industrial Societies* (Cambridge and New York: Cambridge University Press, 1980). An important theoretical statement about the political and economic dynamics of dual economies, with special reference to France and Italy.

Ronald H. Chilcote et al, *Transitions from Dictatorship to Democracy: Comparative Studies of Spain, Portugal, and Greece* (New York: Crane Russak, 1990). Essays interpret the transitions from a leftist or Marxist perspective, focusing upon social and economic factors.

Giuseppe Di Palma, *To Craft Democracies: An Essay on Democratic Transitions* (Berkeley, Calif.: University of California Press, 1991). This work by a leading scholar of Italian politics focuses on the political process during the transitions.

John Higley and Richard Gunther, editors, *Elites and Democratic Consolidation in Latin America and Southern Europe* (Cambridge and New York: Cambridge University Press, 1992). Contains useful chapters on Italy, Spain, and Portugal.

E. J. Hobsbawm, *Primitive Rebels: Studies in Archaic Forms of Social Movement in the 19th and 20th Centuries* (New York, W. W. Norton, 1965). A classic work which includes studies of "social bandits" in southern Italy, anarchism in Andalusia, and peasant communism in Sicily.

Tony Judt, editor, *Resistance and Revolution in Mediterranean Europe, 1939–1948* (London and New York: Routledge, 1989). Includes useful essays on communist partisan movements in Italy and Greece.

Guillermo O'Donnell, Philippe C. Schmitter, and Laurence Whitehead, editors, *Transitions from Authoritarian Rule: Southern Europe* (Baltimore: Johns Hopkins University Press, 1986). Interprets the transitions from a liberal perspective, focusing on the political process rather than social or economic factors.

Stanley G. Payne, *A History of Spain and Portugal*, two volumes (Madison: University of Wisconsin Press, 1973). The most comprehensive comparative history of Spain and Portugal, presenting parallel accounts of developments in the two countries. The second volume covers the period since the eighteenth century.

Stanley G. Payne, *Fascism: Comparison and Definition* (Madison: University of Wisconsin Press, 1980). A comprehensive and perceptive analysis of fascism, including accounts of Italy, Spain, and Portugal.

Geoffrey Pridham, editor, *The New Mediterranean Democracies: Regime Transition in Spain, Greece, and Portugal* (London and Totowa, N.J.: Frank Cass, 1984). This volume and the following one contain useful essays by reputable scholars on the democratic transition and later consolidations.

Geoffrey Pridham, editor, *Securing Democracy: Political Parties and Democratic Consolidation in Southern Europe* (London and New York: Routledge, 1990).

Howard J. Wiarda, *Corporatism and National Development in Latin America* (Boulder, Colo.: Westview Press, 1981). Chapters 4 and 5 provide a comprehensive discussion of the "Iberic-Latin tradition" and the corporative model in Southern Europe as well as Latin America.

Allan M. Williams, *Southern Europe Transformed: Political and Economic Change in Greece, Italy, Portugal, and Spain* (London: Harper and Row, 1984). A useful, if conventional, comparative discussion.

ITALY

Judith Chubb, *Patronage, Power, and Poverty in Southern Italy: A Tale of Two Cities* (Cambridge and New York: Cambridge University Press, 1982). An innovative and sophisticated analysis of clientelist politics, focusing upon and contrasting Palermo and Naples.

Alexander De Grand, *The Italian Left in the Twentieth Century: A History of the Socialist and Communist Parties* (Bloomington: Indiana University, Press, 1989). A comprehensive and conventional account of its topic.

Guiseppe Di Palma, *Surviving with Governing: The Italian Parties in Parliament* (Berkeley, Calif.: University of California Press, 1977). A thorough account of the party dynamics in the Italian parliament, focusing upon the political process rather than social and economic factors.

Paolo Faraeti, edited by S.E. Finer and Alfio Mastropaolo, *The Italian Party System* (New York: St. Martin's Press, 1985). A comprehensive and informative analysis of the topic, with more attention to social and economic factors than the above work by Di Palma.

David Forgacs, *Italian Culture in the Industrial Era, 1880–1980* (Manchester and New York: Manchester University Press, 1970). An innovative analysis of the interactions between industrialization, popular culture, and politics in Italy.

Francois Gay and Paul Wagret, *L'Economie de l'Italie* (Paris: Presses Universitaires de France, coll. "Que sais-je," #1007, 1991). Explores regional and sectorial differences in the Italian economy.

A. James Gregor, *Italian Fascism and Developmental Dictatorship* (Princeton: Princeton University Press, 1979). An original analysis which argues that Italian fas-

cism was an attempt to overcome the distinctive problems of a lateindustrial-
izing country.

Paul Guichonnet, *Histoire de l'Italie* (Paris: Presses Universitaires de France, coll.
"Que sais-je," #286, 1969, fifth edition, 1989). A compact overview and
periodization of Italian history.

Stephen Hellman, *Italian Communism in Transition: The Rise and Fall of the Historic
Compromise in Turin, 1975–1980* (Oxford and New York: Oxford University Press, 1988). A thorough analysis of the dilemmas of the Communist Party,
focusing on Turin.

H. Stuart Hughes, *The United States and Italy*, third edition (Cambridge, Mass.:
Harvard University Press, 1979). A concise, respected, and useful history of
modern Italy. (There is much less emphasis on the United States than the title
suggests.)

David I. Kertzer, *Comrades and Christians: Religion and Political Struggle in Communist Italy* (Cambridge and New York: Cambridge University Press, 1980). An
excellent analysis of the paradoxes of the struggle between the Communist
Party and the Catholic Church in a working-class district of Bologna.

Norman Kogan, *A Political History of Postwar Italy: From the Old to the New Center–Left* (New York: Praeger, 1981). A standard political history from a liberal perspective.

Peter Lange and Mario Regini, editors, *State, Market and Social Regulation: New
Perspectives on Italy* (Cambridge and New York: Cambridge University Press,
1989). Innovative and informative analyses of the tensions between the state
and the market in Italy.

Peter Lange and Sidney Tarrow, editors, *Italy in Transition: Conflict and Consensus*
(London and Totowa, N.J.: Frank Cass, 1980). Useful essays by leading
scholars of Italian politics.

Joseph La Palombara,, *Democracy, Italian Style* (New Haven, Conn.: Yale University Press, 1987). An informed and sophisticated interpretation of the paradoxes of Italian politics, emphasizing the real strengths of the Italian way of
democracy.

Robert Leonardi and Douglas A. Wertman, *Italian Christian Democracy: The Politics of Dominance* (London, 1989). The most comprehensive and balanced
recent analysis of the Italian Christian Democratic Party.

Clara Maria Lovett, *The Democratic Movement in Italy, 1830–1876* (Cambridge,
Mass.: Harvard University Press, 1982). A detailed analysis of the leaders of
the democratic or radical movement during the Risorgimento and of its failure.

Denis Mack Smith, *Italy: A Modern History* (Ann Arbor: University of Michigan
Press, 1959). The standard history of modern Italy, providing an account that
is comprehensive and conventional.

Denis Mack Smith, *Italy and Its Monarchy* (New Haven: Yale University Press,
1989). The definitive history of the Savoyard monarchy.

Denis Mack Smith, *Mussolini* (New York: Knoph, 1982). The major recent
biography of Mussolini.

James Edward Miller, *From Elite to Mass Politics: Italian Socialism in the Giolittian*

Era, 1900–1914 (Kent, Ohio: Kent State University Press, 1990). A thorough analysis of the origins of mass politics in Italy.

Robert Putnam, *Making Democracy Work: Civic Traditions in Modern Italy* (Princeton: Princeton University Press, 1993). Argues that longstanding civic traditions from as far back as the medieval epoch have an impact on the quality of contemporary political life in many regions of Italy.

Luisa Quartermaine, editor, *Italy Today: Patterns of Life and Politics*, second edition (Exeter: University of Exeter, 1987). Useful essays by leading British scholars of Italian politics; the diverse topics include the changing economy, the steel industry, coalition politics, and the Vatican.,

Donald Sassoon, *Contemporary Italy: Politics, Economy, and Society since 1945* (London and New York: Longman, 1986). Particularly good on new social subjects such as women and youth; valuable data on regional differences and politics.

Sidney Tarrow, *Democracy and Disorder: Protest and Politics in Italy, 1969–1975* (Oxford and New York: Oxford University Press, 1989). This work by a leading scholar of Italian politics is distinguished by its use of advanced and quantitative methods of political science.

Sidney Tarrow, *Peasant Communism in Southern Italy* (New Haven, Conn.: Yale University Press, 1967). An innovative and highly-regarded analysis of how the Italian communist party became dependent upon and was transformed by the peasantry in southern Italy.

SPAIN

Salvador Aguilar et al, *Interest Associations in the Spanish Transition*, Barcelona: Jaime Bofill Fundacion, 1988). This is an informative account of the structure, policies, and orientation of a variety of business and other interest groups.

Salvador Aguilar, *Sindicalisme y Canvi Social a Espanya 1976–88*. Four volumes of a projected six volume series thus far including: Vol. II. Els Contextos de L'accio Sindical; Vol. IV. Els Liders; Vol. V. Els Treballadors; Vol. VI. Epileg: La Vaga General del 14-D. (All published in Barcelona, Jaime Bofill Fundocion, 1990). These four volumes are the best comprehensive treatment of the Spanish trade union movement in any language.

Bartolomé Bennassar, *Histoire des Espagnols*, two volumes (Paris: Armand Colin, 1985). Covers Spain following the collapse of the Roman Empire all the way to the post-Franco settlement.

Albert Broder, Gérard Chastagnet, and Emile Temime, *Histoire de l'Espagne Contemporaine de 1808 á nos jours* (Paris: Aubier-Montaigne, 1979). Historical analysis that in large measure seeks to explore economic underdevelopment and the weakness of industrialization in Spain.

Raymond Carr and Juan Pablo Fusi Alzpurua, *Spain: Dictatorship to Democracy*, second edition (London and Boston: Allen and Unwin, 1981). An informative account from a liberal perspective of the transition period of the 1970s.

246

Raymond Carr, *Spain, 1808–1975* (Oxford: Clarendon Press, and New York: Oxford University Press, 1982). The standard history of modern Spain, providing an account that is comprehensive and conventional.

Richard P. Clark, *The Basques, the Franco Years and Beyond* (Reno: University of Nevada Press, 1979). Along with Stanley Payne's *Basque Nationalism* (1975) in the same publisher's series, this is the main English language text on ttwentieth century Basque history. Payne ends his narrative in 1937; Clark takes the story up through the 1970s.

Colloque de Bordeaux, *Dix ans de démocratie constitutionelle en Espagne* (Paris: Editions du CNRS, 1991). Based on a conference held in March 1990 and introduced by Dmitri Georges Lavaroff, this book focuses on legal and constitutional questions surrounding democracy, the Basque question, media policy, and the functioning of parliament.

Michel Drain, *L'Economie de l'Espagne* (Paris: Presses Universitaires de Paris, 1968, sixth edition, 1991). Explores the structures of the contemporary Spanish economy, as well as the role of tourism as a motor of development in many regions.

Robert M. Fishman, *Working Class Organization and the Return to Democracy in Spain* (Ithaca: Cornell University Press, 1990). This is probably the best-researched discussion in English on trade unions and politics in the transition and post-transition periods.

Richard Gillispie, *The Spanish Socialist Party: A History of Factionalism* (New York: Oxford University Press, 1989). This is a readable and useful survey of the evolution of the Socialist Party.

Frances Lannon and Paul Preston, editors, *Elites and Power in Twentieth-Century Spain: Essays in Honor of Sir Raymond Carr* (Oxford: Clarendon Press, and New York: Oxford University Press, 1990). Useful essays by leading scholars, on both the Civil War era and the contemporary era.

Maria Goulemot Maeso, *L'Espagne: De la Mort de Franco à l'Europe Des Douze* (Paris: Minerva, 1989). By a writer trained in economics at the Universities of Madrid and Paris, she provides much useful economic and poll data, chapters on the political system, economy, the army, the Church, and the Basque question.

Thierry Malinak, *Les Espagnols de la Movida à l'Europe: La decennie socialiste* (Paris: Centurion, 1990). An exploration of Gonzalez-era Spain by *Le Monde's* longtime Madrid correspondent.

Joan Martinez-Alier and Jordi Roca Jusmet, "Economia politica del corporativismo en el estado español: Del Franquismo el posfranquismo" *Revista Española de Investigacions Sociologicos*, no. 41, *Enero-Marzo* 1988. This is an excellent critique of the first years of the González regime, illustrating the negative impact of its economic policies.

Jacques Maurice and Carlos Serrano, *L'Espagne au XXe Siècle* (Paris: Hachette, 1992). Part of a new series covering modern Spain.

Stanley G. Payne, *The Franco Regime, 1936–1975* (Madison: University of Wisconsin Press, 1987). This work, by the leading American historian of modern Spain, presents a comprehensive and definitive biography of Franco; it focuses upon political history rather than social and economic developments.

Stanley G. Payne, *Spanish Catholicism: An Historical Overview* (Madison: University of Wisconsin Press, 1984). An especially comprehensive, perceptive, and balanced account of its topic.

Paul Preston, *Franco: Biography* (London: Harper Collins, forthcoming, 1994). A new and massive (over 1000 pages) biography which has already generated much advance discussion in Spain.

Paul Preston, *The Triumph of Democracy in Spain*, (London and New York: Methuen, 1986). A perceptive analysis of the transition by a leading British historian of Spain.

Jaume Rossinyol, *Le problème national catalan* (Paris: Mouton, 1974). A massive tome that is a revised version of the writer's doctoral thesis at the Université de Nantes.

Jose Maria Torlosa, *El 'cambio' y la Modernizacion* (Alicante, 1985). This book focuses on several issues (NATO, etc.) which reflect the rightward shift in Spanish Socialist policies.

Pierre Vilar, *Spain: A Brief History* (Oxford: Pergamon, 1977). English translation of the second edition by the distinguished French historian of Catalonia. Excellent for main historical outlines and periodization.

Jaime Vicens Vives, *An Economic History of Spain* (Princeton: Princeton University Press, 1969). While Spanish economic history has been dominated by the scholarship of non-Spaniards (Earl J. Hamilton, Robert S. Lopez, and Julius Klein from the U.S., Pierre Vilar and Pierre Chaunu from France), Jaime Vicens Vives (1910–1960) of the University of Barcelona produced the most accessible general overview. Covers pre-Roman Empire to the end of the nineteenth century.

Evolucion Social en España, 1977–1987. (Madrid: Instituto Sindical de Estudios, 1988). This is excellent source of statistical data on social conditions in Spain from the late 1970s to the late 1980s.

RECENT WORKS ON BARCELONA AND ITS LEADING ROLE IN MODERN SPAIN

Sebastian Balfour, *Dictatorship, Workers, and the City: Labour in Greater Barcelona Since 1939* (Oxford and New York: Oxford University Press, 1989).

Robert Hughes, *Barcelona* (London: Harvill, 1992). Discusses the creative achievements of Barcelona in art and architecture.

Temma Kaplan, *Red City, Blue Period: Social Movements in Picasso's Barcelona* (Berkeley: University of California Press, 1992). Among the leading feminist historians and scholars of Spanish anarchism, she explores intellectual and art history, as well as political and social movements in Barcelona from 1888 to 1939.

Cristina and Eduardo Mendoza, *Barcelona Modernista* (Barcelona: Planeta, 1989).

J.K.J. Thomson, *A Distinctive Industrialization: Cotton in Barcelona, 1728–1832* (Cambridge: Cambrige University Press, 1993). This monograph poses the important question why Catalonia became "the one Mediterranean exception to the tendency of early industrialization to be concentrated in northern Europe." Downplaying technological leadership, he suggests the significance of an active state and the very social acceptability of industry among the Catalans.

Michael Seidman, *Workers Against Work: Labor in Paris and Barcelona during the Popular Fronts* (Berkeley: University of California Press, 1991). Comparison of Paris and Barcelona during the 1930s; it demonstrates widespread worker resistance to "productivist" ideologies of both Marxists and anarchists.

PORTUGAL

Albert-Alain Bourdon, *Histoire du Portugal* (Paris: Presses Universitaires de France, coll. "Que sais-je?," #1394, 1970, second edition 1977). Compact introduction to Portuguese history.

António Rangel Bandeira, "The Portuguese Armed Forces Movement: Historical Antecedents, Professional Demands, and Class Conflict," *Politics and Society* 6,1 (1976): 1-56. An historical survey of the role and actions of the Portuguese Armed Forces during the twentieth century, which shows how the colonial wars in Africa aggravated internal contradictions and provoked the coup of 25 April 1974.

Nancy Gina Bermeo, *The Revolution in the Revolution: Workers' Control in Rural Portugal* (Princeton: Princeton University Press, 1986). A major study on rural workers in southern Portugal during the aftermath of the 1974 coup.

Thomas Bruneau, *Politics and Nationhood: Post-Revolutionary Portugal* (New York: Praeger, 1984). An overview of politics in Portugal prior to 1974.

Ronald H. Chilcote, editor, *The Portuguese Revolution of 25 April 1974: Annotated Bibliography on the Antecedents and Aftermath* (Coimbra: Centro de Documentacão 25 de Abril, Universidade de Coimbra, 1987). The major sources on the revolutionary events surrounding the coup of 25 April 1974, including 1116 books and pamphlets and 1047 periodical references.

Charles Downs, *Revolution at the Grassroots: Community Organizations in the Portuguese Revolution* (New York: State University of New York Press, 1989). A scholarly study, based on dissertation field work, of popular community organizations, with a focus on the Setúbal area.

Hugo Gil Ferreira and Michael W. Marshall, *Portugal's Revolution: Ten Years On* (Cambridge: Cambridge University Press, 1986). A summary and descriptive account of the decade after 25 April 1974, including the verbatim publication of interviews with major participants.

John J. Hammond, *Building Popular Power: Workers and Neighborhood Movements in the Portuguese Revolution* (New York: Monthly Review Press, 1988). A major study, drawing on interviews and important documentation, of the popular labor and workers commissions in the period after 25 April 1974.

Lawrence S. Graham and Harry M. Makler, editors, *Contemporary Portugal: The Revolution and Its Antecedents* (Austin, Texas: University of Texas Press, 1979). This volume contains essays by many of the leading American scholars of

Portuguese politics; it is especially strong in its political, social and economic analyses of the Salazar-Caetano era.

Phil Mailer, *Portugal: The Impossible Revolution* (New York: Free Life Editions, 1977). Firsthand reporting, including appendices of useful documents, of events during the revolutionary period of 1974–1975.

Jacques Marcadé, *Le Portugal au XXe Siècle, 1910–1985* (Paris: Presses Universitaires de France, 1988). Chapters on Portuguese political structure and evolution, the Church, the Portuguese countryside, agrarian reform, industrialization, the legacy of empire, and current foreign policy. Provides a useful chronology.

Antonio Henrique de Oliveira Marques, *Historia de Portugal*, two volumes (Lisboa: Palais Editores, 1972, seventh edition, 1977). A detailed history by a distinguished Portuguese historian.

Daniel Nataf and Elizabeth Sammis, "Classes, Hegemony, and Portuguese Democratization," chapter 3, pp. 73–130, in Ronald H. Chilcote et al, *Transitions from Dictatorship to Democracy: Comparative Studies of Spain, Portugal, and Greece* (New York: Crane Russak, 1990). Departs from, reassesses and updates the analysis of Nicos Poulantzas, *Crisis of the Dictatorships* (1974).

Walter C. Opello Jr., *Portugal: From Monarchy to Pluralist Democracy* (Boulder: Westview Press, 1991). A useful general overview of Portugal, with emphasis on politics during the twentieth century.

D. L. Raby, *Fascism and Resistance in Portugal: Communists, Liberals and Military Dissidents in the Opposition to Salazar, 1941–1974*. (Manchester: Manchester University Press, 1988). A major study of the Salazar-Caetano dictatorship.

Christian Rudel, *La Liberté Coulleur d'Oeillet: Histoire du XXe Siècle Portugais* (Paris: Fayard, 1980). A political history by the Iberian and Latin American correspondent for *La Croix*; he previously produced a book on Salazar.

Gervase Clarence Smith, *The Third Portuguese Empire 1825–1975: A Study in Economic Imperialism* (Manchester: Manchester University Press, 1985).

Douglas L. Wheeler, *Republican Portugal: A Political History, 1910–1926* (Madison: University of Wisconsin Press, 1978). A thorough and definitive, if conventional, account of the republican era that preceded the Salazar regime.

GREECE

Richard Clogg, editor, *Greece in the 1980s* (New York: St. Martin's Press, 1983). Useful essays by reputable scholars of Greek politics.

Richard Clogg, *Parties and Elections in Greece: The Search for Legitimacy* (Durham: Duke University Press, 1987). This work, by the leading British historian of modern Greece, focuses upon political processes.

Richard Clogg, *A Short History of Modern Greece*, second edition (Cambridge and New York: Cambridge University Press, 1986). A useful but conventional overview of modern Greek history.

Douglas Dakin, *The Unification of Greece, 1770–1923* (New York: St. Martin's Press, 1972). A comprehensive and conventional account, focusing upon political and diplomatic history.

Georges B. Dertilis, editor, *Banquiers, Usuriers et Paysans: Réseaux de crédit et straté-gies du capital en Grèce, 1780–1930* (Paris: Editions La Découverte, 1988). Explains networks of investment, the immobility of the Greek economy in the late nineteenth century, and the limited penetration of industrialization in the twentieth. Contains a substantial bibliography of economic literature in Greek, French, and English.

Kevin Featherstone and D.K. Katsoudas, *Political Change in Greece: Before and After the Colonels* (New York: St. Martin's Press, 1987).

Christos Ioannov, "The Manufacturing Workers in the Trade Union Movement, 1974–1984," in *Social Classes, Social Change and Economic Development in the Mediterranean*, Proceedings of the Foundation for Mediterranean Studies, 1986. A fine empirical survey of the industrial working class in the post-military period.

Yorgos A. Kourvetaris and Betty A. Dobratz, *A Profile of Modern Greece: In Search of Identity* (Oxford: Clarendon Press, and New York: Oxford University Press, 1987). A short introduction to modern Greek politics and history; particularly strong on culture and literature.

William W. McGrew, *Land and Revolution in Modern Greece, 1800–1881: The Transition in the Tenure and Exploitation of Land from Ottoman Rule to Independence* (Kent, Ohio: Kent State University, 1985). A thorough account of the agrarian issue and the social bases of Greek politics in the nineteenth century.

William Hardy McNeill, *The Metamophosis of Greece since World War II* (Chicago: University of Chicago Press, 1978). A perceptive and sensitive interpretation of Greek politics, at the national, city, and village levels, by a distinguished historian of European history.

George Th. Mavrogordatos, "The Greek Party System: A Case of Limited but Polarised Pluralism," *West European Politics*, number 7, (1984), pp. 156–169. A useful description of party politics and cleavages.

George Th. Mavrogordatos, *Stillborn Republic: Social Coalitions and Party Strategies in Greece, 1922–1936* (Berkeley: University of California Press, 1983). An innovative work analyzing the social bases of clientelism, cleavages, and coalitions in interwar Greek politics.

Mark Mazower, *Greece and the Inter-War Economic Crisis* (Oxford: Clarendon Press, 1991). Thorough analysis of the economic bases and dynamics of interwar Greek politics.

Andreas Moschonas, *Traditional Middle Strata: The Case of Greece* (Athens: Foundation for Mediterranean Studies, 1986). (In Greek.) A major empirical survey of the structure and orientation of the middle strata.

Nicos Mouzelis, *Modern Greece: Facts of Underdevelopment* (London: MacMillan 1978). The best overall survey of the Greek political economy from a "dependency" perspective.

George Yannopoulis, *Greece and the EEC* (New York: St. Martins, 1985). Provides useful data and discussion on Greek entry into the European Community.

Eastern Europe: Comparative Studies

Timothy Garton Ash, *The Uses of Adversity: Essays on the Fate of Central Europe* (New York: Random House, 1989). Perceptive and sensitive interpretations of Eastern European nations in the twilight of the communist era.

Misha Glenny, *The Rebirth of History: Eastern Europe in the Age of Democracy* (London: Penguin Books, 1990). A concise but comprehensive overview of the region by the Central European Correspondent of the BBC.

Stephen R. Graubard, editor, *Eastern Europe....Central Europe....Europe*, special issue of *Daedalus*, volume 119, number 1 (Winter 1990). Innovative and sophisticated essays on the politics and culture of Eastern Europe.

Stephen R. Graubard, editor, *The Exit from Communism*, special issue of *Daedalus*, volume 121, number 2 (Spring 1992). Includes an essay by Juan Linz and Alfred Stepan comparing Spain, the Soviet Union, and Yugoslavia; and one by Fabio Luca Cavazza on the paradox of Italian communism.

Barbara Jelavich, *History of the Balkans*, two volumes (Cambridge and New York: Cambridge University Press, 1983). The standard history of the Balkans since the eighteenth century; provides an excellent comparison between Ottoman and Habsburg rule and also a useful comparison between the communist states and Greece during the Cold War era.

Joseph Rothschild, *East Central Europe Between the Two World Wars* (Seattle: University of Washington Press, 1974). The standard history of Eastern Europe between the wars.

Joseph Rothschild, *Return to Diversity: A Political History of East Central Europe since World War II* (New York: Oxford University Press, 1989). A comprehensive and balanced history of the communist era.

Jacques Rupnik, *The Other Europe: The Rise and Fall of Communism in East-Central Europe* (New York: Pantheon Books, 1989). A sophisticated and sympathetic understanding of the distinctive features of Central European history.

Hugh Seton-Watson, *Eastern Europe Between the Wars, 1918–1941*, third edition revised (New York: Harper and Row, 1967). This work, by the leading British scholar of Eastern Europe of his generation, was for many years the standard history of its topic.

Hugh Seton-Watson, *The East-European Revolution*, third edition (New York: Praeger, 1964. The standard account of how the communists took power in Eastern Europe in the 1940s.

Robert Lee Wolff, *The Balkans in Our Time* (New York: W. W. Norton, 1967). Presents both an excellent and concise history of the Balkans and a thorough and detailed analysis of how the communists took power in the Balkan states; particularly strong on Tito's Yugoslavia.

INDEX